ROYAL REPUBLICANS

French Naval Leaders at the Paris Air Show
National Archives Photo

RONALD CHALMERS HOOD III

ROYAL REPUBLICANS

The French Naval Dynasties Between the World Wars

Louisiana State University Press
Baton Rouge and London

Designer: Albert Crochet
Typeface: Linotron Trump Mediaeval
Typesetter: G & S Typesetters, Inc.
Printer and binder: Edwards Brothers, Inc.

Publication of this book has been assisted by a grant
from the Andrew W. Mellon Foundation.

Library of Congress Cataloging in Publication Data

Hood, Ronald Chalmers.
  Royal republicans.

  Bibliography: p.
  Includes index.
    1. France. Marine—History—20th century.
  2. Sociology, Military—France—History—
  20th century.   3. France. Marine—Officers.
  4. France—History, Naval.   I. Title.
  VA503.H66   1985   306'.27   81-21331
  ISBN 0-8071-1211-9

In memory of
Paul Philippe Bolduc
(1911–1978)
Who brought it all alive, from the Petit Tailleur
to Proust, in old Classroom 36. Merci.

Ainsi, toujours poussés vers de nouveaux rivages,
Dans la nuit éternelle emportés sans retour,
Ne pourrons-nous jamais sur l'océan des âges
Jeter l'ancre un seul jour?

ALPHONSE DE LAMARTINE, *Le Lac*

Contents

Preface   1

Introduction   Historical Burdens of a Naval Tradition, 1690–1918   7

Part I   Social Foundations

Chapter 1   Bourgeois Roots   19

Chapter 2   Aristocratic Dreams   33

Part II   Family and Career Values

Chapter 3   The French Naval Household: Mothers and Sons   53

Chapter 4   As Fathers Did Before: The Life of a Knight Errant   75

Part III   The Officer Corps *Engagé*

Chapter 5   Temptations from the Right   105

Chapter 6   What Do We Do with the Legislature?   128

Chapter 7   *La Politique d'Abord*   148

Chapter 8   Denouement: Vichy and Beyond   173

Conclusion   188

Appendix   Composition of the French Naval Officer Corps in
            1936   195

Bibliographical Essay   199

Acknowledgments   215

Index   217

Illustrations

Admiral Descottes-Genon   48
"Chicago"   56
Admiral and Madame Hector Violette   61
Mariage à la mode navale   65
Naval leaders at the Invalides   86
The AEN ball   89
Hands across the sea   99
Neptune offrant à Louis XIV l'empire de la mer   100
The Salaün-Violette staff   110
Georges Leygues   130
Pierre Varillon   151
Admiral Darlan and President Lebrun   158
Pétain and Darlan   181
De Gaulle and his admirals   184

Tables

Table 1   Social Origins of Students at the *Grandes Écoles* Compared with General Population, 1920–1939   23

Table 2   Geographic Origins of Students at the *Grandes Écoles*, 1920–1939   30

Table 3   Nobility in the *Grand Corps*   36

Table 4   Flag Officers, 1919–1939   38

Table 5   Marriages, Family, and Children in the Naval Officer Corps, 1924–1940   41

Table 6   Academic Preparation for *Grandes Écoles*, 1932–1939   44

Table 7   Partisan Success with Naval Legislation, 1920–1935   133

Table 8   Party Solidarity on Naval Legislation, 1920–1935   134

Table 9   Voting Similarity on Naval Legislation, 1920–1935   134

Table 10   Regional Cohesion on Naval Legislation, 1919–1935   137

ROYAL REPUBLICANS

Preface

Paris during the summer of 1967 was still politically tense. Only five years after the withdrawal from Algeria and one year before severing military ties with NATO, the French armed forces were lost between two different roles—the *force coloniale* of the past and the *force de frappe*, yet to be. I had the fortune that summer to live in the home of a French officer who had just returned from a life overseas, frustrated by what he saw before him. I was also halfway through a French language major at Annapolis, where one of my advisors was a French naval officer who found this transition from old to new roles equally difficult. Seeing these men and their friends struggle for a new identity persuaded me that there was more than just an interesting summer vacation ahead of me. Reading the French naval officers' memoirs that were appearing in the bookstores at that time added to an impression of the French navy that surprised me because it differed so much from what I knew in the United States. For the French naval officers, World War II, the two colonial wars that followed, and all the related bitterness were topics of heated debate.

To study the French naval officer corps and its role in the demise of the Third Republic, I needed to expand my research beyond the printed works on the interwar era and explore the roots of naval isolation firsthand. These men and their families placed an inordinate emphasis on personal alliances, genealogy, and traditional habits, which influenced their outlook on modernization and change. Evidence of these attitudes came largely from private sources, which Frenchmen make a habit of concealing from researchers.

Of all French institutions, the navy remains one of the least explored by contemporary scholars. Most of what we know is a by-product of some other institutional or political study in which naval personnel played a subordinate role, generally lost to the reader in masses of detail and secondary evidence. Apart from some romanticized biographies, very little is known of the officer corps itself and its role in French society and statecraft. We are reminded of these men, perhaps, as tools of Jean-Baptiste Colbert's maritime policies, as the frequent losers in battles described by Alfred Thayer Mahan, and as minor officials in Jules Ferry's empire building after Sedan. One might also recall that Admiral de Grasse had a very fortunate afternoon with his fleet near the Chesapeake Bay, that Admiral Pierre de Villeneuve had an equally disastrous day off the Spanish coast; and that François Darlan was, indeed, a French admiral as well as a politician. Outside observers of the French often have problems understanding their military institutions. Comments that Frenchmen do not look like sailors or that Balzac's and Proust's sketches of soldiers are unbelievable, reveal the chasm to be bridged. This work is designed to fill some of the void and to add to the growing body of literature on civil-military relations in France.

Studies of European military and naval institutions in the past few years have turned away from the traditional combat narratives, focusing instead on human and political problems. A disproportionately large number of these works are written by scholars of modern Germany who have had the unique fortune since 1945 of unlimited access to archival material. Gordon Craig's exploratory work on the Prussian army opened new doors for such later scholars as F. L. Carsten and Holger Herwig who examined social problems in the German army and navy, respectively. Others, like Michael Lewis and Stanley Payne, have looked at military elites in Britain, Spain, and other Western nations. More recently, Peter Karsten's *The Naval Aristocracy* raised the ire of many naval historians in the United States. Yet when all the smoke had cleared, his argument stood firm. Perhaps the battle of the scholars is too recent for final conclusions on this thesis.

In spite of tight controls over primary sources, students of French military institutions have made major headway in studies of the army officer corps. Philip Bankwitz' very personal study of Maxime Weygand set a trend followed by Jan Tanenbaum's biography of

Maurice Sarrail. Judith Hughes and Robert Paxton have written further volumes on the military in politics during the 1920s and the Vichy years, reaching substantially different conclusions about the same group of men.

In all these works, however, French naval officers have been overlooked. Such an oversight seems natural when we remember the dominant role played by the army in defense matters while the navy remained in the shadows, often an object of ridicule. Yet this unknown and apparently unimportant group of officers gained national prominence seemingly overnight. Rising from insignificance in the French ports, these men, under the direction of a powerful admiral, became a leading bloc at Vichy. No one has yet explained why the navy was so slow to join the Gaullist movement, which army officers turned to far more quickly.

For several reasons an examination of the French naval officer corps in the period from 1919 to 1940 seemed productive. During these two decades, the navy experienced very rapid growth accompanied by internal political turmoil. Moreover, there is a fine body of material dealing with other aspects of French history from the same era. Major works by David Thomson, Eugen Weber, François Goguel, René Rémond, and Theodore Zeldin have invited others to test their theories on political developments during the interwar years. Many of these writers owe part of their success to the methodology developed by social scientists who have contributed to *La Revue française de sociologie* in France and the Inter-University Seminar on Armed Forces and Society in the United States. Some scholars with official connections have obtained special access to the personnel dossiers of post-1945 naval officers in the hope that their research might provide some assistance to a confused and depressed officer corps.

The old fifty-year rule has been lifted in most French archives, permitting access to materials up to the Vichy era. Unfortunately, the dossiers on those whom I studied will remain sealed until after the year 2000, delaying a detailed statistical analysis of those officers who served between the world wars. Most other forms of documentation were accessible including retired politicians and naval officers of the era who wanted to talk and, in several cases, to show me their private papers. These circumstances and the virtual absence of published research on the interwar French navy encouraged the present work. It is time to see how Darlan's public record compares with that of his associate and rival Weygand.

In addition to both primary and secondary published material, research for this work covered a variety of unpublished sources in the United States and France. Diplomatic and naval attaché correspondence provided a framework but left many unanswered questions. The archives of the Ministry of Marine, now at Vincennes, provided further insight into the subject; yet they too were incomplete largely because of widespread destruction on the eve of the French surrender in June, 1940. These documents have hardly been examined by scholars and they certainly merit greater attention for the rich detail they provide on the inner workings of the Ministry of Marine between the world wars. Elsewhere, private sources proved invaluable in filling the gaps left by incomplete records. Papers of the semiofficial Association amicale des anciens élèves de l'École navale, the naval academy's alumni society, were of help in developing social portraits of the naval families as were the private papers of individual officers of all ranks. Finally, interviews with former officers and their families and with political leaders rounded out the written and oral evidence.

In trying to understand the French naval officers, I asked myself the following questions. Was the officer corps a haven for aristocrats with unrepentant royalist sympathies? How did family traditions and education shape officer corps opinion? What sort of issues divided the officers into cliques? How did these men differ in attitude from their army counterparts? Finally, how did these men achieve such enormous political power in 1940, and why did responsible political leaders fail to stop them before civil-military relations collapsed? During my research, it became clear that the French naval community thrived in a world of traditions that had changed very little in more than two centuries. The social isolation of its leaders influenced the navy's political role during the summer of 1940 as the Third Republic staggered through its death throes.

The problem facing the French navy and its leaders between the world wars was one of great social conflicts aggravated by stark political and economic problems which few in or out of uniform comprehended at that time. A better understanding of who these men were and what they stood for should make their public role understandable and, I hope, contribute to a more complete knowledge of modern French military institutions.

Two very special sources, of help that is, were my advisors, C. Stewart Doty at the University of Maine and Louis M. Greenberg at the University of Maryland, who saw me through my two degrees. Each devoted that little extra bit of attention, from lengthy sessions on style to dinner in Paris while I was frantically completing my research, that made it all possible. Their patience in getting me to dig out of myself what I knew but couldn't explain was probably what made the difference in the end. All their efforts would have gone for naught if it hadn't been for three friends from an unlikely place, Major General Joe McLernan and Colonels Reilly Love and Bruce Brown all of the United States Marines. Their understanding of my interests, which did not fit the Marine norm, was greatly appreciated, and I hope I earned the trust they had in me. Many thanks.

Last, and far from least as an absolutely indispensable source of help and support, was the girl I married, known to our French friends as Madame Lucy. Accompanying me on what she expected to be summer vacations in France, it became clear from our arrival in Paris that she would play an integral role in the research. Trained as an actress, her stage presence made the difference in many hours of interviewing the French men and women in this story. It was through her, I later discovered, that my own credentials were checked out by some who believed that if the wife is all right then the husband cannot be all that bad either. Her sense of the dramatic was perfect. Wearing a black dress with black seamed stockings, black gloves and, for those critical moments, a black mantilla, Madame Lucy added the perfect genealogical touch in this rarefied atmosphere; she is the daughter of a Catholic American admiral. Leaving nothing to chance, she also wore some medals about her neck: Saint Christopher, for the travelers we surely were, and Saint Jude for the hopeless case I would have been without many good interviews. As a convert to Calvinism through very strong maternal influence, she stimulated the interest of a few very anxious French women who wondered how she could survive in America without the Virgin. For them, she had an excellent little speech that went over nicely. Somewhere along the way, she also picked up a third medal: Saint Genesius for the actors we sometimes were, concluding late afternoon interviews over cocktails of imported "Bourbon" and delightful chats with our French naval hosts about "le bon vieux temps." Merci, Lucy.

INTRODUCTION
Historical Burdens of a Naval Tradition
1690–1918

In a republic known as Marianne, there existed a navy called La Royale. A French admiral recently explained how these conflicting symbols could exist side by side and how his navy of the 1970s is the cultural heir to those of Louis XIV and even of President Émile Loubet.[1] Generations of French naval officers were imbued both at home and in their professional lives with a fairly uniform view of their own naval past. This view came to play an important role in their career development as though the mixture of legend, folklore, and history became a standard by which these naval officers would measure their twentieth-century lives. Regardless of the individual officers' perspectives, their ties with the past have always been vital in providing the philosophical foundation of their vocation. It is a way of thinking that David Thomson saw as a chronic problem throughout modern French history. He warned contemporary Frenchmen to avoid measuring current problems with antiquated yardsticks lest the issue at hand be "left in suspense or lost by default."[2]

In the French navy, this advice went unheeded. Its officers shared a generally pessimistic view of history, and they strove to prevent repeating it. At the heart of their soul searching was the quest for a way to avoid the recurring problem of losing their fleet just on the eve of some great successful venture.[3]

Officers and sympathetic writers have declared that each gen-

1. Admiral Marc François de Joybert, Preface to Jean Randier, *L'Éperon et la cuirasse* (Paris, 1972), 5, Vol. I of *La Royale*, 2 vols.
2. David Thomson, *Democracy in France Since 1870* (5th ed.; London, 1969), 52.
3. Louis Nicolas, *Du moyen âge à 1815* (Paris, 1964), 8–9, Vol. I of André Reussner (ed.), *La Puissance navale dans l'histoire*, 3 vols.

eration of French naval personnel worked quietly and diligently against enormous odds, building up their fleet to the point where it could provide the state enormous rewards. Success came normally through the destruction of an archenemy at sea or the seizure of some rich colony from under a rival's nose. Then, as the tale goes, some major crisis—from storm to battle—ruined the fleet just when a great victory was possible, ending the hopes of a generation or more of French sailors. Perhaps worst of all, these disasters embittered the officers who never had more than one chance in a lifetime to fight a great battle at sea.

French midshipmen over the years have learned that their fleet was destroyed five times in two centuries either at the hand of a foreign power or through some domestic crisis. First in 1690, and later in 1763, 1789, 1870, and finally in 1942, the country was left without a force at sea to protect Marianne or her predecessors from threats to their frontiers, colonies, and trade.[4] A few individuals have gained fame for their diligence in putting a navy together in spite of the odds against success. The name of Jean-Baptiste Colbert stands above all others. Among French officers, he is revered as the founder of the Ministry of Marine. Under his skillful direction, the fleet was built from nothing into a major instrument of European power in the latter half of the seventeenth century. In true baroque style, however, Colbert was more interested in achieving prestige and glory on the seas than in destroying France's maritime rivals.[5] It is appropriate that in a navy frequently weighed down by a massive bureaucracy ashore, the father figure is a bureaucrat of the first order and not a sea captain or buccaneer as in the British and American naval traditions. Alas, Colbert died soon enough to miss the Sun King's decision to dry-dock the whole fleet

4. This theme was expressed by Admiral Paul Auphan, *La Marine dans l'histoire de France* (Paris, 1955), 69 *et passim*; Admiral Paul Auphan and Jacques Mordal, *The French Navy in World War II*, trans. A. C. J. Sabalot (Annapolis, 1959), 1–7; Claude Farrère, *Histoire de la marine française* (Paris, 1934), 194 *et passim*; René Jouan, *Histoire de la marine française* (Paris, 1950), 21 *et passim*; Espagnac du Ravay [Louis de La Monneraye], *Vingt Ans de politique navale, 1919–1939* (Grenoble, 1941), ix–19; Charles de La Roncière, *Histoire de la marine française* (6 vols.; Paris, 1920), V, 327 *et passim*.

5. Claude Farrère, *Jean-Baptiste Colbert* (Paris, 1954), Chaps. 7–9; Auphan, *Marine dans l'histoire*, 206; La Roncière, *Marine française*, Chap. 14; Nicolas, *Puissance navale*, 137–39.

to save money for his war in Europe. French naval officers have blamed this act on Louis' abnormal bias toward his field armies and his vast ignorance of France's maritime needs.

Rebuilt in time for the Seven Years' War, the fleet by 1763 was once again devastated, this time by piecemeal deployment against larger British forces. The recovery was swift, however, for by the 1770s the French navy was strong enough to challenge Britain in the American War of Independence.

French naval officers took credit for plucking the flower of Britain's empire from her, but they regarded their victory as pyrrhic. Within months after Yorktown, the French fleet was again destroyed in battle. More important, the war led to the financial ruin of France, contributing directly to what many naval officers felt was the worst of all national disasters: the French Revolution. The fleet was again rebuilt in 1789 but was the object of revolutionary excesses. Officers have been quick to attribute the demise of their navy to the Committee of Public Safety, which purged royalist sympathizers from its ranks. They see Villeneuve as the hopeless pawn of Napoleon's ignorance and the inheritor of an institution weakened by the Terror.[6]

French officers skim over the first half of the nineteenth century, for it was a period of little maritime activity. The fleet supported the initial conquest of Algiers, participated in some colonial exploration, and returned Napoleon's body from Saint Helena. Activities declined to such a level that one official proposed to get rid of the navy altogether. With the growth of industrialization, however, Napoleon III harnessed technology for naval interests. Once again, France was second only to Great Britain on the seas. But she lost her position very soon in the Franco-Prussian War when warships were stripped of their crews to man the trenches against the German invaders and later to overcome the Commune.

More relevant to naval officers searching for historical lessons was the recent past, beginning with the Third Republic. Many officers in the 1920s knew this regime from childhood or through stories told by their parents—that is, from first- or at most second-

6. Auphan, *Marine dans l'histoire,* 106–78; Farrère, *Marine française,* 225–59; Jouan, *Marine française,* Chaps. 6–8; Nicolas, *Du moyen âge à 1815,* 307–99.

hand experience. National problems encountered after 1870 were real, tangible, and oftentimes still unresolved in the twenties, giving eager officers a reason for personal involvement. With little to do in European waters, naval officers competed in the search for new colonies. As early as 1871, they were writing articles encouraging others to forget the loss at Sedan and join in expanding French power overseas for, said one, "history has no other lessons than conquest."[7] The colonial mission was a natural one for the navy. Since the days of Colbert, the Ministry of Marine had the responsibility for the navy, the colonies, and the Colonial Army, as well as the merchant and fishing fleets. Individuals who had no opportunities at home or who foresaw only boredom in French home ports sought careers abroad. They saw the gathering of colonies not so much as a profit-making enterprise but as a vehicle for establishing French prestige worldwide.[8]

In the colonies, the navy performed two functions. As an extension of a policy of association, local defense squadrons were manned by mixed crews of French naval officers and native sailors. In addition, the Ministry of Marine refined the policy of assimilation by making colonial administrators of naval officers. In their capacity as colonial governors, the admirals brought the fruits of the French *mission civilisatrice* to the natives.[9] While the French army oversaw North Africa, the navy assumed the lead role in Indochina. Admiral Amédée Courbet became a near folk hero in naval circles after successful conquest of the region, and soon after the colony became known as "the admirals' preserve."[10] Elsewhere, naval officers became deeply involved in the acquisition of territory in Central Africa and Madagascar as the tricolor followed naval conquerors like Pierre Brazza, Henri Rivière, and Auguste Penfentenyo

7. "La Cochinchine en 1871," *Revue des deux mondes*, XCVII (January, 1872), 204–18.

8. Auphan and Mordal, *French Navy*, 2; James A. Bising, "The Admirals' Government: A History of the Naval Colony That Was French Indochina" (Ph.D. dissertation, New York University, 1972), ii–vi; Henri Brunschwig, *French Colonialism, 1871–1914: Myths and Realities*, trans. William Glanville Brown (London, 1964), 16.

9. Raymond F. Betts, *Assimilation and Association in French Colonial Theory, 1890–1914* (New York, 1961), Chaps. 6–8.

10. Bising, "Admirals' Government," iv–vi; John Munholland, "The Emergence of the Colonial Military in France, 1880–1905" (Ph.D. dissertation, Princeton University, 1964), 7.

de Kervéreguin. These and other naval officers thrived on the free-dom from government control and the detachment from political squabbles back home.[11]

On November 12, 1890, it was Charles Cardinal Lavigerie, prelate of North Africa, who decided to test the Vatican's rapprochement with Paris in a speech to the Mediterranean fleet. The audience seemed ideal; the naval officer corps was known to be fervently Catholic, and its social involvement in the colonies likely gave this group a reformist image. To the cardinal's surprise, his famous toast fell on deaf ears. Lavigerie's appeal for adherence to republican institutions followed by his monks' band's playing of La Mar-seillaise stunned the wardroom. The Bonapartist officer hosting the ceremony, Admiral Victor Duperré, left no doubt how ideo-logically distant his officers were from much of French public opinion.[12]

As these officers rejected the cardinal's invitation to join the Ralliement and support the republic, so too did they resent the leg-islation separating church and state in 1905. Starting in the mid-1890s, moderate cabinets began to include radical ministers of ma-rine who were personally involved in achieving social reforms in the navy. They attempted to alter long-standing customs and tradi-tions of the officer corps.[13] By ministerial edict religious benedic-tion of warships was stopped, nuns were no longer permitted to serve as nurses in the naval hospitals, and new warships began to be named for heroes of the republic. All this led to an endless outcry from an officer corps accustomed to an intermingling of religious and maritime traditions. More now than ever before, the officers were polarized, subject to what some perceived as unprecedented Jewish or Masonic influence in the government.[14]

11. Munholland, "Colonial Military," 51.
12. D. W. Brogan, The Development of Modern France, 1870–1939 (Rev. ed.; 2 vols.; New York, 1966), I, 262; John McManners, Church and State in France, 1870–1914 (New York, 1973), 71–72; D. Shapiro, "The Ralliement in the Politics of the 1890's," in D. Shapiro (ed.), The Right in France, 1890–1919: Three Studies (Carbondale, Ill., 1962), 13.
13. Jean Jolly (ed.), Dictionnaire des parlementaires français: notices biogra-phiques sur les ministres, députés, et sénateurs français de 1889 à 1940 (8 vols.; Paris, 1960–77), VI, 2120–21, 2280–89, VII, 2637–38.
14. McManners, Church and State, 133; Pierre Chevalier, La Maçonnerie: église de la république, 1877–1944 (Paris, 1975), 93, Vol. III of Histoire de la franc-maçonnerie française, 3 vols.; Admiral Jean Decoux, Adieu marine (Paris, 1957),

If the lessons to be learned had been unclear before, they were no longer. Officers thought Émile Combes' naval policies "looked like a new Trafalgar," and some threw their tainted gloves into the ocean after shaking hands with his minister of marine, Camille Pelletan.[15] He and the next two holding the naval portfolio, Edouard Lockroy and Jean Marie de Lanessan, were deeply committed to rapid modernization of an archaic bureaucracy incapable of responding to crises. But because these three tried to alter traditions, they received almost no cooperation from the officer corps. Perhaps the French naval legacy reached a new low point when the chief of staff informed his minister of marine that the navy could not help in the Fashoda crisis because it was not ready to fight either an offensive or a defensive war.[16] (Little difference it would have made to Major Jean-Baptiste Marchand, who was stranded in the Sahara's wastelands, one thousand miles from the Mediterranean.)

Despite bitter feelings over the British success at Fashoda, the government finally redirected naval energies toward some badly needed reforms. The colonies became a separate portfolio while the Colonial Army and coastal defenses eventually went to the minister of war. More difficult to change, however, was the archaic naval administration, which one insider called "a vegetating organism."[17] It was twice the size of the British admiralty yet supported a fleet less than half the Royal Navy's strength.

Britain remained the arch-rival and greatest potential threat. The French officers at naval headquarters in rue Royale continued to prepare plans for the destruction of the Royal Navy even after Paris

---

10–11; Paul Masson, *Le Juif dans la marine: étude de moeurs administratives* (Paris, 1891), *passim*; Louis V. Méjan, *La Séparation des églises et de l'état* (Paris, 1959), 55.

15. Decoux, *Adieu marine*, 10; Hélène de David-Beauregard, *Souvenirs de famille* (Toulon, 1970), 30.

16. Jean-Marie de Lanessan, *Nos forces navales* (Paris, 1911), 29–31; Auphan, *Marine dans l'histoire*, 212; Thomas M. Iiams, Jr., "Gabriel Hanotaux at the Quai d'Orsay: The Foreign Policy of France, 1894–1898" (Ph.D. dissertation, Columbia University, 1960), 106.

17. Jean Abrial to parents, November 18, 1898, in Admiral Jean Abrial Papers, Private Collection; Lieutenant X, *La Guerre avec Angleterre: politique navale de la France* (Paris, 1900), viii–ix; U.S. Naval Attaché Reports, June 22, 1899, January 3, 1902, both in Record Group 38, Series 98, National Archives; Admiral Henri Salaün, *La Marine française* (Paris, 1934), 77–86, 104, quotation from 89.

and London concluded a diplomatic entente in 1904. For generations they had tried to achieve a Mediterranean balance of power.[18]
Thus, Théophile Delcassé became a hero to many naval officers
when he took over the Ministry of Marine long enough to secure
the Anglo-French naval accord of 1912. His officers supported this
move because it guaranteed French dominance of the Mediterranean, which they saw as far more important than the Atlantic,
where the British fleet and naval interests prevailed.[19]

Naval personnel remembered the First World War as another period of sacrifice and missed opportunities. Officers recalled the
mundane duties of transporting the Colonial Army to Europe, protecting the convoys from submarines, and guarding against an Aus-
trian naval menace that never really materialized. The Dardanelles
campaign involved the French navy in the same routine fashion, far
from home and not really involved in the important part of the war.

Despite these duties of surveillance and siege, the French naval
officers felt slighted, for they had never engaged a major opponent
at sea. Some naval officers even felt guilty about the navy's comparatively small wartime role, which they measured in loss of life.
Naval deaths amounted to a mere twelve thousand, whereas the
army lost nearly two million men. The handing over of the navy's
shipyards to the army for manufacture of arms for the western front
aggravated naval frustrations even further and left officers feeling
that the fleet was no more than a peacetime luxury to the government, which had no qualms about setting it aside during real national emergencies. Loss of the shipyards for four years also meant
that repair and maintenance of the fleet could not be performed.
This produced additional bitterness and, by late 1918, a fleet too
rusty to operate at sea. The officers felt they had come through an
exhausting war with little recognition for their sacrifices in protecting the Atlantic and Mediterranean sea lanes. It was they who
had made it possible for the army to get the necessary supplies and
reinforcements from abroad to hold out along the Marne. As in numerous earlier wars, the French naval officers believed that they

18. Auphan, *Marine dans l'histoire*, 213.
19. U.S. Naval Attaché Reports, February 10, 1913, in RG 38, Ser. 98, NA; Luigi
Albertini, *The Origins of the War of 1914* (2 vols.; London, 1952), I, 274.

had sacrificed their institution for the good of the country without due rewards.[20]

Many came to believe it was the officer corps, far more than either the enlisted personnel or a few parliamentary supporters, that held the navy together. More than just a band of comrades, the officers saw themselves as a special class of men, descended from a select number of French families that traditionally provided their sons to the navy. Jean-Baptiste Colbert, while serving as Louis XIV's minister of marine, established the patrimonial relationship between these families and the naval officer corps. He recruited his officers very carefully while turning the ministry itself into a family office for his own heirs as well.[21]

The officer corps was divided from the start into two distinct halves: those who went to sea and took command, or the *grand corps*, and those who made up the shore-based administrative services, or the *petits corps*. These two branches were as distinct in their social makeup as they were in the type of work performed. From the earliest days, the *grand corps* routinely came from noble and Breton families, a tradition that one admiral called a "social necessity."[22] This custom survived into the twentieth century, jealously guarded by the officers themselves. It was widely believed that these officers inherited special qualities needed to command ships and men.

The aristocracy had been denied the right to conduct commercial or mercantile activities, a privilege relegated to the bourgeoisie. The naval officer corps continued this detachment from modern economic activities as well. Rather than seek individual profits, they threw themselves into colonial matters for the sake of adding to national prestige.[23] If recent analysis of American and

20. Auphan and Mordal, *French Navy*, 6–7.
21. La Roncière, *Marine française*, 356–57; Auphan and Mordal, *French Navy*, Chap. 1; Geoffrey Symcox, *The Crisis of French Sea Power, 1688–1697: From the 'Guerre d'Escadre' to the 'Guerre de Course'* (The Hague, 1974), 2, 23; Admiral Jurien de La Gravière, *Souvenirs d'un amiral* (Paris, 1860), epilogue; Commander Jacques Bodin, Interview, November 24, 1977.
22. Ministère de la marine, *Annuaire de la marine* (Paris, 1878–1940), provides details on the various branches of the officer corps including names and schools of each member. Paul W. Bamford, *Fighting Ships and Prisons: The Mediterranean Galleys of France in the Age of Louis XIV* (Minneapolis, 1973), 95–113, 298–318; Symcox, *French Sea Power*, 23–29, 68; Bodin Interview.
23. Here, I am comparing the aristocratic values of the seventeenth through the

British naval officers is correct, then the French counterparts are a far different lot. American and British officers were drawn from the same socioeconomic classes as their compatriots in banking, commerce, and industry.[24] French naval officers, however, frequently enjoyed high status without any claim to wealth, in the tradition of the chivalrous but impoverished *hoberaux*. Although we know that the bourgeoisie gained access to the *grand corps*, these "new" men were not immune to the economic plight of the landed French aristocrats. They retained only the appearance of means long after the family fortunes disappeared. Of course there were exceptions to this trend of poor men gravitating toward the navy, as we shall see. Nevertheless, the social and economic frustrations that bourgeois and aristocratic officers suffered in the twentieth century recall the fate of the petty nobility on the eve of the French Revolution.

This tradition was markedly different from that of the *petits corps*. There, bourgeois customs and a heritage of separate social development kept these men at arm's length from the *grand corps*. Squabbles between the two halves of the naval officer corps were endemic, and special vocabularies grew up to describe how each felt about the other's company.[25]

Steeped in the traditions of the French naval past, the *grand corps* portrayed itself as "one of the last lay orders," recalling Colbert's dependence on the Knights of Malta to command his fleet.[26] Belief in their peculiar social foundations was as important to the officers as belief in the grandeur of the French navy. The two qualities were inseparable. And although many interpretations of the navy's historical origins were possible, the pessimistic view prevailed in the wardrooms and naval schools of the 1920s. Returning

nineteenth centuries as expressed in the two notes above and with the values of the French nobility seen by Pierre Goubert, *The Ancien Régime: French Society, 1600–1750*, trans. Steve Cox (New York, 1973), 162–92.

24. For the social foundation of the American and British navies, see Peter Karsten, *The Naval Aristocracy: The Golden Age of Annapolis and the Emergence of Modern American Navalism* (New York, 1972); Michael A. Lewis, *England's Sea Officers: The Story of the Naval Profession* (London, 1939).

25. Symcox, *French Sea Power*, 23–29; Lieutenant François de Mury, "Nos officiers de marine," *Revue politique et littéraire*, XVII (February, 1902), 132–36; Mury, "Un dernier mot," Charles de Neubourg, "Les Officiers de vaisseau," both in *Revue politique et littéraire*, XVII (March, 1902), 265–66, 261–65.

26. Admiral Pierre Le Bris, "A.E.N.," in *Gala de la marine, 14 février 1935* (Paris, 1935), n.p.; Bamford, *Fighting Ships and Prisons*, 95–101.

from a depressing war, the officers were confirmed in their interpretation of naval history. It was a gray cloud that was to influence
their thought and behavior over the next two decades.

One reserve officer who spent his life teaching at the École supérieure de guerre navale drew the following conclusion about how
France treated her navy over three centuries: "If sometimes she
loved her sailors dearly and suffered bitterly from all their losses,
she never considered them her eldest children and never gave them
the support which might have permitted them to give her the top
position in the world."[27] The officers approached the future in 1919
having learned in the classroom and the wardroom that they were
ignored and forgotten by the rest of the country. Looking back over
three centuries of an uneven past to the glorious days of the seventeenth century, they sadly asked themselves, "*Mais où sont les
neiges d'antan?*"

27. Jouan, *Marine française*, 313.

PART I
Social Foundations

Le marin n'a pas de place dans la société, et ne doit pas en avoir. Croyez-vous qu'un officier de la Marine se forme comme un employé de banque, ou comme un marchand de drap? Pour former un homme qui ait le sens de la mer, il faut deux ou trois générations de marins.

Louis Guichard

CHAPTER 1
Bourgeois Roots

The absence of a conscript tradition in the navy set this service apart from the other French armed forces and their claims to better represent the national will through the draft. The experiences of the French Revolution and later the Prussian army's successes of the 1860s led many countries to form conscript armed forces to better defend themselves. The French navy, however, remained the small professional service, *la marine du métier*, it had been since its beginnings under Louis XIV. Based on career officers and enlisted personnel, with almost no reserve, the size of the navy varied little from peace to war.[1]

Dominating the officer ranks were the *officiers de marine*, or line officers, who made up about half the entire naval officer strength. This branch, or corps as the French called it, averaged 2,300 men of all ranks, rising only to 2,600 on the eve of the Second World War. The members existed solely to command men, ships, and major installations ashore. They were firmly in charge of all aspects of naval administration and dominated the major naval staffs.[2]

Beneath these officers were another seventeen distinct branches commonly referred to as the *petits corps*. Officers of these corps filled engineering, medical, and other support positions within the

1. Richard D. Challener, *The French Theory of the Nation in Arms, 1866–1939* (New York, 1952), Chap. 1; Theodore Ropp, *War in the Modern World* (Rev. ed; New York, 1962), Chap. 7; Philip Bankwitz, *Maxime Weygand and Civil-Military Relations in Modern France* (Cambridge, Mass., 1967), Chap. 3.
2. The volumes of Ministère de la marine, *Annuaire de la marine* (Paris, 1920–39), contain annual personnel strength figures. See also Office of Naval Intelligence, Naval Attaché Report, Paris, October, 1932, E-5-a, 16682-A, in National Archives.

naval hierarchy as technical experts.[3] During the 1920s and 1930s, the *officiers de marine,* or *grand corps* as they liked to call themselves, amounted to 45 percent of the total officer corps, while the several engineering corps made up 27 percent; the medical corps, 9 percent; and the administrative corps, the remaining 19 percent. All the line officers, a majority of the engineers, and half the administrative specialists were eligible for sea duty. The remainder were permanently stationed ashore in the shipyards and on the largest staffs.

The shore-based officers, like civil servants, tended to remain in one position for lengthy periods, serving as advisors to men in the *grand corps.*[4] The incorporation of these men, who would have been civilians in other navies, into the uniformed establishment was consistent with the practices of the *ancien régime.* Jean-Baptiste Colbert and the ministers of marine who succeeded him were intent upon establishing a totally self-sufficient navy under royal patronage. Seagoing officers were aided from the start by special services, including a corps of hydrographers, who prepared the nautical charts, and engineers charged with ship construction. Many of these auxiliary corps dated from the eighteenth century, while others were added with the advent of new maritime technology.[5] By nationalizing all support services, from shipbuilding to map making, the Ministry of Marine demonstrated its historical distrust of the private sector.

Habits changed slowly in the navy as they did in other French institutions. Parliament criticized an antiquated system of keeping one officer on active duty for every twelve sailors, four times the ratio of officers to soldiers in the French army.[6] Criticism, however,

3. See Ministère de la marine, *Annuaire de la marine,* for details on the various corps. For unofficial popular names of the corps, see Lieutenant François de Mury, "Nos officiers de marine," and "Un dernier mot," both in *Revue politique et littéraire,* XVII (February, 1902), 132–36 (March, 1902), 265–266.

4. ONI, Naval Attaché Report, Paris, series of reports for 1932, E-5-a, 16682, NA; Ministère de la marine, *Annuaire de la marine* (1920–1939).

5. Charles Braibant, *Un bourgeois sous trois républiques* (Paris, 1961), 325; Geoffrey Symcox, *The Crisis of French Sea Power, 1688–1697: From the 'Guerre d'Escadre' to the 'Guerre de Course'* (The Hague, 1974), 26–27.

6. *Journal officiel de la République Française. Chambre des Députés. Débats parlementaires,* February 27, 1925, pp. 1396–97, November 13, 1926, pp. 3401; "Chronique des marines française et étrangères," *Revue maritime,* XCVII (December, 1927), 804–805.

did not lead to desired changes. The navy remained a professional service with a permanent officer corps and long-term enlisted men drawn on a rotating basis from the merchant and fishing fleets. A sailor served one year of every five in the navy, reverting to merchant seaman status for the next four years. This policy of self-containment effectively shut the navy off from the national labor force and the problems the army encountered with conscription.

Administrative law dictated that only the *officiers de marine* were eligible for command. They were further set apart from the other naval officers because they were the only ones who attended the École navale. The minister of marine reserved this *grande école*, equivalent to the army's Saint Cyr, solely for educating career line officers. Some engineers and administrators attended the École polytechnique and the less fashionable École des arts et métiers, but the line officers had the distinct privilege of attending an exclusive *grande école*.[7] Different promotion criteria for École navale graduates set these men even further apart from their *petits corps* associates years after the French army integrated all officers into a single bloc. Even those few line officers educated somewhere other than the École navale received second-class treatment. These men came either from the École polytechnique or, in very rare instances, from the enlisted ranks, and they made up less than 5 percent of the *grand corps*. Although in every other respect they were identical to their peers from the École navale, they were handled for promotion as members of the auxiliary corps, and few ever reached top rank.[8] In 1935 there were only seventy living *officiers de marine* who were Polytechnique alumni. Only one was an admiral.

Those naval officers of other corps who did not attend a *grande*

---

7. Captain André Benoist, Report, May 16, 1928, in Série 1BB2¹, Carton 86, Archives de la marine; ONI, Naval Attaché Report, Paris, October, 1932, E-5-a, 16682-A, NA; Charles de La Roncière and G. Clerc-Rampal, *Histoire de la marine française, illustrée* (Paris, 1934), 390–91; "Chronique des marines," *Revue maritime,* CI (March, 1929), 384–90; Vice Admiral Charles Drujon, "Le Commandement et le matériel dans la marine nationale," Admiral L. Jouch, "Recrutement et formation des ingénieurs méchaniciens de la marine nationale," both in *Revue nautique,* n.v. (January, 1937), n.p.

8. Raoul Girardet and Jean Pierre Thomas, *La Crise militaire française, 1945–1962: aspects sociologiques et idéologiques* (Paris, 1964), 15; *Annuaire de la Société amicale de secours des anciens élèves de l'École polytechnique* (Paris, 1935), S 26–S 28 (1937).

école received their commissions through competitive examinations after graduation from a technical or secondary school. A few, such as the paymasters, were promoted to officer status from the enlisted ranks. In most of these cases, careers were restricted to narrow technical fields.[9]

Administrative regulations were not the only way to separate the *grand* from the various *petits corps*. École navale alumni, unlike most other officers, tended to come from families with generations of ties to the navy.[10] A study by the Naval General Staff emphasized the importance of these historical ties between certain select families and the *grand corps*. "Atavism and surroundings certainly play a very large role. Many young men, sons, nephews, or cousins of seafarers living either in a totally nautical setting or at least in one with maritime connections, grow up with the idea of one day coming into the Navy. [They wish this] without really knowing why, simply because they never imagined they could do otherwise."[11]

Who were these men and from what sorts of backgrounds did they come? Naval officers and writers have often alluded to how different they were from the remainder of the French public. These sources remind us that the officer had very little in common with the man in the street. Statistics offer us some better insights into the social backgrounds of these men and how they differed from other sectors of French society.

The percentage figures in Table 1 represent the social origins of 1,139 of 1,876 graduates of the École navale and 2,555 of 4,751 graduates of the École polytechnique between the world wars. These figures for the two major *grandes écoles* commissioning naval officers are compared with the occupations of all employable men in France for the same period. The contrast between the two schools' figures offers some idea of how the naval officers differed from the elites in business and industry, traditionally recruited from Polytechnique.

Looking at these figures, we see first that Navale had one-third

9. ONI, Naval Attaché Report, Paris, October, 1932, E-5-a, 16682-A, NA.
10. Lieutenant Raymond de Villaine, to École navale alumni, October 18, 1920, in Archives de l'Association amicale des anciens élèves de l'École navale.
11. Commander Stanislas de David-Beauregard, Report, March 20, 1921, p. 15, in Sér. Ca, Car. 34, Archives de la marine.

Table 1.   Social Origins of Students at *Grandes Écoles* Compared with
General Population, 1920–1939

Occupations	Fathers of École Navale Students	Fathers of Polytechnique Students	All Employable Men
Military officer	29	16	–
Military enlisted	2	1	3*
High-level employee or liberal profession	10	15	3
Commercial or industrial manager	19	28	8
Mid-level employee	26	34	11
Manual worker	1	3	38
Farmer	12	2	36
Other	1	1	1

SOURCES: *Bulletin de l'Association amicale des anciens élèves de l'École navale* (Paris, 1920–39); *Bulletin de la Société amicale et de secours des anciens élèves de l'École polytechnique* (Paris, 1920–39); Commander Loïc Abrial, Interview, July 28, 1975; Admiral Paul Auphan, Interviews, June 5, 1974, May 30, 1975; Commander Jacques Bodin, Interview, November 24, 1977; Admiral René Godfroy, Interview, July 2, 1975; Admiral Paul Ortoli, Interview, July 4, 1974; Institut national de la statistique et des économiques, *Statistique générale de la France: résultats statistiques du recensement général de la population, 8 mars 1931* (Paris, 1931), 8 *et seq.* (which contains census figures for 1926 and 1931).

NOTES: Figures represent the nearest whole percent in each category. Figures are derived from a survey of 61 percent of École navale graduates and 54 percent of École polytechnique graduates for the period. Employment categories are based on those used in a statistical analysis of all midshipmen entering the French naval officer corps between 1945 and 1960. See Guy Michelat and Jean Pierre Thomas, "Contribution à l'étude du recrutement des écoles d'officiers de la marine, 1945–1960," *Revue française de sociologie*, IX (April–June, 1968), 51–70.

* This figure represents a consolidation of both enlisted men and officers.

fewer sons of the highly paid and those from prestigious liberal professions. In contrast with those who attended Polytechnique, significantly fewer going to Navale came from homes of commercial or industrial managers. Both schools attracted substantial numbers from *grand bourgeois* families, those whose lineage and prominence dated from the early nineteenth century. As for the sons of the *moyenne bourgeoisie* coming from the homes of mid-level *fonctionnaires* and business employees, the École navale recruited 25 percent fewer than Polytechnique. These families also had status and reputations dating from the nineteenth century but gained political power as a class only under the Second Empire. Boys from these strata attending Navale came from homes of lesser wealth and prestige than their counterparts at Polytechnique. The concentration of the well-to-do was natural at the latter school which had always provided the technocratic and business elite of the country.

Among students from nonbourgeois homes, the difference in the social origins of the two student bodies is also apparent. The Navale recruited two-thirds fewer sons of manual workers than did the better known engineering school, but at both schools working-class students are virtually unrepresented. Alumni and faculty can usually recall only one or two midshipmen from such homes in any one class.[12] The weak urban ties of the naval officer corps and its traditional links with the landed class are also apparent in these figures. Navale attracted six times as many rural youth as did Polytechnique, and all of these students came from landed families. The peasantry was excluded by educational disadvantages that will be discussed later on.

Greatest of all the gaps between the social foundations of these two schools was in the reliance on military families. One of every three students at the École navale was the son of a military careerist. Most of these were sons of officers, three-quarters of whom were in the navy. The remainder—only 7 percent—had fathers either in the army or the Colonial Army, which had close ties with the navy. Until 1900, both the navy and the Colonial Army had been part of a single Ministry of Marine and Colonies. Even in the 1930s, officers of these two institutions were often the only noticeable French presence in remote overseas possessions.[13] These two military services were also similar in their reliance on career officer and enlisted personnel. The Metropolitan Army had been a conscript service since Napoleon.

The social profile of the École navale graduates is even more unusual when alumni are compared with middle- and upper-class families listed in the censuses. Two to three times the national average of upper bourgeois families were represented at the Navale,

12. Jacques Godechot, Interview, June 25, 1975; Loïc Abrial Interview; Auphan Interviews.

13. D. W. Brogan, *The Development of Modern France, 1870–1939* (Rev. ed.; 2 vols.; New York, 1966), I, 217–18.

while the working classes, which made up one-third of all employed Frenchmen, provided almost no future *officiers de marine*. The figure for farmers' sons attending Navale is much smaller than the national average, but only because the national figures lump landowners and peasants together as a single figure. Were the two separated, the proportion of landowners in France would come much closer to the 12 percent figure among École navale students. Moreover, by the 1920s, the navy had stepped up its recruitment of boys with technical skills, found more often in the urban areas. These skills were in greater demand as naval technology grew more complex and the Paris staff expanded. Over the years, the Ministry of Marine and the Naval General Staff enlarged their power by assuming many of the duties formerly performed at lower levels of command. In this respect, the centralization of resources and power was part of a national trend.

The larger number of boys from military homes at the École navale also differed widely from the national average. Military families were ten times better represented among Navale students than in the French population as a whole. This disparity would be even greater if census reports separated military families into officer and enlisted categories. Thus, like Saint Cyr but unlike Saint Maxient, the École navale definitely encouraged the sons of officers to follow in their fathers' footsteps. At Saint Cyr, 16 percent of the students between 1920 and 1939 were sons of alumni; at École navale, the percentage was 15. In comparison, only 10 percent of the students at Polytechnique were attending their fathers' alma mater.[14]

If the entire army officer corps is considered, a much greater disparity between naval and other military homes is apparent. The school of Saint Maxient also graduated line officers, but the student body came from less prestigious homes than their peers at

14. *Bulletin de l'Association amicale des anciens élèves de l'École navale* (Paris, 1920–39), hereinafter cited as *Bulletin de AEN; Bulletin de la Société amicale et de secours des anciens élèves de l'École polytechnique* (Paris, 1920–39), hereinafter cited as *Bulletin de SEP; Bulletin de la Société amicale et de secours des élèves et des anciens élèves de l'École spéciale militaire de Saint Cyr* (Paris, 1920–39). On an average, the École navale graduated 114 each year, while the École polytechnique graduated 218, and Saint Cyr, 366 annually.

Saint Cyr, and most were former enlisted men. They represented over half the new military officers commissioned each year after World War I.[15] In the navy, however, it was much more difficult for enlisted men to gain access to the officer corps. The École des élèves-officiers, the navy's equivalent to the army's Saint Maxient, evolved into a school, not for enlisted men, but for civilian youth who had failed the entrance exam for Navale. Boys were permitted to enlist specifically for entry into this school where they could make a final attempt for the École navale through a far easier exam. This admission procedure supplanted the career sailors for whom the school was founded. By 1933, the institution was virtually closed; only two of twenty-two applicants were admitted. The navy's program for commissioning enlisted men remained insignificant even after 1936, when the minister of marine sought unsuccessfully to expand the program.[16] Moreover, graduates of the École des élèves-officiers had no chance of rising to high rank. In reality, the school existed to produce specialized line officers who performed menial but necessary work at sea, freeing the École navale graduates for command and more elegant duty ashore.[17]

At the École polytechnique the students shunned the *corps des officiers de marine*, though it was available to them. Appointment to the various corps was based on class standing, those graduating highest having the first choice of careers and assignments. The navy annually reserved approximately twelve positions in the *grand corps* for Polytechnique students, but they were rarely filled. Instead, the top students vied for admission to the navy's engineering fields. The *corps de génie maritime*, responsible for the design of warships, was very popular among the top graduates in each class. In 1929, for example, only two graduates chose commissions as *officiers de marine*, but fifteen young men, every one in the top fifth of his class, joined the *corps de génie maritime*, filling all the available slots.[18]

15. Jan Tanenbaum, *General Maurice Sarrail, 1856–1929: The French Army and Left-Wing Politics* (Chapel Hill, 1974), 20.
16. ONI, Naval Attaché Reports, Paris, Series of January 21, 1932, May 11, 1933, and October, 1937, E-5-a, 16682-A, August 14, 1936, E-5-a, 20257, all in NA.
17. Benoist, Report, May 16, 1928.
18. *Bulletin de SEP*, November 15, 1929, and 1920–39 *passim*.

From the mid-1920s, however, economic pressures on military officers began to change the *grand corps*. The interwar years saw constant and oftentimes massive inflation. In the ten-year period from 1914 to 1924, the French consumer price index quadrupled.[19] By 1929 the average cost of living had risen by a factor of 5.5 in Paris and 6.6 in the Midi and Brittany over the 1914 index. These figures continued to rise even further after 1930, when the delayed impact of the worldwide depression reached France.[20] Yet military salaries were never adjusted to maintain purchasing power.

On their fixed salaries, which changed only with promotion, the military professionals were among those Frenchmen least able to adjust to new postwar living conditions. Their plight appeared so miserable that a scholar called them the "professional proletariat" because of the substandard life-styles which many of them had to adopt. Several scholars have concluded that the purchasing power of the French officers of the 1920s had dropped to about one-third that of their forebears of equal rank serving in the 1780s. Though the problem was grave and had serious impact on officer retention in all the armed forces, little was done to improve the situation until 1939.[21]

The attrition problem among career naval officers became so alarming that the alumni society at École navale conducted a study of the economic predicament facing its members in hopes of bringing pressure for reform. Considering only the expenses of food, shelter, and clothing, the study revealed that officers could not make ends meet on their salaries alone. If the additional family ex-

---

19. Paul Marie de La Gorce, *La République et son armée* (Paris, 1963), 241.

20. Ministère du travail, *Bulletin de la statistique générale de la France*, IX (October-December, 1929), 62–63, XXI (October-December 1931), 42–43.

21. Robert F. Byrnes, *The Prologue to the Dreyfus Affair* (New Brunswick, N.J., 1950), 264, Vol. I of *Anti-Semitism in Modern France*, 1 vol. to date. Elsewhere, a French economist found that the purchasing power of the working class grew by 300 to 400 percent between 1820 and 1949 while that of the mid-level civil service and military officers (colonels or navy captains) remained the same over the entire period. Jean Fourastié, *Machinisme et bien-être: niveau de vie et gendre de vie en France de 1870 à nos jours* (Paris, 1962), 52–55, and Table X; Theodore Zeldin, *Ambition, Love, and Politics* (Oxford, 1973), 122–23, Vol. I of *France, 1848–1945*, 2 vols. See also Cost of Living Study, January, 1933, in Sér. FMF-SE, Cars. 33, 23, Archives de la marine. The first attempt to link salary hikes to the cost of living came in the winter of 1938–39.

pense of education was added to the budget, the average household deficit would reach twenty thousand francs annually.[22]

The study divided officers into two groups: those who had outside capital, in the form of inheritances or dowries, that enabled them to survive and those who did not. It concluded that officers in the latter category were either resigning from the navy, falling hopelessly into debt, or practicing the socially unacceptable vices of speculation or a part-time job. Only the lucky few with private incomes were able to enjoy a high standard of living. For the most part, officers became obsessed with thrift, pigeonholing their savings at home and generally avoiding all institutions of credit.[23]

Among the *officiers de marine*, the greatest impact of the economic squeeze was on officers from naval families, which traditionally had very little money. Such men were often forced to resign and seek employment elsewhere. Their sons, who in other times would have been destined for the École navale, began turning to other professions in which economic survival was less at issue. This exodus threatened to take from the *grand corps* its unique "benefits of certain traditions and the hereditary spirit of the sailors' life."[24] The pleas for reform were met, however, with new regressive tax laws, raising an ensign's taxes fourfold, doubling a lieutenant's, and adding 30 percent to a captain's portion. The new tax bill of 1938 struck hardest those who could least afford to pay at a time of substantial economic distress.[25]

The gaps at the École navale caused by reduced numbers of boys from traditional homes were filled by sons of the Parisian upper and middle bourgeoisie, who were already socially acceptable within the officer corps. Navale and Polytechnique became equally dependent on this new source of manpower after 1918. At both schools, boys from such homes made up one-third of each graduating class. Some were sons of officers who adopted Paris as their home after years of duty at the Ministry of Marine. Others cited in Table 1 were from families with historical ties to the capital city. One of

22. *Bulletin de AEN*, supplement to XXVII (January, 1927), 9–10. Figures vary according to rank and numbers of children.
23. Hélène de David-Beauregard, *Souvenirs de famille* (Toulon, 1970), 174.
24. *Bulletin de AEN*, supplement to XXVII (January, 1927), 10.
25. ONI, Naval Attaché Report, Paris, November 21, 1938, C-10-j, 15373-H, NA.

every three Parisians attending the École navale, or 11 percent of the entire student body, came from homes in the exclusive sixteenth *arrondissement*, thus contributing further to the elitist image already suggested by family ties and noticed by writers like Proust. Those coming from these prestigious households also were likely to have some independent financial means. Naval salaries alone could never support a family in this quarter of Paris after World War I.

As for those officers from Brittany, the Midi, or the west, they came from the rural or small-town settings common in these regions of France. While Navale attracted more boys from these three areas, Polytechnique drew more heavily on the industrial east and north. Navale also took in less than half the foreign and colonial students that Polytechnique attracted. The incomplete statistical evidence from Saint Cyr for the same period indicates the student body was even less urban than that of the other two schools.

At the École navale, one of nearly every five midshipmen came from Brittany, which had been the preferred recruiting ground for French naval officers since the seventeenth century.[26] The school itself, after all, was located in Brest. Although somewhat diminished, the Breton mystique survived within the navy, and those with historic names like Penfentenyo de Kervéreguin, Le Guen, and Rodellec de Portizic remained symbols of the *grand corps*. In the enlisted ranks, the proportion of Bretons remained well over 70 percent throughout the entire interwar period. In 1920 alone, 40 percent of all sailors came from the Finistère Department, while fewer than 7 percent came from noncoastal districts. The admirals considered this proportion of Breton sailors vital.[27] One senior officer explained how these sailors, stationed at the school, helped mold the midshipmen from diverse backgrounds into a homogeneous body. For twenty-two months, these sailors were the only people, apart from officers, whom the midshipmen saw while isolated aboard the school ship, *Borda*, in Brest harbor.[28]

26. Symcox, *French Sea Power*, 24.
27. David-Beauregard, Report, March 20, 1921.
28. Vice Admiral Georges Laurent, "Les Traditions de la marine militaire" (Speech presented before the Académie de la marine, June 18, 1937, in "Esprit de la marine" Collection, Bibliothèque de la marine).

Table 2.   **Geographic Origins of Students at
the *Grandes Écoles*, 1920–1939**

Region	École Navale	Polytechnique
Paris	34	39
Brittany	18	8
Midi	30	9
West, Southwest	10	11
North, Northeast, East	6	28
Other	2	5

SOURCES: *Bulletin de AEN* (1920–39); *Bulletin de SEP* (1920–39). Additional information is from the Archives de AEN, containing dossiers of private correspondence between the secretary general of the association and two hundred naval families after 1918.

NOTE: Figures represent the nearest whole percent in each category.

Concern over the diverse origins of the midshipmen stemmed from long-standing mistrust between officers from Brittany and those from the Midi. Those from the Mediterranean coast formed the second largest bloc in the Navy, perpetuating the traditions of the French galley fleet which Louis XIV had staffed with officers from the south.[29] The Bretons were perceived as characteristically stoic and independent men, but their peers from the Midi were thought of as a more emotional lot. By the twentieth century, the two traditions were blended together, producing an image of Breton toughness with a dash of that religious zeal of the old Mediterranean galley fleet.[30]

Yet, naval officers were encouraged to develop roots in Paris though they may have been reared in a port city. Specialization led to extended tours of duty on the Naval General Staff in Paris where power was highly centralized. As the gap between salary and the cost of living grew, mobile life-styles became a thing of the past. Duty in Paris was highly coveted, and on alternate tours at sea, officers frequently left their families behind instead of moving them to Toulon or Brest.[31]

29. Paul W. Bamford, *Fighting Ships and Prisons: The Mediterranean Galleys of France in the Age of Louis XIV* (Minneapolis, 1973), 95.
30. Braibant, *Un bourgeois*, 337.
31. *Ibid.*, 342 *et passim*; Bodin Interview.

The picture we have developed shows a *corps des officiers de marine* composed largely of the urban bourgeois and sons of provincial landowners. By comparison with other national elites, the naval officer corps had few wealthy members apart from those who married into money. After 1918 these officers, who had formerly been on an economic par with the elite of the sixteenth *arrondissement*, could claim only the special prestige of an elite. Still, the most significant characteristic of this group of men is the number who came from families tied for generations to the military. Young men with a naval tradition in their families were better represented at Navale than those without it. Of all those attending the school between the world wars, one of three was the son of a career officer in one of the armed forces, one of five was the son of a naval officer, and one of seven was the son of an École navale alumnus. Even in 1940, 25 percent of the Navale graduating class came from career military households.[32] And over half of all midshipmen came from either the Mediterranean or Breton coasts.

How different this was from the pecking order of the German navy in its heyday on the eve of World War I. From a social point of view, the German naval officers were "newly arrived" in French eyes. The absence of a German naval heritage and a shortage of aristocrats in the officer ranks made for poor social status at home and abroad. Of this the German naval officers were painfully aware, and they made extraordinary efforts to compensate by trying to create tradition overnight. It just might have been envy gone wild which led the German naval band to play *La Marche Lorraine* as the Kaiser hosted a reception for the officers of a French warship docked alongside his personal yacht in 1899. After the incident, the insulted French captain lectured his subordinates on the need to exercise self-restraint. Said one officer in a letter home, "These are painful duties which one must know how to perform, above all when they are in the interest of the country."[33]

Perhaps the German naval officers would have been more at

32. *Bulletin de AEN* (October, 1938), 17.
33. Admiral Jean Abrial to parents, July 8, 1899, in Admiral Jean Abrial Papers, Private Collection. On this aspect of the German navy, see Holger H. Herwig, *The German Naval Officer Corps: A Social and Political History, 1890–1918* (Oxford, 1973), Chaps. 3 and 4.

home with their counterparts in the French army, which was well on its way to becoming a meritocracy in most branches except for the cavalry. The French navy was another sort of service. Depending on old and established sources for recruits, the navy maintained its patrimonial lineage in the *grand corps*. Though these people could no longer depend on royal favor to protect their family interests as under the *ancien régime*, they remained an aristocracy of power if not of birth. A career in the navy's *grand corps* in particular still followed in a family from generation to generation. There was little interest in change.[34]

34. Braibant, *Un bourgeois*, 336.

CHAPTER 2
Aristocratic Dreams

Indications that contemporary French naval officers leaned more toward aristocratic than bourgeois life-styles comes as no great surprise. Long-standing ties between the navy and the nobility date from the mid-seventeenth century and were not overlooked by succeeding generations of officers. Originally, aristocrats were recruited for the more exclusive branch serving aboard the Mediterranean galleys. Only later did this class of officer find its way to the Atlantic fleet.[1] By the mid-eighteenth century, after the galleys were scrapped, the single, consolidated officer corps became the private domain of the nobility, far more exclusive than the army officer corps of the day, in which commissions were routinely purchased by the bourgeoisie. In the navy of the *ancien régime,* young men could not even aspire to a commission without patents of nobility in hand.[2]

Although the First Empire opened many doors to men with talent, the line officer corps maintained its traditional composition. The Bourbon and future Republican officer corps were symbolically joined under Louis Philippe's son, the Prince de Joinville, who spent his life in the navy, rising to the rank of admiral.

To understand the navy of the twentieth century, it is important to know how much the aristocratic tradition carried over into mod-

1. Paul W. Bamford, *Fighting Ships and Prisons: The Mediterranean Galleys of France in the Age of Louis XIV* (Minneapolis, 1973), 95; and Geoffrey Symcox, *The Crisis of French Sea Power, 1688–1697: From the 'Guerre d'Escadre' to the 'Guerre de Course'* (The Hague, 1974), 29.
2. Walter L. Dorn, *Competition for Empire, 1740–1763* (New York, 1940), 117; G. Lacour-Gayet, *La Marine militaire de la France sous le règne de Louis XIV* (Paris, 1905), 42.

ern times. The issue extends beyond the obvious matters of blood and marriage to include social relationships between naval families and professional associations between aristocratic and bourgeois officers.

The informal alliances between the navy and the aristocracy took many forms. Line officers in particular, regardless of social origins, went out of their way to show off their connections with the nobility. Vice Admiral Antoine Schwerer spoke with pride of his family's relationship with the Bourbons, dating from the Franco-Prussian War when the pretender served under the elder Schwerer, disguised as an American of French extraction. Admiral Jean Decoux also spoke often of the personal friendship he established on his own with the royal family during the 1920s. Much publicity was made of titled socialites who christened warships named for heroic ancestors who served in the navy. Even an American officer attending the École supérieure de guerre navale in Paris during the 1930s found that his ability to mix socially with aristocratic naval officers was possible only because he was the protégé of his own landlord who came from the same class.[3]

Marcel Proust first drew attention to the social position of modern French naval officers in his novel on *la belle époque*. He showed how much disdain these men expressed for the ordinary Frenchman in those years when growing awareness of the human condition was matched by the refusal of established families to open the doors to new faces. Although half Jewish himself in a highly anti-Semitic circle, Proust described how he, as the character Swann, was accepted into the inner circle of the Duchesse d'Orleans because he was mistaken for the nephew of a famous French admiral. These same friends also spoke contemptuously of several army generals rising from less exclusive homes who broke and now threatened to topple ancient social barriers.[4]

3. Admiral Antoine Schwerer, *Souvenirs de ma vie maritime, 1878–1914* (Paris, 1933), 166–69; Admiral Jean Decoux, *Adieu marine* (Paris, 1957), 263–64; Admiral Jean Abrial, Note, April 3, 1929, in Admiral Jean Abrial Papers, Private Collection; Office of Naval Intelligence, Naval Attaché Report, Paris, August 20, 1937, A-5-a, 15151, in National Archives, written by Major G. Dessez, U.S. Marine Corps, who attended the two-year course as an exchange officer.
4. Marcel Proust, *A la recherche du temps perdu* (3 vols.; Paris, 1947), I, 340–41

In fact, the *grand corps* lived a life not far from the one Proust depicted. The officers stood apart from the mainstream of French society. In the years after the First World War, this mood was set by men whose social standards had not been shaken by the trauma of battle and who continued to live in the vanishing fantasy world Proust so well described.

There is no doubt that the nobility had somewhat declined in strength within the *grand corps*. Among entry-level officers the proportion of nobility decreased by two-thirds over sixty years while a slower decrease at the senior ranks likely demonstrated the self-protective nature of any bureaucratic promotion system. If the proportion of admirals with titles declined more quickly than the proportion of captains, this is attributable to the greater political pressures involved in choosing men for flag rank. The decline of aristocratic presence in the *grand corps* went faster over the thirty-five years from 1905 to 1940 than during the first thirty-five years of the Third Republic, reflecting changes both in the promotion system and in the recruiting patterns for the exclusive École navale. Even so, those senior officers from aristocratic homes remained well out of proportion to the size of this class throughout France. Although the aristocracy represented less than 1 percent of the total French population in the 1930s, it constituted 17 percent of the senior naval officers in the *grand corps*.

Although the number of aristocrats in the officer corps diminished over time, the more traditional image was always best preserved at the top. Only the top few admirals were handpicked by the minister of marine with the advice and consent of other cabinet members. Direct involvement of civil authorities in the promotion of more junior officers varied with each cabinet and the public reputations of individual officers concerned. The practice became emotional when the Dreyfus case inflamed civil-military relations and when ministers of marine under Charles Dupuy, Pierre Waldeck-Rousseau, and Justin Combes focused on modernizing naval administration and separating naval customs from religious prac-

---

(*Le Côté de Guermantes II*), 457 (*Sodome et Gomorrhe II*), III, 643 (*Le Temps retrouvé*).

Table 3.   **Nobility in the *Grand Corps***

	1874	1906	1936
Admirals	37	33	14
Captains	19	18	18
Ensigns	21	14	10
Midshipmen	18	11	6

SOURCES: Mattei Dogan, "Les Officiers dans la carrière politique du Maréchal MacMahon au Général de Gaulle," *Revue française de sociologie*, II (1962), 92; ONI, Naval Attaché Report, Paris, August 14, 1936, E-5-A, 20257, NA; Ministère de la marine, *Annuaire de la marine* (Paris, 1874, 1906, 1936).
NOTE: Figures represent the nearest whole percent.

tices.[5] The rapid turnover of governments, however, precluded radical changes in the social composition of the officer corps and led only to a gradual reduction of aristocrats.

The proportion of genuine nobles in the naval officer corps is difficult to ascertain. Genealogists have filled volumes with ancient feuds between those who claim titles and those who, with equal vigor, dispute their right to bear those titles.[6] Here, a title's validity is of much less importance than the fact that a particular family chose to use it, thereby assuming the trappings common to true and false nobles alike. Both groups chose to set their families apart publicly from other Frenchmen by claims to a privileged birth long after the Bourbon monarchy and all chances for a restoration had faded away.

Claims to noble titles grew throughout France during the early twentieth century, with a noticeable increase after 1918. The Ministry of Justice sometimes authorized the addition of the particle *de* to family names. In other cases, arrangements could be made with town mayors for the addition of this *particule nobiliaire* at the time of birth or marriage. Other families were authorized to use the particle with further addition of a relative's name to preserve

5. President Gaston Monnerville, Interview, June 24, 1974; Mattéo Connet, Interview, July 10, 1974.
6. See, for example, D. Labarre de Raillicourt, *La Noblesse française* (Brussels, 1970); de Raillicourt, *Origines des faux titres portés à l'annuaire nobiliaire française* (Paris, 1971).

those that would otherwise have been lost because of wartime casu-
alties. One scholar concluded that by the armistice of 1918, there
were three times as many false titles in France as genuine ones.[7]
Even more titles appeared as gifts offered for services rendered
or as expressions of personal friendship by foreign powers such as
Monaco, San Marino, Spain, and the Vatican. As an example, Admiral Abrial's father was awarded his title by the Pope in 1905 when,
as a government inspector, he refused to implement the laws separating church and state institutions. He lost his comfortable job in
the process but gained the hereditary title of Comte de Romain.
Elevation to the peerage made him the social equal of his wife who
bore a Bourbon title first awarded her family by Charles X.[8]

The concern for titles was not isolated in the naval officer corps.
French society accorded the nobility great prestige. Both the bourgeoisie and the nobility of the period attached great importance to
the whole issue of rank and class status. In naval circles, however,
titles were considered particularly chic, and those who held them
stood a notch above officers without them. Because of the greater
relative importance of the title in naval circles than in the society
as a whole, officers underscored their aristocratic ties more within
than outside their professional milieu.[9]

At the senior ranks, the *grand corps* maintained a far more aristocratic image than any other branch of the naval officer corps. The
percentage of noble admirals shown in Table 4 is close to that given
in Table 3, though the data were extracted from different sources. In
other respects, the figures shown in Table 4 tend to undercut the
image of an officer corps made up largely of aristocratic naval families. It is clear that only a minority of admirals claimed titles.
Moreover, there is a disparity between the figure in this table,
which indicates that half the top officers came from naval families,
and that in Table 1, which showed only 29 percent of the midshipmen coming from these same houses. This reflects the tempo-

7. Philippe du Puy de Clinchamps, *La Noblesse* (Paris, 1968), 109–12; Theodore
Zeldin, *Ambition, Love, and Politics* (Oxford, 1973), 16, 403–406, Vol. I of *Modern
France, 1848–1945*, 2 vols.
8. Raymond Abrial, Genealogy, in Jean Abrial Papers.
9. Bernard Paquet, Interview, June 30, 1975; Commander Jacques Bodin, Interview, November 24, 1977.

Table 4.   **Flag Officers, 1919–1939**

	Nobility	Naval Family	Elitist Professional Ties	High Society Ties
Officiers de marine (École navale)	13	50	33	7
Génie maritime (École polytechnique)	0	50	60	8
Corps de santé (École de santé de la marine)	2	25	50	0
Commissariat (Écoles des arts et métiers)	0	20	60	0

SOURCES: Ministère de la marine, *Annuaire de la marine* (1919, 1925, 1930, 1935, 1939); Albert Dauzet, *Dictionnaire etymologique des noms de famille et prénoms de France* (Paris, 1951); *Bottin mondain* (Paris, 1919, 1925, 1930, 1935, 1939); *Tout-Paris: annuaire de la société parisienne* (Paris, 1919, 1925, 1930, 1935, 1939).

NOTES: Figures represent the nearest whole percent. They do not add up to 100 percent.

rary efforts to broaden the recruiting for the École navale as well as the advantages of naval family ties in getting to the top. As for family ties with other professional groups elsewhere in French society, the admirals of the *grand corps* had the strongest links with men holding prestigious honorary jobs, such as consulships and presidencies of clubs, and with members of the nobility who chose to be recognized for their titles rather than their occupations in the social registers of Paris. These same naval officers also came largely from the western part of France, where aristocratic ways survived in the relative isolation of Brittany and the Loire Valley.

Even the *petits corps* reflected the inbreeding caused by overdependence on a small number of families. A significant minority of the admirals of the *commissariat*, the navy's supply, administrative, and legal officers, came from naval homes. As a corps, they were one of the most exclusive, having numerous ties with prominent lawyers, politicians, and a few leading engineers. Their counterparts in the *corps de génie maritime*, the navy's shipbuilders, came as often from naval families as did the admirals of the *grand corps*. Consistent with the career preferences of students at the École polytechnique, those who chose *génie maritime* had more family connections with wealth than did their peers from the École navale. The families of the naval engineers received their money from banking, big business, and large engineering firms, and they frequently bore the title baron, common under the Second Empire when the French technocratic elite emerged in grand style. The *corps de génie maritime* was also the only branch of the naval officer corps to have noticeable ties with Jewish families. As for the medical officers, they had the strongest links with the intellectual community and the civil service.

It is clear from a comparison with the figures for midshipmen shown in Table 1 that elitist ties were strongest at the senior ranks. The naval officer corps had become a refuge for those who wished to avoid the egalitarian forces burgeoning elsewhere in French society. The *officiers de marine* often had little money, but the admirals of this corps nevertheless tried to present the image they felt was appropriate to their rank. Those stationed in Paris found a way to join the more exclusive and costly social clubs, gravitating toward Cercle de l'union, Union artistique, Cercle de l'union inter-allié, Aéro club, Auto club, and of course, le Yacht club. They paid their dues with private money from inheritances or with special funds for official entertainment. It is possible that clubs interested in having naval officers as members waived part of the fees, but this is only speculation.

These officers were far less likely to evidence any form' of conspicuous consumption. Very few of the admirals listed in *Tout-Paris*, the elitist social guide to the city, indicated that they owned an automobile, for example, even though these machines were marks of great prestige because of their cost and scarcity. Symbols of status were important to admirals from aristocratic and bourgeois homes alike, but because there was often little money to spare French naval officers expressed their elitism in other ways. Application of quantitative methods has helped to identify certain characteristics that naval families shared with the aristocracy and that set them apart from those whom they considered beneath them.[10] The entire way of life for these traditionalists were rooted

10. Guy Michelat and Jean Pierre Thomas, "Contribution à l'étude du recrutement des écoles d'officiers de la marine, 1945–1960," *Revue française de sociologie,*

in the *ancien régime* and based on values preserved in conservative Catholic homes. At its foundation were three special requirements: the head of the household must pursue the right profession; the nuclear family should be large; and the children should be educated privately. Preferred occupations among these families were the military, the law, and executive positions in the civil service or big business. The children in these families, averaging four or more per couple, attended private Catholic or military schools, thus avoiding the masses educated in the French public school system and especially the wage-earning classes. Traditionalist families felt the need to isolate themselves in order to preserve their special way of life.

Within the navy, there was a higher concentration of families living this way in the *grand corps* than in any of the other branches of the officer corps. Following the traditional interests of the aristocracy, these officers chose command of men over any interest in technology. Machinery and logistics they left to their more bourgeois peers in *génie maritime* and the *commissariat*. This trend is clear from the figures in Table 4, which show six times the proportion of nobility among admirals of the *grand corps* than in any other branch of the navy.

The Catholic church in France encouraged large families, forbidding abortions and most forms of contraception. Catholic traditionalists, such as the strongly religious Frenchmen organized under retired General Noël de Castelnau, also discouraged sex education. For a man, success in life was partly measured by the number of sons able to carry on the family name and profession.[11] Each successive generation learned these values not only in the home but in the Catholic schools that so many attended. Although comparatively small in number, these schools were very influential in perpetuating the social values held dear by the families patronizing them.

IX (April–June, 1968), 51–70. Their work was inspired by the research of Morris Janowitz, *The Professional Soldier: A Social and Political Portrait* (New York, 1960), and the ongoing work by Raoul Girardet on French military sociology. See also Zeldin, *Ambition, Love, and Politics*, 16.

11. Zeldin, *Ambition, Love, and Politics*, 299.

Table 5. **Marriages, Family, and Children in the
Naval Officer Corps, 1924–1940**

Aristocratic Marriages	
Bride only	19%
Groom only	14%
Both	6%

Naval Marriage Patterns	
Between a naval and another *grande école* family	20%
Between two naval families	16%
One family with two or more generations of naval ties	13%

Size of Naval Families	
Two or more children	46%
Three or more children	23%

SOURCE: Marriage and birth announcements printed in the *Bulletin de AEN* (1924–40).

The *Bulletin de l'Association amicale des anciens élèves de l'École navale* served as a kind of social register where marriages between alumni and daughters of fashionable homes were published. The announcements were not intended to be all-inclusive but to provide a consistent image of the officer corps. The semi-official magazine was entirely managed by École navale alumni and edited by a secretariat, elected by class presidents, under the direction of Admiral Pierre Le Bris. He and another officer had founded the society in 1920 to meet perceived threats to the separate identity of the line officer corps.[12] They felt the need to defend their elite status through the publication of statistics on their births, marriages, and education and, through this data, to set themselves apart from and above ordinary Frenchmen.

In the sixteen years between 1924 and 1940, the *Bulletin* an-

12. Lieutenant Raymond de Villaine to members, October 18, 1920, in Archives de l'Association amicale des anciens élèves de l'École navale, hereinafter cited as Archives de AEN.

nounced 201 marriages. In most cases, if titles were not involved on either side of a union, then other prestigiouş connections existed to be passed on to the offspring of the marriage. Half of the marriages announced perpetuated a naval heritage or joined two families with long ties to the *grandes écoles*. Daughters of naval officers appeared as frequently as did sons.[13]

Such naval marriages tended to produce more children than the national average of 1.8 children per couple. Among École navale alumni there were an average of four children per family.[14] The education of these children was a most important matter, for secondary schooling was one of the three most important criteria for gaining access to the *grand corps*. Moreover, education was also an essential ingredient in preserving the aristocratic way of life in France well into this century.[15] Among naval officers, preference was for education at a private Catholic school. To prepare adequately for the entrance examination at the École navale, as at most *grandes écoles*, special two-year post-*lycée* courses were necessary. Such courses, whether offered by private or public schools, were all quite expensive, and they shared Navale's elitist image. But if the money could be found, the payoff was great. Once a student entered a *grande école*, his chances of graduation were very high, and employment was guaranteed upon graduation. Neither of these was true at the regular universities. The fact that the alumni society at Navale regarded secondary school tuition as a large but unavoidable part of a naval officer's budget shows what was expected during the interwar years.[16]

Most of the secondary schools that offered the preparatory courses for the *grandes écoles*, and for Navale in particular, had similar reputations. Prospective midshipmen and their parents chose preparatory schools according to their success in getting boys admitted to the École navale as well as by their ideological reputa-

13. *Bulletin de AEN* (1924–40).
14. Ministère de l'économie nationale, *Statistique des familles en 1936* (Paris, 1945), xv. The largest families came from the rural areas, notably Brittany. "Rapport sur la 'situation matérielle' de l'officier de marine," *Bulletin de AEN*, XXVII (January, 1927), 4; letters to the secretary general, in Archives de AEN. The dossiers on two hundred member families for the interwar period provide sociological data.
15. Michelat and Thomas, "Recrutement des écoles d'officiers," 54.
16. "Situation matérielle," 10.

tions.[17] Boys from naval homes had little difficulty adapting themselves to the confessional practices at Catholic institutions. Lycées
like the Janson de Sailly and Stanislas tended to attract wealthy
bourgeois families concerned about social elegance. Saint Charles,
in north-central Brittany, attracted sons of poorer religious families, typical of the local population at that time. To the south, in the
Vendée, was the Prytané Militaire, better known as La Flèche for
the town in which it was located. Affiliated with the Ministry of
War, the school was unique among the preparatory schools for
the *grandes écoles*. It was open only to the sons of military professionals of all ranks and prepared young men for all four of the
military schools: Saint Cyr, École navale, the École de l'air, and
Polytechnique. The whole environment at La Flèche was military,
producing students who set themselves apart from other midshipmen once at the École navale. Graduates of La Flèche who went on
to Navale also came from rural backgrounds where religion was less
important than among the more socially prominent midshipmen.

The figures in Table 6 support the image of the École navale as
a haven for the Parisian bourgeoisie with a mixture of rural youth
from Brittany and the Midi. Saint Louis in Paris, one of the largest
and best known of the state-owned *lycées*, prepared one-third of all
young men going on to Navale during the 1930s. Three other public
lycées, in the naval ports of Brest, Toulon, and Lorient, together
prepared another third of the midshipmen of this period. These
three preparatory courses had poor academic reputations among
the naval officers but were convenient for the less wealthy residing
in these towns. La Flèche, dominated by boys intent on Saint Cyr,
prepared only one-tenth of those who went on to Navale. Finally,
among the important preparatory schools was Sainte Geneviève,
a small but very posh and influential Jesuit school in Versailles.
Though far smaller than Saint Louis and other schools, Sainte Geneviève continued an old tradition of close ties with the navy by providing one-fifth of all boys entering the École navale between 1932
and 1939.

17. Admiral Paul Auphan, Interviews, June 5, 1974, May 30, 1975; Admiral Réné
Godfroy, Interview, July 2, 1975; Commander Jacques Bodin, Interview, November
24, 1977; Commander André Sauvage, Interview, September 10, 1977; Sauvage to author, January 1, 1978, in my possession.

Table 6.   Academic Preparation for Grandes Écoles, 1932–1939

Preparatory School	École Navale	Polytechnique
Saint Louis	32	20
Sainte Geneviève *	21	9
La Flèche	10	3
Brest	10	—
Toulon	8	—
Stanislas *	5	5
Lorient	5	—
Saint Charles *	3	—
Janson de Sailly	2	7
Chaptal *	—	4
Louis le Grand	—	13
Other Parisian schools	0	12
Other provincial schools	4	26
Schools abroad	0	1

SOURCES: *Bulletin de AEN* (1932–40); *Bulletin de la Société amicale et de secours des anciens élèves de l'École polytechnique* (Paris, 1932–40).

NOTES: A dash indicates course not offered. Figures represent the nearest whole percent.

* Private school.

The Jesuit influence throughout the career military and civil service in France was substantial. During the Second Empire, the Society of Jesus was permitted to reestablish schools, and the order quickly opened three dozen *collèges* and *écoles préparatoires*. From their inception, these schools were geared toward educating the elite of the country. The latter institutions were designed specifically to prepare young men for the *grandes écoles*. As one scholar saw them, the schools served as "transmission belts," passing Jesuit-educated students to the top of French government and society. The elitist aims of these schools were achieved by careful screening of applicants, the less promising of whom were passed on to other Catholic schools. Among the Jesuit schools, Caousou in Toulouse specialized in preparing boys for Saint Cyr, while Sainte Geneviève prepared young men for all the *grandes écoles* but with a special emphasis on Navale. For several years when the course for Navale was moved to the Isle of Jersey, a substantial number remained at Sainte Geneviève because of its excellent scholastic reputation overall.[18]

Parents believed that two years of the highly structured routine at Sainte Geneviève prepared their sons well for a life of virtual isolation aboard the École navale's school ship, *Borda*, anchored in Brest harbor.[19] Boys aspiring to naval careers between the world wars had fathers who recalled their own years at Sainte Geneviève when the school was packed with those avoiding the newly secularized public *lycées*.

From a different perspective, we can examine the success of each school preparing young men for the École navale. Of all those who took the exam after two years' preparation, one-third from La Flèche, one-quarter each from Sainte Geneviève and the *lycée* in Brest, and one-sixth from Saint Louis were admitted to Navale. Other schools were less successful or prepared less than 5 percent of the midshipmen admitted during the 1930s.[20] Thus, the specialized military and Jesuit schools appear to have been best able to prepare a student for a career in the navy's *grand corps*. At the Brest *lycée*, boys taking the reputedly poor course there had help from the outside. The AEN hired a local priest who tutored officers' sons trying for Navale. Boys admitted to this program by the secretary general of the AEN came from homes with historical ties to the navy but without the means to pay for the better *cours préparatoires*.[21]

A very different profile of Polytechnique arises from these statistics. Saint Louis and Louis le Grand, traditional havens for the sons of the Parisian bourgeoisie, prepared one-third of all students attending Polytechnique, while virtually none came from the military school at La Flèche. One-fourth came from schools in the

18. John William Langdon, "Social Implications of Jesuit Education in France: The Schools of Vaugirard and Sainte Geneviève" (Ph.D. dissertation, Syracuse University, 1973), 7–8, 74, 151–52.

19. ONI, Naval Attaché Report, Paris, August 14, 1936, E-5-a, 20257, NA.

20. *Bulletin de AEN* (1932–40); *Bulletin de la Société amicale et de secours des anciens élèves de l'École polytechnique* (1932–40); hereinafter cited as the *Bulletin de SEP*.

21. Secretary general of the AEN to Madame Saint-Raymond, April 10, 1923, in Archives de AEN.

North, Northeast, and East, equal to the numbers of students with homes in those regions. The preference for Polytechnique among the wealthy is reflected in the figures for Stanislas and Janson de Sailly, both very expensive institutions. These two schools sent twice the proportion on to Polytechnique as to Navale. Finally, the very strict and religious life-style at Sainte Geneviève was far less attractive to those boys choosing engineering and business careers than to those looking for a life at sea. Less complete data on scholastic origins of boys at Navale and Polytechnique show that the same patterns existed as far back as 1920.[22]

Between the world wars, the *corps des officiers de marine*, which dominated the navy, came largely from the bourgeoisie.[23] However, these men perpetuated a life-style more akin to the *noblesse d'épée* among the seagoing officers and the *noblesse de robe* among those stationed ashore. Although only a minority claimed noble titles, the social conventions of that group pervaded the entire officer corps, going well beyond the point of mere snobbishness. Both believers and nonbelievers saw in the *grand corps* a twentieth-century order of knighthood whose romantic existence sustained timeless social and ideological values. Seeing themselves as an "international order, semi-religious, semi-military," they believed they were the heirs to the Knights of Malta whom Colbert frequently hired to staff Louis XIV's Mediterranean galley fleet.[24] On the eve of World War II, the officers still expressed the classic contempt for the bourgeoisie and its reliance on profit-making enterprises for survival. One such officer was singled out by his messmates as the greatest living symbol of the aristocratic naval officer, combining a noble heritage with attitudes that had all but vanished from other walks of life. "D'Estienne d'Orves was a superb figure of Christian chivalry; fearless, beyond moral reproach, straightforward, of the race who knew the Roman arenas, of those who fought

22. The *Bulletin de SEP* kept complete statistics on each class from 1927, while the *Bulletin de AEN* started only in 1922. Before that date, information published on the new classes entering Navale was incomplete.

23. Charles Braibant, *Un bourgeois sous trois républiques* (Paris, 1961), 342; Nerée [pseud.], "La Marine et le régime," Pt. 3, *Action française*, August 21, 1924, pp. 1–2.

24. Admiral Paul Auphan and Jacques Mordal, *The French Navy in World War II*, trans. A. C. J. Sabalot (Annapolis, 1959), 2–3; Braibant, *Un Bourgeois*, 337, 340.

in plumed helmets and white gloves or who died in the last square at Waterloo. Transcending goodness, generosity, faith and moral rectitude, he was also inflexible and humorless. His restlessness and Boy Scout zeal clashed with the dry and carefree spirit of [officers from different backgrounds]."[25]

The uniform adoption of aristocratic attitudes by both the bourgeois and the noble officers is reminiscent of what Franklin Ford saw in pre-Revolutionary French officialdom. Among the *officiers de marine*, those who belonged to the third estate clearly wished to rise to the second, even though the latter no longer had legal existence.[26] Nevertheless, there were definite social conventions for those who wished to rise.

Clear rules for assimilating the bourgeoisie into the French armed forces date from 1750. In that year, Louis XV signed into law a code for ennobling officers for good and faithful service. This was all part of a tradition whereby the French crown could grant power and status to cooperative followers when old ones proved too hostile. Custom also allowed the elevation of a deserving officer to the nobility based on his birth, marriage, and number of friends at court.[27] The idea that birth has something to do with an officer's abilities to command regiments and ships carried over into the present century. One man with very close ties to the *grand corps* between the world wars said its members viewed themselves as "the proprietors of the Navy by hereditary means."[28] Even as late as the 1930s, only a small percentage of Frenchmen had the chance to attend École navale and become a line officer. The navy was not yet a meritocracy.[29]

The aristocratic officer corps preserved itself by erecting barriers to changing social values and by continuing traditional patterns of recruitment. The *grand corps* successfully maintained a way of life

25. Roger Barberot, *A bras le coeur* (Paris, 1972), 33.
26. Franklin Ford, *Robe and Sword: The Regrouping of the French Aristocracy After Louis XIV* (Cambridge, Mass., 1953), 250–51; Zeldin, *Ambition, Love, and Politics*, 17.
27. Louis Tuetey, *Les Officiers sous l'ancien régime: nobles et roturiers* (2nd. ed.; Paris, 1980), 367–72, 339–52; Lacour-Gayet, *Marine militaire*, 605–72 *et passim*.
28. Braibant, *Un Bourgeois*, 336.
29. Mattei Dogan, "Les Officiers dans la carrière politique du Maréchal MacMahon au Général de Gaulle," *Revue française de sociologie*, II (1962), 91.

Portrait of a Naval Aristocrat: Admiral Descottes-Genon
The living image of a French naval aristocrat, Rear Admiral Descottes-Genon, with his romantic flair and his reputation as a successful sailor, was a model for young officers to emulate. *Office of Naval Intelligence Photo*

undisturbed by many of the developments in the rest of French society.

It is possible to draw a social profile of the French naval officer between the world wars. If we set aside the shore-based administrative officers, seen as the modern *noblesse de robe*, the remaining corps fall into three groups. First were the several engineering corps, drawn largely from Polytechnique, though a very few rose up from the ranks. Graduates of that school shared the image of its other alumni who went into big business and the civil service. Next were the specialized corps coming from the medical and law schools. These men served in the *corps de santé* and the *commissariat* and shared many social values with the *grand corps*. Of all those educated in the *grandes écoles* or equivalent institutions, substantial numbers came from naval families.

These men had about twice the number of children as an average French household of the era, and they often came from rural areas removed from the mainstream of French society. A growing minority came from Paris, but many of them were sons of rural-born officers who adopted the city while stationed there for many years. The *génie maritime* officers from Polytechnique had firmer roots in the capital city, and the titles borne by engineers were very likely to date from the Second Empire.

Unlike the engineers, whose wealth and naval ties dated from the 1860s, the line officers from Navale had many sixth- and seventh-generation officers, families like the de Trogoffs, Penfentenyo de Kervéreguins, and Niellys. It was such men whose personal fortunes were the smallest among all the officers but whose claims to noble lineage were the strongest. True or false, these titles were marks of distinction that could still attract young women from wealthy bourgeois homes seeking the perfect match with a young and dashing aristocrat. The officers did not forget their roots. They sent their children to the same schools they had attended, undeterred by any public pressure toward a democratization of public education. Pride in the family and its social position and in the prestige of a naval commission were still very strong in the *grand corps*. Even in 1939, members still preferred to remain outside the mainstream of French society, preserving a special way of life for their own children.

PART II
Family and Career Values

Si la France n'est pas et ne veut pas devenir une Puissance secondaire, elle le doit d'abord à ces foyers militaires où, depuis plusieurs générations parfois, les familles s'imposent les plus durs sacrifices pour faire de leurs fils des officiers. Je sais combien cet état d'esprit reste vivace dans le corps des officiers de marine que l'on a pu appeler "notre dernier ordre laïque."

Vice Admiral Georges Durand-Viel

CHAPTER 3
The French Naval Household
Mothers and Sons

A retired French naval officer explained how his father, Jean, had chosen the navy as a career in the days of the Dreyfus affair. Jean came from a large family that had no maritime tradition. But his father was a senior bureaucrat with the Ministry of Education near Toulouse, married to a woman from a well-known aristocratic family. The two decided very early what professions their children would adopt. Because of Jean's serious nature and love of the ocean, his parents decided he would be a perfect naval officer and informed him of their choice when he was still in primary school. From that day on, they groomed him for the École navale, and Jean accepted their decision with no questions asked. In French households of that day, mothers ruled, and therefore, it was Jean's mother who prepared her son for his life in the navy's elite *corps des officiers de marine.* Jean Abrial went on to become an admiral, distinguishing himself in the early days of World War II. In the way his career was selected for him, he was typical of his generation; the son acted out the will of his parents.[1]

As products of a common culture, the naval families shared many social traditions with Frenchmen in other walks of life. The strenuous demands of the navy upon the family, however, were unique and led naval personnel to develop day-to-day habits not found elsewhere. The result was a maritime subculture blossoming in the port cities and wherever else naval families congregated.

1. Commander Loïc Abrial, Interview, July 28, 1975. On the role of French women, see Theodore Zeldin, *Ambition, Love, and Politics* (Oxford, 1973), Chap. 13, esp., 361–62, Vol. I of *Modern France, 1848–1945,* 2 vols.

Wives and children, as well as the officers and sailors, were fully integrated into this peculiar way of life.

A career in the French naval officer corps meant a life in an all-male environment occasionally interrupted by short interludes with one's family. An officer's primary concern was for his physical and emotional survival in his demanding profession, and family affairs, by necessity, often took second place. Regulations gave officers sweeping powers to establish local work routines in the fleet and in naval installations ashore. Those serving aboard warships had the most arduous life of all. Even while the ship was in home port, a sixteen-hour workday with only Sundays free was common. Submarine crews had an easier life in port, for no one lived aboard the cramped vessels and work hours tended to be short. Most comfortable of all was staff duty ashore, though even there professional duties intruded deeply into the home. Staff officers performed many of their administrative tasks in the evening hours to the detriment of family life.[2] These exhausting work habits came as much from an overdose of the work ethic as they did from a chronic shortage of personnel.

When an officer went to sea or transferred to the colonies, his already reduced family life came to an abrupt end. Generally, the Ministry of Marine discouraged wives from following their husbands overseas.[3] Deployments away from France varied in duration but averaged two years. During this time husband and wife had only the remotest chance of getting together. They had nothing but a slow and unreliable postal system with which to keep each other abreast of family affairs. Commander Stanislas David-Beauregard's career was typical for French naval officers before World War II. Marrying a woman from his hometown of Toulon, he immediately departed for duty at sea. With the exception of short visits, he was

2. Hélène de David-Beauregard, Souvenirs de famille (Toulon, 1970), 126; Commander Stanislas de David-Beauregard, Personnel Report, March 20, 1921, pp. 32, 41, in Série Ca, Carton 34, Archives de la marine; Loïc Abrial Interview; Admiral René Godfroy, Interview, July 2, 1975; Commander Jacques Bodin, Interview, November 4, 1977.

3. Madame Jean Violette, Interview, July 18, 1975; Bodin Interview. Admirals Jean Abrial and Jean Decoux affirmed the all-male society that existed away from home. See the Admiral Jean Abrial Papers, Private Collection; Jean Decoux, Adieu marine (Paris, 1957).

away from Toulon for twelve years.[4] Living what one wife called the life of "perpetual separation," navy families experienced the very antithesis of the stable and static life patterns of most French homes.[5] Even officers of the Metropolitan Army took their families to their duty stations throughout Europe and to Algeria.[6] In the navy, however, lengthy periods of isolation at sea or in the colonies offered few of the normal distractions from professional life available to others. Consequently, naval officers tended to immerse themselves totally in their careers. For many, the navy was both job and hobby, and social life suffered from these compulsive work habits. Mixed gatherings were few and far between, even when officers were stationed at home—another significant contrast to the elaborate pattern of entertaining commonly followed by army families.

Duty in Paris provided the only major opportunity for naval officers to associate with Frenchmen from other walks of life. Poor salaries and high prices restricted significant civilian contacts to high ranking and independently wealthy officers who could afford expensive pastimes. Status-conscious members of Parisian high society apparently felt that the scarcity of admirals in the city enhanced the prestige of having them in one's circle of friends.[7] In the coastal towns, group activities largely gave way to life either in the ship's wardroom or at home. Long workdays with little time off helped reduce night life to an occasional reception at the Naval Prefecture or the annual ball sponsored by the Association amicale des anciens élèves de l'École navale for members only.[8]

When not involved with the family or the church, officers spent their limited off-duty hours with the same kinds of distractions

4. David-Beauregard, *Souvenirs*, Chap. 3 and p. 163.
5. *Ibid.*, 162; André Siegfried, "Approaches to an Understanding of Modern France," in Edward Mead Earle (ed.), *Modern France: Problems of the Third and Fourth Republics* (Princeton, 1951), 7–9; Zeldin, *Ambition, Love, and Politics*, 15–16.
6. Colonel Raymond Abrial, Interview, June 27, 1975; Madame Jean Violette Interview.
7. *Bottin mondain* (Paris, 1919, 1925, 1930, 1935, 1939); *Tout-Paris: annuaire de la société parisienne* (Paris, 1919, 1925, 1930, 1935, 1939). Comments on the prestige value of having admirals as friends come from interviews with Madame Roger Houzel (née Durand-Viel), June 24, 1974, July 10, 1975, and from limited access granted to the papers of her father, Admiral Georges Durand-Viel.
8. *Bulletin de l'Association amicale des anciens élèves de l'École navale* (Paris, 1920–39), hereinafter cited as *Bulletin de AEN*.

"Chicago" French Style
The old quarter of Toulon had been the favorite night spot for French
sailors and the home of many naval families for generations. Known
simply as Chicago, this part of town suffered heavy damage during World
War II. *National Archives Photo*

which other Frenchmen sought when they were away from home
and family. Gathering points of the interwar years included a wide
variety of brothels, each catering to different ranks. Most famous
were those in the "Chicago" district of Toulon, named·for its dark
alleys and racy entertainment reminiscent of what Frenchmen

thought the American namesake was like during Prohibition. To these brothels, restaurants, and bars near the waterfront went the fleet sailors and a few young officers in search of excitement. Most officers, however, turned instead to the more sedate private or semiprivate establishments farther from the harbor.[9] The culture and climate of the Mediterranean encouraged this form of night life more in Toulon than in any other naval port. Elsewhere, in more somber and isolated surroundings, officers spent more time at home.

At sea or in the colonies for as much as three-quarters of their careers, some naval officers openly took on surrogate wives who performed all the housekeeping functions of the real spouse left back in France.[10] The officer's concubine, often a native of the colony in which he served, was also an additional protection from an occasionally hostile population. Wives generally knew of their husbands' homes away from home, but closed their eyes to the practice. Many felt it to be the best way to keep the lonely men off the street and out of trouble. Some wives were even friendly acquaintances of the mistresses. Such tolerance of extramarital affairs, so frowned upon in many other Western cultures, was widespread in French culture in any case. It was not just the navy wife who believed that her husband would have "a few little adventures in the course of a long life" but that he would "always come back to his own" afterwards. And in some cases, both husband and wife engaged in the same practice quite openly. To the great surprise of foreign military associates bound by more rigid moral codes, French naval couples, like French couples generally, found it easy to segregate marriage from romantic love.[11]

9. Charles Bos, "L'Opium dans la marine," *La Vie maritime et fluviale*, May 10, 1913, pp. 193–94; Michel de Saint-Pierre, *La Mer à boire* (Paris, 1951), 87–88; Bernard Paquet, Interview, June 30, 1975; Commander André Sauvage, Interview, September 10, 1977; Zeldin, *Ambition, Love, and Politics*, Chap. 6; Decoux, *Adieu marine*, 43.

10. David-Beauregard, *Souvenirs*, 126; Jacques Baroche, *Sexualité de la femme mariée: la française et l'adultère* (Paris, 1973), 293–97; Baroche, *Comportement sexuel de l'homme marié en France* (Paris, 1969), 146, 176.

11. Sauvage Interview; Bodin Interview; Bernard Paquet, Interview, June 30, 1975; Commander Ivan Fleuriot de Langle provided extensive information on the French naval officers' ways of life in a course on the French navy which he taught at the U.S. Naval Academy from 1967 to 1970. See also Zeldin, *Ambition, Love, and Politics*, 305–307; Baroche, *Sexualité de la femme*, 293–97; Baroche, *Comporte-*

Although extramarital affairs were part of an acceptable code of conduct, divorce was strictly forbidden. Naval couples who chose to ignore this deeply felt conviction by seeking legal separation found themselves ostracized by their friends and fellow officers. In one case, a naval prefect, senior commander of the navy's shore facilities in the Toulon region, married a divorcée. As prefect, this admiral had numerous official social responsibilities, but when his subordinates learned of his wife's divorce, some of them refused to attend any social gatherings at which she was present. They were appalled at the idea of bringing their wives into the presence of a woman who had broken Church law and was presumed an excommunicate. This convention was so strong that even those wives who sought divorce after desertion by their husbands encountered the same barriers just when help was most needed.[12]

Setting up housekeeping with a native girl was only part of the fairly complete integration of naval officers into foreign cultures. Unlike other colonizers, Frenchmen eagerly assimilated local customs, language, and dress; they blended in easily, and experienced little racial conflict except in North Africa. Moreover, the mix of naval officers and indigenous peoples was all the more possible because the navy did not maintain walled garrisons for its personnel. A mixture of French officers and native sailors made up the colonial patrol squadrons. One of the better-known naval officers who spent his career immersed in colonial life was Victor Ségalen. A novelist, he wrote about his experiences in the Pacific islands and Indochina, where he spent many years as a naval surgeon, writer, and amateur archeologist. Like many others in the navy who fell in love with the exotic life of primitive lands, he never fully adjusted to his native France and did all he could to remain abroad.[13]

Another well-publicized example of a French officer's life away

---

ment sexuel de l'homme, 176; Warren Tute, The Deadly Stroke (New York, 1973), 65; Sanche de Gramont, The French: Portrait of a People (New York, 1969), 388.

12. Loïc Abrial Interview; Paquet Interview; David-Beauregard, Souvenirs, 170; Gautier and Varneg dossiers, in Archives de AEN.

13. Admiral Hector Violette Papers and Photographs, Private Collection; Madame Jean Violette Interview; Loïc Abrial Interview; Commander Georges Débat, Interview, June 22, 1976; Paquet Interview. On Victor Ségalen, see his novels plus Paul Roux, Correspondance Saint-Pol–Roux, Victor Ségalen (Limoges, 1975); "Revival for Adventuring Artist," International Herald-Tribune, June 10, 1975, p. 16.

from home set a standard for others to follow. Count Eugène de Jon-quières, who preferred to use his title rather than his official rank of vice admiral, spent several years in Indochina and Tahiti. He later went to Berlin in 1905 as naval attaché where his lineage and pro-fessional reputation made him a natural friend of the kaiser. Jon-quières' wife chose to remain at home in Toulon, as many naval wives did, preferring familiar surroundings and her own circle of friends to life in a foreign capital. Her choice did not handicap her husband, although social responsibilities were paramount in the German court. It was common knowledge in French and German circles that the admiral relieved his solitude with French chorus girls from traveling musical shows. When the presence of his wife was essential at special social functions, Jonquières arranged for her to visit Berlin only long enough to make her appearance. As for the chorus girls, the admiral flaunted them in public for all, even the kaiser, to see.[14]

Behavior like this was neither a public embarrassment nor an impediment to Jonquières' incredible career. French naval officers looked upon themselves as members of a class that could manage these affairs as a normal pastime with no adverse effect on their professional lives. It was an attitude that was widespread through-out other European military services in the years before World War I. But after that time French naval officers continued the same practices in public when greater discretion prevailed elsewhere. Years after his death, Jonquières remained the model officer others wished to emulate.[15]

Many stationed in Indochina acquired the local opium habit, which some brought back to France. In the home ports, notably Toulon, opium dens, or *fumeries*, sprang up in private homes and brothels where officers gathered in the familiar oriental decor they had come to prefer. The drug habit caused only minor scandal in French naval circles. Officers were quite open in using drugs before

14. Decoux, *Adieu marine*, 88–89.

15. *Ibid.*; Bodin Interview. Proust described how admirals and generals were treated differently by members of the pretentious and decadent high society of Paris. See Marcel Proust, *A la recherche du temps perdu* (3 vols.; Paris, 1947), I, 340–41 (*Le Côté de Guermantes II*), 457 (*Sodome et Gomorrhe II*), III, 643 (*Le Temps retrouvé*).

1914, as they were in many habits acquired in the colonies. But their wives tended to frown on the drug habit, for they saw it as a black mark on the family's reputation. The Ministry of Marine did little to penalize the offenders and avoided witch hunts of suspected drug abusers.[16]

Because these men were committed to careers that kept them away from home so much, the raising of their families was left to their spouses. At first, young couples found the adjustment to separation fairly difficult, but most adapted well to the demands of living apart. The family had to survive without the father as a reliable influence for stability. At the same time, the church placed great pressure on these men and women to raise large families in spite of social and economic hardships. This placed additional burdens on the wives who bore the dual responsibilities of mother and father in families twice the average size for France.[17] Although French mothers in all walks of life enjoyed the role of family matriarch, those married to naval officers played it to the fullest extent.

Like Madame Jonquières, most wives preferred to settle in one place where children could be reared in stable surroundings. Official policy, which was opposed to French families in the colonies, encouraged this preference for hometown life.[18] Only a few spouses had the wanderlust of their seafaring husbands. Those who did, adapted quite well to native customs in good naval fashion.[19] But very few wives could hope to set up the traditionally well-organized French household in the sparsely developed empire. In such places as Dakar and Saigon, one had to adapt to local custom.

Although the nuclear family was the norm in the French navy, ties remained strong among the many relatives living in the same town. Economic austerity after 1918 made it rare for three generations to share the same roof. Even when an officer's parents moved into his home, the young wife retained the unchallenged role of

16. Office of Naval Intelligence, Naval Attaché Reports, Paris, May 21, 1908, E-5-c, 8421, E-5-b, 692A, in Record Group 38, Series 98, National Archives; Paquet Interview.

17. Ministère de l'économie nationale, Statistiques des familles en 1936 (Paris, 1945), xv; "Rapport sur la 'situation matérielle' de l'officier de la marine," Bulletin de AEN, XXVII (January, 1927), 4.

18. Henry Bordeaux, Le Mariage: hier et aujourd'hui (Paris, 1921), Chap. 8.

19. Madame Jean Violette Interview; Admiral Hector Violette Papers.

Admiral and Madame Hector Violette in Tunis
Like many French naval officers, Admiral Violette adapted well to life
in the colonies. His wife's partiality to overseas travel and adventure,
however, was a rare quality for a naval wife. *Violette Family Photo*

household matriarch.[20] Cut off from many other pursuits outside
the home, these naval wives cultivated this role well. Total involvement in domestic affairs helped them accept the lengthy separa-

20. Archives de AEN. From a sample of two hundred families, 1919–40, only 1
percent had more than two generations living under a single roof.

tions from their husbands. Many of these women believed themselves to be a caste apart from other French women and passed on the matriarchal traditions to their own daughters. Only a few naval wives broke away from these customs by developing interests outside the home. Involvement in politics was almost unheard of. This was all part of the limitation which French law and naval custom placed upon women interested in careers. The horizons of the naval wife were normally limited to raising her children and assisting her husband in his career.[21]

Of all their domestic tasks, none was more important to these women than bearing and rearing children, a priority that accorded well with traditional Catholic beliefs and with official policy. After 1918 the French government began a public relations campaign to stem the declining birth rate, and the navy played its part by offering decorations to prolific wives of servicemen. Madame Bernard Paquet received recognition after giving birth to her sixteenth child.[22]

Few couples made any connection between postwar economic constraints and the need to reduce the number of offspring. Instead, many thought it better to raise several children in poverty than few in greater comfort. Birth control methods beyond abstention and the use of surrogate partners attracted little interest and were, in any case, forbidden by the church. Wives expected husbands to assume any burden for family planning. When financial difficulties arose, women focused on how to spread scarce assets even thinner. The idea of sacrifice was paramount, and most women were unlikely to insist on many comforts and pleasures. The most significant variable expense was the cost of education, for only through an expensive preparatory school could a boy gain entrance to the

21. Admiral Hector Violette Papers; Admiral Georges Durand-Viel Papers. Of the leading naval figures of the interwar years, I found only three who appear to have treated their wives as intellectual and social equals: Hector Violette, Henri Salaün, and Louis Le D'O. My list may not be all inclusive, but it indicates the general tendency of Frenchmen of that era to treat their spouses as inferior in many areas. The same habit was analyzed by Zeldin, *Amibition, Love, and Politics*, Chaps. 6, 8, 13; David-Beauregard, *Souvenirs*, 36.

22. Paquet Interview; Nerée [pseud.], "La Marine et le régime," Pt. 2, *Action française*, August 19, 1924, pp. 1–2; *Bulletin de AEN* (1924–40). See also de Gramont, *The French*, 404–10.

École navale. Mothers focused their dreams on their sons; it was the sons who were expected to carry on the family name and the dynastic tradition of service in the navy. Their success was the fundamental badge of family success, and the women pursued it as though an end of traditional affiliation with the navy somehow meant ruin for the lineage.

Daughters, however, required little formal education.[23] They were expected to marry and raise naval families of their own, and their mothers tried to find them suitable husbands. Madame Lesqueru, wife of an officer and daughter of a Breton admiral, had eight sons and three daughters. She married off two of her girls to military officers, and a third eventually became a nun. Madame Rouvier, daughter of a naval officer and wife of a naval officer, married her only daughter to yet another naval officer after educating her entirely at home. She did this to save money for her son's schooling in hopes that his costly preparation would lead to an appointment to the École navale. Another navy wife, Madame Savidan of Nantes, wrote in despair to the secretary general of the École navale alumni society, asking him to "open horizons for her" in the case of a troublesome daughter. The girl eventually became a nun in the order of Saint Vincent de Paul after some maternal prodding. In Flanders, Madame Wackernie persuaded three of her five daughters to take the veil.[24]

The daughters in naval households had few alternatives. Most, like their mothers before them, dreamed of marrying an officer and raising a large family. If they found no suitable groom in the navy or some other elite circle, these girls sought refuge and security in a convent as was the custom in many Catholic homes of the era. Many women made this choice after 1918 when money and eligible bachelors were both scarce. The ideas of a professional life or of serious academic interests still were not reasonable goals for these women.

If a girl could find the right husband, she would be assured a life

23. Odon de Comminges, Lesqueru, Nicolas, Louel de Keraugue, Rouvier, and Savidan family dossiers, all in Archives de AEN.

24. Lesqueru, Rouvier, and Wackernie family dossiers; Madame Savidan to Secretary General, January 7, 1936, all *ibid.*

in familiar surroundings. Mothers, therefore, kept a close watch on the young graduates of the École navale and even of Saint Cyr in the hope of securing a good name and perhaps some money to go along with it. The proper match required an elegant wedding in which the two families would be joined in fashionable dignity preferably in the prestigious military setting of the chapel at the Invalides or the École militaire in Paris. Naval families, though clearly disturbed that these two baroque shrines belonged to the army, put aside interservice rivalries for the nuptial celebration. For these solemn wedding masses, the two chapels were considered neutral territory, appropriate for navy and army weddings alike.[25]

Normally, a priest in the family or one affiliated with the navy celebrated the marriage. At Jean Abrial's wedding, his cousin the Abbé Ardant presided and gave a sermon on the popular subject of "God, Country, and Family, the three greatest loves which should fill the heart of a Christian and a sailor."[26] At the wedding and throughout the naval couple's life, religion bound family and profession together.

Weddings were also often the highlights of the social season. The domestic and even the international press offered wide coverage of important unions. One such event was the marriage of Ensign Paul Nivet to Andrée Doumer, granddaughter of Senator Paul Doumer, soon to become president of France. The leading personalities of both the navy and the army, many of whom shunned other public gatherings, turned out for the wedding and reception in full regalia.

Sons were also expected to marry well, but parents were most concerned that they choose the proper career. Again, mothers provided the major influence through firm guidance of their sons. The acceptable range of occupations was quite narrow; if a son could not enter the navy, the family preferred that he join the civil service. Naval families considered government positions prestigious investments. Salaries were modest but steady, and pensions were guaranteed between the world wars when few other occupations

25. Loïc Abrial Interview; Commandant Jacques Vernet, Interview, May 2, 1975.
26. Admiral Jean Abrial, note on his second marriage of February 7, 1907, in Jean Abrial Papers. See also *Bulletin de AEN*, marriage announcements, 1920–1940, *passim*.

Mariage à la Mode Navale
Ensign Paul Nivet married Andrée Doumer in a traditional naval ceremony.
The leaders of the military and naval officer corps including General Henri
Gouraud and Admiral Georges Robert turned out for the reception.
National Archives Photo

provided this economic security.[27] The strongest family influence was exerted on boys in the traditionally large naval families where many children needed to find employment. In these cases, mothers' persuasive skills were rigorously tested. All the critical talents of balancing resources, evaluating child potential early, and gathering support at just the right moment came into play. Sons and mothers from naval households remained consistent in their choices of careers throughout the 1920s and 1930s.

Among boys from naval homes interested in military service, the first choice was the École navale. If they failed to gain entrance there, they turned next to a career in the navy's *corps de santé*. Although the medical corps was out of the mainstream of command, admission meant a free education at the Ministry of Marine's excellent École de santé in Bordeaux and a marketable skill in civilian life after retirement. Moreover, the historical affiliation of leading families with this corps created a naturally hospitable atmosphere for sons and brothers of *officiers de marine*.[28] In this instance, the normal pecking order between the *grand corps* and the various *petits corps* did not hold true.

If a boy failed entrance to these two corps he was likely to try for the École polytechnique with hopes of serving in the navy's *corps de génie maritime*. This choice offered the same benefits as the medical corps with the additional incentives of very little sea duty and few family dislocations once settled near a shipyard. Life in this branch of the navy was so comfortable that Polytechnique alumni looked on it as civilian rather than true military employment.[29] Some naval families had reservations about this school because of its reputation as a haven for agnostics and wealthy Jews in addition to its affiliation with the army. But such qualms usually subsided even in the most traditional naval homes when a son received his admission notice. The reputation of the *corps de génie*

27. Comments by naval officers and their wives confirmed the findings of Zeldin, *Ambition, Love, and Politics*, 114.
28. Admiral and Madame P. Bonnel, Interview, June 4, 1974; Admiral Louis de La Monneraye, Interview, July 23, 1975; Paquet Interview; Boidron, Carion, Piquet, Poitevin, and Truc family dossiers, all in Archives de AEN.
29. *Bulletin de la Société amicale et de secours des anciens élèves de l'École polytechnique*, IX (November 15, 1929), 29–33.

maritime dated back many years; it was renowned among the world's shipbuilders and naval architects. The quality of French warships designed and built by these men was always superb. This followed the French tradition of excellence in specialized industries where quality received greater emphasis than quantity.[30] In addition, graduates of Polytechnique could choose to enter the navy's *grand corps* instead of a more technical field such as *génie maritime*. Those boys who could not get into any of the prestigious branches, including the *commissariat*, would try for Saint Cyr, the clergy, the civil service, or perhaps a career in law.[31]

Madame Saint-Raymond, a naval widow from Toulouse, raised her six sons by working part-time for various charities. Her first and fourth boys attended Sainte Geneviève in hopes of life in the navy. When they failed to score high enough on the École navale exams, they successfully competed for positions at Saint Cyr followed by army careers. Her second son became a priest, and her third was admitted to École navale on his second try with some good recommendations from friends in the *grand corps*. Her fifth son, whom Madame Saint-Raymond felt had less potential than his brothers, remained at home and attended a local vocational school. Two of Jean Abrial's sons also tried for the École navale. Raymond scored too low on his mathematics exam for consideration but did well on the easier Saint Cyr tests. He was admitted and pursued a career in the army, while his two younger brothers chose the prefectoral corps and the navy. In Lyon, Madame Foillard, whose father and husband died in military service, had four boys to rear on her own. The eldest went to École navale and later married the daughter of a navy captain. Her second attended the military preparatory school, La Flèche, also in hopes of admission to Navale. Like Raymond Abrial, he failed his admission examination but passed the one for Saint Cyr, leading to a life in the army. Inadequate funds for

30. J. H. Clapham, *The Economic Development of France and Germany, 1815–1914* (4th ed.; Cambridge, 1968), 232–33; W. O. Henderson, *The Industrial Revolution in Europe: Germany, France, Russia, 1815–1914* (Chicago, 1961), 177, 182–83; Tom Kemp, *Industrialization in Nineteenth Century Europe* (Edinburgh, 1969), 74–75; Charles P. Kindleberger, *Economic Growth in France and Britain, 1851–1950* (Cambridge, Mass., 1964), 308–309.

31. Evidence gathered from the two hundred family member dossiers available at the Archives de AEN.

reeducation helped guide him in his choice. Madame Foillard's third son became a monk, and her youngest chose the law.[32]

Madame Requin of Saint Raphael in the Midi carefully steered her three sons in the same traditional directions. Her eldest chose the École centrale after he was turned down by the École navale. She had difficulty accepting his failure to get into the navy, writing "As for my three sons, I wished to make sailors of them all as their father wished so much." In Paris, Madame Quesnel had the same reaction to her son's failure to pass the Navale exam when he missed a minor question on history during his final oral interview. The boy was later admitted to Polytechnique, to his mother's dismay.[33]

Madame Lesqueru sent her three eldest sons to École navale and Saint Cyr. Madame Savidan recovered from her "maternal torments" only after her three sons completed Saint Cyr, got their army commissions, and married girls she approved of. Madame Nicolas expressed the same relief in thanking several naval officers for their help in getting her son into the army's second preparatory school, Saint Maxient. All three of her daughters upheld family tradition by marrying young naval officers.[34]

Mothers and sons made determined efforts to continue traditions of family service in the military. Madame Rouvier went through great personal anguish trying to get her only son into the École navale. The boy was the family's only chance to maintain the link between the Rouvier family and the *grand corps*. She explained her worries, as did so many naval wives, in a letter to the secretary general of the Association amicale des anciens élèves de l'École navale. "He adores the Navy," she wrote. "He represents the seventh generation of sailors in the family. Surely, you can imagine how happy I would be to see him enter the profession of his father, following in the footsteps of his ancestors." Unfortunately for

---

32. Saint-Raymond and Foillard family dossiers, both *ibid.*; Raymond Abrial Interview; Loïc Abrial Interview.

33. Madame Requin to Secretary General, February 22, 1929, in Requin family dossier, Madame Quesnel to Secretary General, May 17, 1934, in Quesnel family dossier, both in Archives de AEN.

34. Lesqueru and Nicolas family dossiers, Madame Savidan to Secretary General, January 7, 1936, all *ibid.*

mother and son, the boy failed to gain admission to Navale, but he stubbornly refused to abandon hope for a life at sea. He decided to enlist in the merchant marine, in the belief that eventually a naval commission would follow. "You can easily imagine how crushed I was to see him enter the Navy by other means than the grand entrance," she said.[35]

Madame Truc's first son had much the same disappointment. He failed to gain admission not only to École navale but to Saint Cyr and twice to the navy's École de santé. He finally settled for the life of a civilian doctor in Toulon, treating naval dependents.[36]

Boys learned from childhood which careers they should seek. Loïc Abrial's parents singled him out as the son best suited for a naval career, and he was told flatly that he "would be a sailor." He never doubted this parental decision and went on to fulfill his family's expectations. His father's devotion to the navy wavered briefly at the time of his first wife's death. After toying with the idea of a monastic life, however, he decided to stay in the navy, eventually rising to the rank of admiral in 1939.[37]

Unlike their mothers, young boys left behind few written documents about their efforts to gain access to the École navale or other military schools. However, the available testimony confirms that young Loïc Abrial's experiences were typical of sons of naval officers in the early 1920s. The importance of family tradition, the romantic attraction of the sea and the colonies, and the lack of interest in alternatives all played their part as so many boys followed their fathers into the French navy. When a boy failed the École navale exam, he and his mother shared the same dismay as childhood dreams were shattered in a single blow.

These mothers came from a very select element of French society. One in five came from an aristocratic family, while one in seven grew up in a naval home and later married into another one.[38] Their responsibilities to the family included not only the living but

35. Madame Rouvier to Secretary General, June 19, December 9, 1931, both in Rouvier family dossier, ibid.
36. Truc family dossier, ibid.
37. Loïc Abrial Interview; Jean Abrial, note, February 7, 1907, in Jean Abrial Papers; Raymond Abrial Interview.
38. See Chapter 1, Table 2.

the dead and future generations as well. Funerals received the same social attention as did weddings. Observers focused on the "beauty" of these last rites, and years later, career highlights of retired officers included the most romantic and vivid recollections of naval funerals.[39] Wives and daughters assumed lifetime vigils against real or imagined detractors of a deceased officer's reputation.

The family home, often an ancient dwelling passed down from generation to generation, stood as a living memorial to past and present family members in the navy. Over the years, the salons became small museums, displaying relics from distant voyages, pieces of ancient uniforms and swords, evidence of that special bond between the family and the fleet. Portraits of naval officers dating back to the *ancien régime* hung prominently around the rooms. Everywhere, small mementos including elephant tusks, arts and crafts of various colonies, and pictures of colonial settings lay interspersed with royal commissions signed by the Bourbon kings. Each item had a complete history to go with it, recounted in great detail by women of the family charged with preserving the family treasures. These women shared the role of the official naval museums in Paris and several port cities; they emphasized the role of the individual hero and the importance of the navy as an exporter of French civilization.[40]

Naval wives also served as the family archivists, as did most French wives of the interwar period. They carefully preserved every scrap of paper, from important letters to social invitations and administrative correspondence. For many women, each document bore equal value not because of content but because each was evidence of the family's achievements and reputation, which had to be

39. Paquet Interview; La Monneraye Interview; Admiral Paul Auphan, Interview, May 30, 1975. Death announcements of naval officers in the *Bulletin de AEN*, 1924–40, reflected the same tone.
40. This is a collective impression based on visits to the homes of Admiral Paul Auphan, Admiral Paul Ortoli, Admiral René Godfroy, Admiral Louis de La Monneraye, Admiral Hector Violette, Admiral Jean Abrial, Admiral M. J. Adam, Commander Loïc Abrial, Madame Roger Houzel, Captain Eynaud de Fey, Commander Georges Débat, Commander Jacques Bodin, and Commander Ivan Fleuriot de Langle. Additional impressions were gained from photographs of other naval homes and from the correspondence of yet other families in the Archives de AEN. The principal naval museums in France are located in Paris and Toulon, with smaller collections in Brest, Lorient, Rochefort, and other French port cities.

carefully protected from detractors. Saving the papers did not automatically mean that interested parties outside the family had access to them. On the contrary, documents customarily passed from generation to generation without ever being shown to strangers. Sometimes widows or the officers themselves burned their private papers, fearing that the contents might tarnish the family image or perhaps contradict a legend passed down by word of mouth for generations.

Although common throughout French society, these protective habits were far more effective in those closed professions dominated by small tightly knit elites.[41] Under such circumstances, a few individuals working together could censor a large amount of information about their group. They could and did destroy evidence in the sincere belief that they were defending the reputations of the family and the navy alike. In the end, however, the desire to create a mantle of protection only blurred that fine line separating official from private matters. When Madame Lambert said that "the Navy was one big happy family," she demonstrated how easily she confused one with the other.[42]

Naval wives, though they dominated their households and raised their children single-handedly, were not known for their skill in managing the family budget. They were members of an elite, accustomed to a more ample prewar life-style, and many of them found it difficult to adapt to the changes that occurred in France after 1918. As inflation reduced their purchasing power, some tried in vain to preserve the good life they had known in the past and squandered the family's savings in the process.[43]

Financial mismanagement brought many naval households to the brink of disaster and beyond, but many had difficulty overcoming the long-standing French distrust of banks and other credit institutions. Wives preferred to squirrel away their money at home as

41. John M. S. Allison, *Lamoignon de Malesherbes: Defender and Reformer of the French Monarchy, 1721–1794* (New Haven, 1938), v–vi. The special handling of family papers was explained in Auphan Interviews, June 5, 1974, May 30, 1975, Godfroy Interview; Houzel Interviews.

42. Madame Lambert to Secretary General, September 1, 1934, in Lambert family dossier, Archives de AEN.

43. Adam de Villiers, Aguier, Bahezre, Bayle, Blondeau, Caillaud, Jehle, Montgolfier, Thomas, Ollivier family dossiers, all *ibid.*

their own mothers had done. One rare naval widow cast aside her misgivings and tried her hand as manager of a small bank. In the end she lost everything, apparently a victim of her own ignorance.[44] Ideas about money and investments remained strongly influenced by traditional Catholic teaching against money lending and usury.[45] Women caught in the vicious circle of insufficient revenue, rampant inflation, and dissipated savings usually turned in desperation to charity. Various naval charities could provide temporary aid, and the government frequently granted licenses for state-owned tobacco shops, a traditional French method of helping the destitute.

If the navy wished to preserve the composition of the officer corps after 1918 as it had been before the war, it needed the support of the officers' wives. The admirals understood and capitalized upon the vital role these women played in supporting their husbands and in encouraging their sons to join up. With the evolution of the Association amicale des anciens élèves de l'École navale as the unofficial guardian of traditions within the *grand corps*, its secretary general became the confidant of many wives and widows. The ties between this active-duty naval officer and these women became the fundamental link between the navy and the traditional homes that provided the kinds of boys sought by the École navale. Mothers and officers both preferred to see a closed system of selection for the *grand corps* and, to a lesser degree, for the *petits corps* as well. Although admission to the *grandes écoles* was possible only through competitive testing, mothers still found naval support effective when trying to get a son admitted to Navale.[46] Madame O'Byrne, a naval widow who was carefully steering her son toward the navy, appealed to the secretary general of the AEN for help in getting him admitted. "I am told," she wrote, "that the new students are designated by the Minister and a recommendation is very helpful. Well, naturally, I do not know anyone at the Ministry. Do you think it would be possible to present my request to the Minister of Marine? I very much wish that he be admitted because a dis-

44. Chaix family dossier, *ibid.*
45. David-Beauregard, *Souvenirs*, 174.
46. Lambert, Orza, Mauger, Nicolas, Ollivier, Peltier, des Portes, Saint-Raymond, Santelli, Souquet, Théroine, Tissot, Varneg family dossiers, all in Archives de AEN.

ciplined environment, tougher than that of a seminary, would be helpful and would sustain his strength of character."[47]

In other cases, the mother looked to the secretary general almost as a confessor, privy to the innermost worries of these proud but often destitute families. The secretary general then became a career planner, a shoulder for lonely women to cry on, and a source of financial aid to families in need. This was all in addition to the official duties of directing an alumni society for a prestigious *grande école*. Mothers from well-known naval families who pleaded for help with their sons appeared to the secretary general "all the more interesting from the historical point of view."[48]

Most officers believed that boys raised in naval homes were better suited for careers in the officer corps than those from other social or professional backgrounds. It was generally believed that such young men had a "stronger sense of command" than other boys, because they were raised in the proper environment. Children from officers' families were perceived as "an elite by birth" and were given more leeway as midshipmen. When they stepped out of line, as Roger Barberot did when he refused his commission as an ensign on graduation from Navale, high-ranking officers tended to interpret their misconduct as a display of natural courage, so sure were they that these boys would return to the fold. The sons of a civilian, on the other hand, especially those from the working class, always remained suspect.[49]

The navy sought out boys who had been raised, like Corneille's Cid, to be *gens du coeur*. The children of officers had learned to thrive on hardships and an unstable home life different from that of a normal French household. Moreover, since so little of the public had any interest in or knowledge of maritime affairs, naval officers believed that a self-regenerative system best suited the need for stable leadership in the fleet. Isolated for centuries, the naval officer corps constituted a group apart from the private sector. Its mem-

47. Madame O'Byrne to Secretary General, June 24, 1926, in O'Byrne family dossier, *ibid.*
48. Admiral Georges Durand-Viel to AEN, March 16, 1939; in Gibon family dossier, *ibid.*
49. Loïc Abrial Interview; Paquet Interview; Saint-Pierre, *La Mer à boire*, passim; Roger Barberot, *A bras le coeur* (Paris, 1972), 10; *Bulletin de AEN* (1923), 8–10.

bers saw the future generations of their own families as the way to keep the navy in the hands of socially acceptable and professionally able men. The inbreeding established under the *ancien régime* was still the preferred method in the 1920s. Naval leaders valued stability even more during an era of political and emotional uncertainty.[50]

Naval leadership revered the family model for its stabilizing influence and its ability to mitigate hardships unique to their way of life. Family separations and substandard living conditions might be overlooked if the officers, their wives and children felt themselves a part of a larger family. "In particular, I am very touched by the solidarity shown among the *officiers de marine*," said Madame Peltier, "and by the *esprit de corps* which unifies them as always."[51] For the time being, this closely knit structure met the needs of the families and of the navy, both fearful of dismantling time-honored customs that served them so well.

50. Personnel Report to Brest Naval Prefect, December 30, 1920, in Carton 34, Vice Admiral Antoine Schwerer, Report on Naval Schools, April 1, 1920, in Carton 36, both in Série Ca, Archives de la marine; Vice Admiral Georges Laurent, "Les Traditions de la marine militaire" (Speech presented before the Académie de la marine, June 18, 1937, in "Esprit de la marine" Collection, Bibliothèque de la marine).

51. Madame Peltier to Secretary General, June 11, 1929, in Peltier family dossier, Archives de AEN; Georges Débat, *Marine oblige* (Paris, 1974), 30.

CHAPTER 4
As Fathers Did Before
The Life of a Knight Errant

Because naval officers spent so much time at sea, they had even less direct influence in the raising of their children than did men in other French homes, where women traditionally played a central role. Yet even though navy wives reared their children alone for long periods of time, the distant husbands remained very strong role models whom the young boys emulated. Naval officers traditionally singled out which sons would prepare for the École navale, and the wives saw to the details of proper education and social acclimatization. Even if these officers had spent more time at home, there is little reason to believe that their children would have seen the navy in any less favorable light. École navale attracted just as many sons of alumni as did Saint Cyr, though army officers spent most of their careers *en famille*. Life with or without father seems to have mattered little to those young men determined to pursue military or naval careers.

In the fleet professional habits complemented the values acquired during childhood at home and school. Prior to World War I, the aristocratic style of life in the *grand corps* resembled that in other European military institutions.[1] After 1918, however, many Western armed forces evolved by necessity away from being the exclusive social preserves of the upper classes. New men from

1. Pierre Chalmin, *L'Officier français de 1815 à 1870* (Paris, 1957), Conclusion; Gordon Craig, *The Politics of the Prussian Army, 1640–1945* (New York, 1972), Chap. 6; Holger H. Herwig, *The German Naval Officer Corps: A Social and Political History, 1890–1918* (Oxford, 1973), 51–52; Theodore Zeldin, *Ambition, Love, and Politics* (Oxford, 1973), 542, Vol. I of *France, 1848–1945*, 2 vols.; E. S. Turner, *Gallant Gentlemen: A Portrait of the British Officer, 1600–1916* (London, 1956), Chap. 1; Gunther E. Rothenberg, *The Army of Francis Joseph* (W. Lafayette, Ind., 1976), 11 *et passim*.

simpler homes entered the officer ranks, often seeking military careers as vehicles for social advancement. This change in recruiting patterns came about partly because massive wartime losses could not be replaced by men from the aristocracy. Moreover, the introduction of more technology into the military services attracted men from bourgeois and working-class homes who had been educated to handle machines rather than to ride on horses. But the French navy did not experience a major loss of life during the First World War, nor did anyone succeed in modifying the traditional recruiting policies of the officer corps.[2] Consequently, men like Capitaine de Boeldieu portrayed in Jean Renoir's film *La Grande illusion* lived on as the role models in the navy's *grand corps*. Officers like him filled command positions in which they set the pattern for others to follow throughout the fleet.[3]

A successful career in the officer corps still depended heavily on one's family and one's connections within the navy. The ministers of marine and the Naval General Staff supported this *status quo* of prewar customs. They believed that these traditions protected officers in the *grand corps* from an invasion of the socially unacceptable among the *petits corps* and enlisted ranks. French businesses and the civil service followed many of these same practices in promoting men within their respective institutions. Custom often required managers to have proper social credentials in addition to the skills needed for their jobs.[4]

Members of the *grand corps* believed that regulations also assured their intellectual superiority over their subordinate officers and men. Only these line officers had the chance for command. They believed that this burden required the assurance that their authority and judgment would never be challenged from below. A commanding officer needed to "impose himself on his subordinates by the superiority of his general culture," acquired in suitable homes and continued in navy schools. As members of the senior

2. Karl Demeter, *The German Officer Corps in Society and State, 1650–1945*, trans. Angus Malcolm (New York, 1965), xiii *et passim*; Alan Bullock, *Hitler: A Study in Tyranny* (Rev. ed.; New York, 1964), 307–308; Craig, *Prussian Army*, 235, 238.

3. Jean Renoir (dir.), *La Grande illusion*, 1937.

4. Captain Charles Ferrand, *Programme naval, études maritimes* (Paris, 1908), 234–53; Zeldin, *Ambition, Love, and Politics*, 113–114.

corps, these officers established the customs and daily regulations governing life within the fleet. If the *grand corps* failed to remain socially and professionally on top, then the entire navy would degenerate into something, said Admiral Jean Ratyé, "like a human body with a weak and unreliable mind."[5] The navy's caste system was evident, even to outsiders, who were surprised that it remained intact while other military institutions at home and abroad were experimenting with opening officer careers to men based on their talent alone. The American naval attaché, for example, wrote: "In naval administration, France demonstrates that she believes there must be a marked distinction between officers who sometimes will be held responsible to the State for major military decisions and those whose duties cannot possibly stimulate the mind to the degree required for such major military responsibilities. . . . Because the line officer is the type that the nation must depend on in great emergencies, he is regarded as a higher type of individual, hence, the necessity for marked distinction to stimulate morale and the highest efficiency."[6]

Officers made frequent private and official pleas to restrict access to the *grand corps* to École navale graduates only. They believed that future admirals could be trained only as they themselves had been trained, in the proper naval setting at Navale. The Naval General Staff recommended that the trickle of graduates from the École centrale and the École polytechnique and the transfer of reservists into the *grand corps* be halted. Authors of these documents assumed that young men from these schools did not have enough nautical experience and were also socially incompatible with graduates from the École navale. There remained some active support for the commissioning of a few enlisted men into the *grand corps* but only for limited duty assignments. Such men were selected to fill specific, tedious jobs in which they would remain, leaving the important positions to graduates of the École navale. Although the enlisted men selected for the officer corps were trained at Navale, they were carefully segregated from their social betters.

5. Admiral Jean Ratyé, "L'Ecole de guerre navale," *Revue maritime*, LXI (January, 1925), 7, 2.
6. Office of Naval Intelligence, Naval Attaché Report, Paris, May, 1933, E-5-a, 17281, in National Archives.

Even though they followed almost identical curricula, the enlisted men and the future line officers were educated separately because of supposed social and intellectual incompatibility.[7]

Attempts to lower the social barriers dividing the officer corps failed because so many believed in the validity of the existing system. A senior officer from the *corps des contrôleurs*, the navy's inspectors, wrote a proposal for comprehensive reform based on trends he perceived in the civilian sector of French society. He recommended direct commissioning of qualified enlisted men into the *grand corps*, considering only individual potential and desire for the job. He believed that the growth of public education, then reaching beyond the old bourgeois classes, was creating "a democratic and egalitarian spirit" among young sailors who now had the chance for the *baccaulauréat*. Although the author's secondary recommendation for higher pay for everyone in the navy received sound endorsement, his main proposal for social reform fell on deaf ears; it was, said one critic, "too theoretical."[8]

This impetus for reform withered away during the early 1920s as traditional prewar customs proved unshakable. Even as late as 1944, attitudes remained unchanged. In the spring of that year, Admiral Georges Robert, secretary general of the École navale alumni society, sent out a letter to all class presidents proposing to extend membership to the *corps des ingénieurs méchaniciens*. Although these officers came originally from the *écoles des arts et métiers*, they spent two additional years at the École navale in a program of study much like that taken by the boys entering the *grand corps*. Because of the similarity of academic preparation and duties aboard ship, these two corps came closest of all to spanning the gap between the *grand* and *petits corps*. Nevertheless, the results of the vote by the alumni was almost entirely one-sided. Of sixty-seven voting class presidents, only nine, representing just 13 percent of the *grand corps*, favored the incorporation of these engineers into

7. Captain André Benoist, Report, May 16, 1928, in Série 1BB2¹, Carton 86, Vice Admiral Antoine Schwerer, Report on Naval Schools, April 1, 1920, in Sér. Ca, Car. 36, both in Archives de la marine; Lieutenant Joseph Lemaresquier, *L'Officier de vaisseau dans la marine moderne* (Paris, 1914), 31–48 *et passim*.

8. Vice Admiral Georges Thierry d'Argenlieu, "Où va notre marine de guerre?" (Report, December 16, 1919, in Sér. Ca, Car. 33, Archives de la marine).

the association. Officers who explained their motives for rejecting the reform believed in the need to preserve the "moral patrimony" of the *grand corps* over the rest of the navy. Admitting one of the lesser corps into their midst would put all officers on an equal footing. For most of the members of the association, "it was inadmissible to accept into the same association those officers who command and others who only have to obey orders."[9] These beliefs stemmed from very strong feelings about the need to separate men who came from different social backgrounds. The *ingénieurs mécaniciens* came primarily from *petit* bourgeois and working-class homes. A few were even sons of navy enlisted men. Boys from aristocratic homes who took the classical *baccaulauréat* in preparation for Navale looked down upon the technical preparation which the others took for entry into the *petits corps*.[10]

In its approach to the professional education of officers, the French navy continued the tradition of social isolation. Regulations at the École navale permitted the midshipmen almost no contact with outsiders during their two years of study. Moving the school ashore from an old sailing ship caused an uproar in the officer corps because contact would be far easier. Only very grudgingly did they accept civilian professors at the school who taught the subjects that naval officers felt unqualified to teach. Officers expected Navale to provide, first and foremost, a proper "moral development" for the midshipmen and, secondly, a "general culture" to reinforce their image of superiority over the sailors and members of the *petits corps*.[11] The idea of theoretical study, devoid of rigid conclusions for students to memorize, frightened many officers involved with the

9. Admiral Georges Robert to class presidents, Spring, 1944, Captain Jean Archambaud to Robert, April 24, 1944, Captain Ferdinand Pellegrin to Robert, April 30, 1944, all in Archives de l'Association amicale des anciens élèves de l'École navale, hereinafter cited as Archives de AEN.

10. Jacques Godechot, Interview, June 25, 1975; ONI, Naval Attaché Report, Paris, August 13, 1936, E-5-a, 20257, and C-10-m, 15380 series, which includes several studies of French education, both in NA.

11. Vice Admiral Merveilleux de Vignaux, Report on the School, December 8, 1922, in Sér. Ca, Car. 36, Archives de la marine; Nerée [pseud.], "La Marine et le régime," Pt. 2, *Action française*, August 19, 1924, pp. 1–2; Commandant François Ollivier, "Armée et marine," *Action française*, November 24, 1929; Espagnac du Ravay [Louis de La Monneraye], *Vingt ans de politique navale, 1919–1939* (Grenoble, 1941), 240–41.

curriculum at Navale. One admiral believed that education of future naval officers should start prior to adolescence if the navy really expected to influence their behavior.[12]

Admission standards remained very tough between the world wars. Only one of every five candidates who applied was finally admitted. It was first necessary to pass one of the toughest batteries of entrance tests for a *grand école*. Only the École normale supérieure in the rue d'Ulm offered an equivalent battery of literary exams.[13] Polytechnique and Saint Cyr required an applicant to pass only a single written exam. At Navale, however, two supplemental written tests in history and philosophy were given in addition to a basic scientific examination, which itself was more difficult than Saint Cyr's. The humanities amounted to one-third of all material tested on the École navale entrance exams. The questions, moreover, were structured in a way that forced the applicants to reveal their personal views on religion and politics. For example, in history questions focused on European revolutions and diplomatic conferences from 1848 to 1870. For the more contemporary period, written and oral questions dealt with the Catholic church, Popes Pius IX and Leo XIII, and the Vatican Council of 1870, which declared papal infallibility. Economics and colonial affairs rounded out the subjects tested.[14]

Those who passed the written tests were interviewed by an examination board composed of both line and medical officers who performed academic and psychological evaluations at a single hearing. They made the final determination on the admissibility of each candidate. As Madame Quesnel complained at the time her son took the test, answers considered improper to very subjective questions on politics and religion could eliminate an otherwise qualified candidate.[15]

The entrance exams at the École navale reflected the curriculum that students would follow. The humanities, for example, were far

12. Captain Aubert du Parc, "Dégénérescence de notre marine de guerre," *Action française*, April 17, 1921, p. 3.

13. *Bulletin de AEN* (October, 1938), 17; Godechot Interview.

14. ONI, Naval Attaché Report, Paris, E-5-a, 16682, series on the curriculum at the École navale, NA.

15. *Ibid.*, August 14, 1936, E-5-a, 20257; Madame Quesnel to Secretary General, May 17, 1934, in Archives de AEN.

more important than at any other of the military *grandes écoles*. Complaints about the curriculum focused on the need to expand the number of "general culture" courses such as French literature and history. Some officers believed the École navale was becoming dangerously technical, teaching things that only subordinates in the *petits corps* needed to know. In their opinion, nautical skills were not the most important subjects taught at Navale.[16] A ministerial decree of 1937 sanctioned these ideas in a formal charter for the school, which emphasized the need to preserve a proper moral environment at the École navale. "Let them study great naval officers, show them the importance of character and the part played by the leader's determination. Instill the concepts of international courtesy used in dealings among warships of the old maritime nations. Make the students understand that French seamen, more than any others, contributed to establish the rules of such courtesy and spread them throughout the entire world. They should hold it an honor to respect them and to preserve such a tradition. Encourage them to cherish classical culture which forms their judgement and provides mankind with his knowledge."[17] Again, culture meant the superiority of the École navale graduate over his associates in the *petits corps*.

This approach, which taught midshipmen "to overcome their collegiate spirit quickly" and "to develop their national pride," was widely supported within the French navy. But outsiders questioned the benefits of this kind of indoctrination. Admitting that the entrance examinations for Navale were more difficult than those for most other *grandes écoles*, an American naval attaché attributed the lack of imagination of French naval officers to their specialized training at Navale. Although this American came from the U.S. Naval Academy at Annapolis, which emphasized the Anglo-American naval tradition, he was amazed by the lack of emphasis on science and engineering at the École navale. The French naval officer, he found, was narrow and often incapable of distinguishing important problems from minutiae. "His mind may be so

16. Captain M. Roman, commanding officer of the École navale, Report, September 1, 1930, in Sér. 1BB[8], Car. 687, Archives de la marine.
17. ONI, Naval Attaché Report, translation of ministerial decree, Paris, August 27, 1937, E-5-a, 16682-C, NA.

logical that when he has overestimated the value of one of his premises, he will stubbornly go on to an obviously unsound conclusion. As for his independence, he is a curious mixture of habit and tradition versus his idea of liberty."[18]

Following the École navale, an officer spent ten or more years at sea before returning as a lieutenant commander to his next professional school, the École supérieure de guerre navale. Admission was by competitive examination, and graduates went on to command the finest warships or to key positions on major staffs. Unofficially, the school screened the student body for officers who appeared suitable for eventual promotion to admiral. The school ranked all applicants according to their "moral fortitude" and "general culture" as demonstrated in a single essay written for the admission board. As at the École navale, the course of study placed greater emphasis on indoctrinating the officer-student than on expanding his technical or managerial knowledge. Formal lectures on naval battles throughout history were the normal fare. Colonial exploits received great emphasis, as did the successful collaboration of French, Spanish, and Italian navies in empire building. The latter theme was part of the general emphasis upon the natural affinity of the Latin peoples for one another, a popular assumption in French naval circles.[19] The French Revolution, however, and the First Empire received scant attention.

A few officers perceived the weakness of this curriculum. They found the material and teaching methods "too ideological," forcing rigid interpretations of events on the students. These officers hoped to create an atmosphere at the school conducive to free thought and exploratory research that would benefit both the navy and the students. Free access to the Ministry of Marine archives was a part of the plan. But this small voice for reform went unheeded, leaving the École de guerre navale unchanged in spirit as well as thought throughout the interwar years.[20]

18. Ibid.; Peter Karsten, The Naval Aristocracy: The Golden Age of Annapolis and the Emergence of Modern American Navalism (New York, 1972), Chap. 2; ONI, Naval Attaché Report, Paris, February 21, 1938, E-4-d, 20997, NA.
19. Bulletin de AEN (January, 1929), 20–21; "Conseil pratique sur le commandement des hommes" (MS, n.d., in "Esprit de Marine" Collection, Bibliothèque de la marine); Captain Maurice Le Luc, Report, October 26, 1927, in Sér. FMF-SE, Car. 28, Archives de la marine.
20. Admiral Georges Mouget, commanding officer of the École de guerre navale,

One of the officers who supported the traditional curriculum was Admiral Raoul Castex. He became the French equivalent to Alfred Thayer Mahan, writing a number of books on naval strategy between the world wars. Although he expanded the study of strategy at the École de guerre navale, his methods included a vigorous defense of the existing pedagogy. He concentrated his efforts on the exclusion of material which did not offer predigested conclusions for the officer-students. Castex felt sure that the pedagogical approach to study found in universities had no place in professional schools, where reality and "extracted truths" held the greatest importance. To "ornament the minds" with theoretical knowledge would only lead to doctrinal confusion in the French naval officer corps.[21]

The tone of the École de guerre navale tended to be xenophobic, reflecting the institutional fear of foreign powers. Naval officers knew their school did not share the international reputation of the French army's equivalent institution, the École supérieure de guerre. Military officers from many countries flocked there to learn firsthand from the heirs of the Napoleonic legend who had halted the German war machine on the Marne and at Verdun. Foreign officers came to absorb some of the French military genius for turning almost sure defeat into stunning victory in spite of incredible odds against success. In contrast, the navy's École de guerre navale stirred little foreign interest. Instead of emphasizing the secrets of success against powerful enemies, the curriculum taught the less glorious methods of naval survival à la française. Historic narratives about Louis XIV's corsairs and Napoleon III's colonial expeditions received the greatest emphasis in the classroom, while major fleet actions were touched only lightly. Trafalgar went unnoticed. This approach relied heavily on French naval heroes whom the officer-students could emulate.[22] It was possible to graduate from

to Admiral Hector Violette, November 11, December 29, 1921, in Admiral Hector Violette Papers, Private Collection.
    21. ONI, Naval Attaché Report (copy of the U.S. military attaché's evaluation of Castex), Paris, E-4-c, 22100, NA. See also file E-5-b, 15172 (French naval officers' opinions on Castex's methods); Castex, Program of Study, October 7, 1937, in Sér. FMF-SE, Car. 34, Archives de la marine.
    22. Archives de la Marine, Program of Study, 1920–24, in Sér. 1BB⁸, Car. 90, Archives de la marine. On the xenophobic tone in the French naval schools, see Georges Débat, *Marine oblige* (Paris, 1974), 30.

the school thinking that protracted warfare, *guerre de course*, was the best alternative for the navy to pursue in any war. Students still learned to keep the fleet in port, thereby tying up the opponent's squadrons in blockades while sending out individual French commerce raiders, submarines, and perhaps an occasional privateer. When the enemy is sufficiently worn down, strike him in his home ports when he least expects it. Since the days of the Sun King, French naval thinking had changed very little. And in fact, the same strategy was applied with a great deal of success by the German navy during both world wars.

Although most naval officers had to work with sophisticated technology, many in the *grand corps* did all they could to avoid *la machine* in their education. They preferred to emphasize the classics instead. Literature and history always formed the basis of their so-called general culture.[23] Without mastery of the abstract, line officers would not feel secure in their positions above technicians who were relegated to lesser chores. "All the splendor and nobility of command are found in this act of making decisions which depend on professional knowledge and sometimes equal amounts of firmness, moral superiority and responsibility."[24]

A strict moral code tied very closely to Catholic teachings stood behind these professional standards. Religion formed an integral part of the French naval officer's life. Apart from the private weddings and funerals, other religious duties were part of the daily routine at sea and ashore. For years, priests blessed new warships at launching ceremonies, and heroes from French naval folklore received honors in religious services. All hands attended Sunday mass aboard ship, and on Good Friday the crew attended a special requiem mass and the ship was decked out in symbolic mourning. Many of these confessional duties came to an abrupt halt early in the twentieth century when laws separating church and state reached the fleet. Officers of middle and senior rank between the

23. Roger Coindreau, "La Vie héroique de René Guilbaud, 1890–1929," *Revue de Bas-Poitou*, n.v. (November, 1958), 2–5; Admiral Paul Auphan, "Les Forces morales chez l'officier" (MS, n.d., in "Esprit de Marine" Collection, Bibliothèque de la marine). Reference to technology as "la machine" comes from several interviews, notably with Admiral Paul Auphan, June 5, 1974.

24. Admiral Raoul Castex, *Questions d'état-major: principes, organisation, fonctionnement* (2 vols.; Paris, 1923–24), I, 1.

world wars recalled these religious ceremonies from their days as midshipmen and remained bitter over their loss.[25] Chaplains disappeared from the fleet for a while but could be brought on in time of war. The École navale managed to retain a chaplain even in peacetime. The minister of marine successfully defended his presence at the school in 1928. When challenged by the Chamber of Deputies, he told the members that the man served only as a moral guide for the midshipmen and not for "proselytizing the cult" of Catholic dogma.[26]

The religious tone within the *grand corps* did not disappear, however. Many of the officers viewed their professional and devotional duties as inseparable, or as one officer said, "as body and soul." Captain Georges Mabille du Chesne explained this in a manuscript submitted for publication to the navy's *Revue maritime*. He remained firmly convinced that only a properly educated practicing Catholic could remain true to his special moral responsibilities. He saw the naval officer primarily as a moral guide for others to follow and emulate. In du Chesne's view, the state had the responsibility to encourage the closest possible integration of official and religious life. He believed that the navy needed to use Catholicism as the foundation for maintaining discipline. Colonial races would only obey their masters, said Admiral Auphan, if they learned Catholic teachings on obedience and remained ignorant of the French Revolution.[27]

A new, more socially responsive form of Catholicism was gaining popularity in many of the *grandes écoles*, but it had few supporters at the École navale. This school remained a bastion of the traditional Catholic thought still in vogue throughout Brittany and in some parts of the French colonies where the navy had the closest

25. Admiral Jean Decoux, *Adieu marine* (Paris, 1957), 9–11. The most important religious services were in May and November. Jean Abrial to parents, October 8, 1896, April 18, 1900, both in Admiral Jean Abrial Papers, Private Collection; Admiral Frix Michelier to Violette, June 2, 6, 1931, in Violette Papers.

26. Minister of Marine J. L. Dumesnil, Speech, in *Journal officiel de la République Française. Chambre des députés. Débats parlementaires*, December 8, 1924, p. 4230.

27. Captain Georges Mabille du Chesne, "Catholicisme et bolshévisme" (MS, December 8, 1926, in Sér. Ca, Car. 27, Archives de la marine); Admiral Paul Auphan, *Les Écheances de l'histoire; ou, l'éclatement des empires coloniaux de l'occident* (Paris, 1952), 309–11.

Naval Leaders at the Invalides Chapel
Leaders of the navy's *grand corps* attend mass at the Invalides. The chapel
there and the one at the École militaire were favorite locations for naval
marriages, funerals, and other special religious events. *National Archives
Photo*

ties. Naval officers remained loyal to the ideas of Bishop Jacques
Bossuet and other prominent thinkers of the classical era.[28]

28. On conservative Catholic thought, see Adrien Dansette, *Religious History of
Modern France,* trans. John Dingle (2 vols.; Edinburgh, 1961); David Shapiro (ed.),
The Right in France, 1890–1919: Three Studies (Carbondale, Ill., 1962); Robert F.
Byrnes, *The Prologue to the Dreyfus Affair* (New Brunswick, N.J., 1950), Vol. I of
Anti-Semitism in Modern France, 1 vol. to date; Malcolm Anderson, *Conservative
Politics in France* (London, 1974).

Converting religious values into secular habits came easily to the officers. They freely expressed their belief in the need for human suffering, personal sacrifice, authority, strong discipline, and the elimination of individuality. They believed that the "marvelous fruits of suffering were offered and received to purify and better the relations among men."[29] The virtue of self-sacrifice divided the elite from the cowardly masses. A code of behavior founded upon these beliefs forbade the questioning of authority and formalized the loyalty oath of ships' crews to their commanding officers.[30] These vows tied the individual sailor in absolute obedience to his commanding officer as did the Prussian oaths that have been cited as the cause of the inflexible behavior of German soldiers. When a new commanding officer was introduced, the ship's company was reminded of its obligation to obey. "Officers and men of [name of ship], you will recognize from today as your commanding officer [his name] here before you and you will obey him in all he orders for the good of the service and the success of the armed forces of France."[31]

The rigid code of ethics tended to isolate the *grand corps* even further from the rest of the navy and the remainder of French society as well. This surfaced as a severe impediment to good working relations when line officers had to cooperate with groups of non-naval people, most of whom they rarely permitted into their inner circle of friends. Journalists and diplomats saw this problem, and even some admirals felt that "the Navy was too cloistered from the rest of the world and that no outside noise was allowed to enter their sacred domain."[32] Most officers defended their isolationist habits by claiming that their profession was so unique that aspiring young men needed many years to be weaned away from harmful civilian habits. This all-encompassing view of their profession ran hand in hand with the lack of outside interests among members of the *grand corps*.

29. Admiral Paul Auphan, *Mensonges et vérité* (Paris, 1949), 19.

30. Vice Admiral Georges Laurent, "Conférence sur le commandement" (MS, August 15, 1931, in Bibliothèque de la marine); Abrial to parents, November 2, 1899, in Jean Abrial Papers; Reprimand of a naval officer who questioned some of his performance evaluations, October 23, 1920, in Sér. Ca, Car. 38, Archives de la marine.

31. Decoux, *Adieu marine*, 125.

32. ONI, Naval Attaché Report, Paris, March, 1937, E-4-c, 22100, NA. See also Mouget to Violette, September 16, 1929, in Violette Papers; du Ravay, *Vingt ans*, xi–xii.

When the navy went before the public, it did so in an attempt to show its independence from all other institutions. The officers were quite happy when the press commented on their tendency toward aloofness from other professional groups. In Paris, where the navy was only a very small minority in a vast array of government bureaucracies, preserving a separate identity was more difficult than in the port cities, where the fleet had no rivals. In the capital, the officers organized themselves to pool their resources when competing for political favor or money from the Parliament. Senior officers chose their friends carefully and planned official appearances to maximize the effect of naval presence. Apart from purely official associations, officers befriended members of the Yacht Club, the Jockey Club, and the Cercle Interallié who shared many social interests with the *grand corps*.[33]

Beginning in 1923, the Association amicale des anciens élèves de l'École navale sponsored an annual ball in Paris for members and close friends. These gatherings began as closed occasions at the Ministry of Marine, but popular response soon outgrew the space there. The balls reached their most extravagant in 1935 and 1936 when the association rented the Paris Opera and staged enormous galas there. Society columns in the domestic and foreign newspapers publicized these events widely. The 1935 program included a conversion of the Opera into a battleship where Simone Simon, Joséphine Baker, and other leading entertainers performed on the simulated foredeck. Actors staged skits portraying highlights of the French navy's past, including the heroic exploits of the Breton corsairs and the conquest of colonies abroad. Dancing followed into the early morning hours in what the *grand corps* claimed to be an enormous success in a city where the navy was hardly known.[34]

These occasions were opportunities to associate with the right sorts of people. Sponsors of the 1935 ball included the Princess de

33. See *Bottin mondain* (Paris, 1919–39), *passim; Tout-Paris: annuaire de la société parisienne* (Paris, 1919–39), *passim*. Special friends were patrons of the AEN's lavish gatherings. See AEN, *Gala de marine, 14 février 1935* (Paris, 1935), n.p. For the ties between the Yacht Club de France and the Navy, see Admiral Georges Durand-Viel to François Darlan, December 24, 1943, in Sér. FMF-SE, Car. 43, Archives de la marine.

34. AEN, *Gala de marine*.

Showing Off the Colors: The AEN Ball
For the Association amicale des anciens élèves de l'École navale ball of
February 14, 1935, the naval officers rented the Paris Opera. "All Paris,
elegant and cosmopolitan was there," a brochure said. *Intransigeant Photo*

Polignac, the Countess de Blois, and the Duchesses de Broglie and de La Rochefoucauld. They and other nontitled friends from literary and political circles represented the most fashionable of "Tout Paris." The president of France and the minister of marine headed the list of honored guests. Front page coverage appeared in the moderate and conservative *Le Figaro, Le Temps, Le Journal des débats,* and in the extreme rightist *Candide, Gringoire,* and *Action française,* to name the most significant.[35]

Officers from the *grand corps* chose their close military friends with the same caution used in picking civilian associates. Extreme prudence marked all their dealings with French army and air force officers. The naval officers feared that too much familiarity with these outsiders might encourage the navy to drop its guard in future power plays among the armed forces. With the exception of a few brief months during 1932, the three military forces remained under separate, autonomous ministries without any central agency to supervise joint affairs. The three military portfolios had technical equality in the Council of Ministers, although tradition made the army the most influential. A delicate *modus operandi* evolved between the separate Naval and Army General Staffs over the years, with each tolerating the other's expertise in specific limited areas. This balance remained undisturbed until 1928, when Premier Raymond Poincaré created the Ministry of Air. Naval leaders immediately perceived this new cabinet post as a threat to their own survival. Funding of naval aviation had always been uncertain, passed back and forth between the navy and air force budgets for years. Programs of the two services were already badly mingled, leaving naval officers with the feeling that money which should have been theirs for new ships had been gobbled up by an untried air force. When press coverage revealed that Pierre Cot, the Popular Front's minister of air, had squandered aviation money, the navy joined in the outcry, labeling the new service both "red" and unreliable.[36]

35. *Ibid.,* including a two-page montage of press clippings on the ball.
36. Du Ravay, *Vingt ans,* 216–26; Auphan Interview, May 30, 1975; Admiral Louis de La Monneraye, Interview, July 23, 1975; Jean La Bruyère, "Revue des questions navales et maritimes," *Revue politique et parlementaire,* CLIX (May, 1934), 353–58; Admiral Paul Auphan and Jacques Mordal, *The French Navy in World War II,* trans. A. C. J. Sabalot (Annapolis, 1959), 15–16.

Eventually, the navy secured its own pilots and aircraft. Nevertheless, power rivalries over money and manpower perpetuated the
bad feelings between the two services, which had as little as possible to do with each other. To make matters worse, the *officiers de
marine* were no friendlier to their own naval aviators. Ship captains
feared moves to create an autonomous corps of naval flyers and
imagined plots to amalgamate with the air force when their backs
were turned.[37]

Senior naval officers were particularly upset with the new Ministry of Air. It was difficult enough getting their point of view across
to the far larger army and to the cabinet; they believed the new
batch of air force generals would tip the balance of power hopelessly against the navy. They never got over the meteoric rise of the
air force from 1914 to full ministry status only fifteen years later
with a budget even larger than the navy's. Officers steeped in centuries of tradition and folklore simply could not grasp the need for a
separate agency charged with the nation's air defenses. The *grand
corps* perceived that aircraft had their place but preferably within
the existing Ministries of War and Marine.

What most exasperated naval officers about the air force was the
absence of tradition and the fact that many flyers came from homes
without any military heritage. The naval officers saw the Air Force
as an upstart service filled with men commissioned from the enlisted ranks, the so-called *officiers de fortune*, having none of the
social prerequisites for officer status. If the naval officers could not
eliminate this kind of upstart, then they could at least ignore it.[38]
But it was not possible to tolerate encroachments on their professional honor. A ten-year dispute arose over a uniform design the air
force wished to adopt, which closely resembled the one worn by
naval officers. The *grand corps* regarded this as an unacceptable
violation of the navy's honor and separate identity. They explained
that the anticipated similarity of naval and air officers would de-
moralize everyone in the fleet. The École navale alumni association

37. Admiral Henri Salaün, *La Marine française* (Paris, 1934), 356–64; Auphan
Interview, May 30, 1975.

38. ONI, Naval Attaché Report, Paris, December 6, 1937 (Report on naval officer
attitudes toward the other armed forces), E-5-a, 17281, NA. The French officer interviewed called his air force counterparts, "beyond the pale, from a social point of
view."

added that the "very blatant similarity," coupled with the slovenly dressing habits common among pilots, would reflect on the navy's image, "to which so many glorious memories and traditions were attached." These complaints failed to stop air force officers from donning their new uniforms.[39]

Friction with the air force, no matter how severe, could never match the deep-seated army-navy jealousies. Both of these institutions guarded equally ancient traditions. Many generations of conflict between them had led to the practice of dividing up spheres of influence as the only way to work together. In the management of the colonial empire, for example, certain colonies remained in the navy's hands to administer while others, primarily those in North Africa, were under army control. Even parts of the *métropole* remained the exclusive domain for naval recruiting, as established by Colbert in the seventeenth century.

Naval officers disliked the way they were perceived by their army counterparts as stepchildren rather than as peers, and ongoing jokes about army officers did nothing to contribute to a better mutual understanding. Officers recalled with bewilderment stories they had heard at the École de guerre navale about the "red pants of 1914." Though all other European armies had adopted some form of camouflage uniform by 1914, French generals sent soldiers to the front in blue coats and crimson pants, the same costume their great-grandparents had worn under Napoleon. Naval officers were appalled at the stupidity of dressing soldiers as walking targets for German sharpshooters and machine gunners. General Pierre Bosquet's dry comment about the charge of the Light Brigade during the Crimean War fit naval opinion of the French army two generations later: "C'est magnifique mais ce n'est pas la guerre." Naturally, feelings were reciprocal. The commander of a French cavalry regiment went out of his way while on maneuvers to test a visiting foreign naval officer's horsemanship. The colonel finally gave up in disgust, unable to understand how someone whom he considered a simple mariner could actually beat him at his own trade. Little did the Frenchman know that he had taken on, not a sailor, but

39. Recommendation against the new air force uniforms, March 11, 1939, in Sér. FMF-SE, Car. 23, Archives de la marine.

an American marine, raised in the hunt country of northern Virginia.[40]

This interservice jealousy had many causes. The army's greater prestige in French homes and within government circles far outstripped anything the navy could muster. This imbalance generated constant friction between naval officers, who refused to accept an inferior status, and army officers, who could not be bothered with problems relating to maritime defense. The long list of military victories on European battlefields far outweighed the French navy's relatively few triumphs at sea. Moreover, the greater importance that Parliament accorded the army produced a budget twice that of the navy. Service prestige received an additional blow from the Ministry of War when in 1915 all the shipyards were handed over to manufacturers of weapons for the army. The desperate need for arms on the Western Front exceeded the secondary requirements for the fleet. The long-term result was a navy that was practically unseaworthy by armistice day in 1918, victim of four years without repair or maintenance. All these irritants, both petty and significant, added to the general feeling among naval officers that their warnings about the need for a maritime and colonial defense were falling on deaf ears in each successive government. Naval officers believed that the cabinets had far greater interest in domestic matters and thought only in terms of the Rhine frontier when considering national security matters.[41]

Naval officers believed that they had to spend an inordinate amount of time every day fending off incursions of army and air force interests into sacred naval domains and in trying to win understanding for French maritime concerns. They viewed the other two armed forces more as domestic enemies than as members of a

40. The red pants story was told to me by Admiral Paul Ortoli, Interview, July 4, 1974, and also appeared in Barbara Tuchman, *The Guns of August* (New York, 1968), 55. Other personal observations about French army-navy rivalry came from Colonel Raymond Abrial, Interview, June 27, 1975; Commander Loïc Abrial, Interview, July 28, 1975; Auphan Interviews; Godechot Interview. Major Robert Dessez, Report on his two years with the French army, in ONI, Naval Attaché Report, Paris, August 20, 1937, A-5-a, 15151, NA. Bosquet cited in Cecil Woodham-Smith, *The Reason Why* (New York, 1960), 238.

41. Hélène de David-Beauregard, *Souvenirs de famille* (Toulon, 1970), 155–57; du Ravay, *Vingt ans*, 173–75; Auphan Interview, May 30, 1975; Loïc Abrial Interview; Admiral René Godfroy, Interview, July 2, 1975.

single profession of arms devoting their collective energies to national security. Naval chiefs of staff initiated numerous fruitless efforts to restore what they dreamed of as a normal balance among the three armed forces. Admiral Darlan led a curious and successful campaign to establish higher ranks at the top for admirals, placing them on a par with their counterparts at home and abroad. Concerned with prestige as well as protocol, he believed that naval officers needed equal status to compete successfully for money and influence. He accomplished this after he was snubbed at the coronation of George VI of England, where he was seated well to the rear of his fellow army and air force chiefs of staff because he was only a vice admiral. Darlan was so junior among the naval dignitaries that he ended up sitting "behind a pillar and after the Chinese admiral," who had more stars on his sleeve but no fleet to show for them.[42]

In protecting their bureaucratic turf against the other armed forces, the admirals worked against the creation of a centralized ministry of defense. The Naval General Staff believed that any consolidation of the military services would further weaken the position of the Ministry of Marine. Naval officers also wanted to limit joint liaison duty and assignment of naval officers to army or air force schools, where ideas could be exchanged free of external pressures.[43] The continuation of three separate services with autonomous staffs perpetuated the tradition established during the seventeenth century when a myriad of bureaucratic and aristocratic groups competed for royal favor.

Naval officers did not spend all their time worrying about domestic threats to the fleet. Attitudes developed at home and shaped by the École navale created a remarkable consensus of opinion about foreigners. Generally, officers had very clear opinions about good and evil, leaving very little room in between for gray issues. Indi-

42. Darlan quoted in Auphan and Mordal, *French Navy*, 17. See also Request to raise ceiling on naval officers' retirement age, July 16, 1922, in Sér. Ca, Car. 27. Various proposals to get higher ranks for admirals, December 7, 1937–August 9, 1939, in Sér. FMF-SE, Car. 24, all in Archives de la marine; Ortoli Interview; La Monneraye Interview; Godfroy Interview.

43. Minister of Marine Georges Leygues to Violette, June 14, 1932, Mouget to Violette, May 17, 1932, both in Violette Papers; du Ravay, *Vingt ans*, 227–28; Vice Admiral Jules Théophile Docteur, *Darlan, amiral de la flotte* (Paris, 1949), 22; Rudolph Binion, *Defeated Leaders: The Political Fate of Caillaux, Jouvenal, and Tardieu* (New York, 1960), 313.

vidual preferences became official policy with great ease among officers raised and educated in very similar environments.

Strong cultural and religious attitudes led naval officers to seek friends among fellow Latin peoples. To be on good terms with Catholic nations was of enormous importance to the more devout. The style of Catholicism in the French navy encouraged members to be highly selective in the choice of friends overseas, feeling secure only in very compatible surroundings. These tastes included an appreciation of the cultural preferences of fellow Latins who had similar life-styles along the Mediterranean littoral. A French naval officer readily understood the family structure and social relations among these neighboring cultures. For him, to be a Latin was second in importance only to being French. Latins formed a special brotherhood of peoples who should forge a bond of mutual trust in a world that threatened their collective survival.[44]

Naturally, the French naval officer believed that France led this federation of Latin peoples, which included Italy, Spain, Portugal, with the South American nations serving as junior members. Top-ranking admirals like Jean Decoux reacted warmly to overtures from any of these countries when they identified France as a "sister nation."[45] These peoples, he felt, had an uncanny ability to see each other's domestic and political dilemmas in the same light. Their special relationship permitted French naval officers to promote cooperation with fellow Latin nations in defense of a common way of life. Any member of this union betraying their special trust to an outsider certainly would have "to pay the great crime of having betrayed Latinity."[46]

According to many naval officers, the greatest threat to the Latin, and to the Frenchman in particular, was the Anglo-Saxon. To defend France against this threat, officers sought for many years to create a diplomatic alliance among France, Italy, and Spain. Outside

44. J. Monlau, "Armée et marine," Action française, September 9, 1928; Eugen Weber, Action Française: Royalism and Reaction in Twentieth Century France (Stanford, 1962), 276. See also Abrial, letters to his parents on contacts with Latin leaders including Salazar, 1932–34, in Jean Abrial Papers.

45. Captain Jean Decoux to French naval attaché in Rome, December 10, 1934, in Sér. FMF-SE, Car. 20, Archives de la marine.

46. Lieutenant X, La Guerre avec Angleterre: politique navale de la France (Paris, 1900), 125.

the navy, however, it was not the Anglo-Saxons who were feared but the Germans.[47] Frenchmen believed they faced a timeless German threat and had come to believe over the years that the animosity between the two peoples was biological. In the fleet, however, there was no practical reason to hate Germany. The two countries were not maritime rivals. The Germans posed no danger to the French colonial empire or to the navy, its chief guardian.[48] The Anglo-Saxon menace, centered in Great Britain, was a test of naval preparedness, and the navy saw it as the greatest threat to national security.

The Englishman had long been the symbol of everything the Latins had to fear. He represented the worst of Protestant and Puritan values. To the Latins, he also appeared arrogant and uncompromising. Moreover, he was a good sailor and had ruined the French fleet more often than French naval officers cared to recall. English society professed such dangerous ideas as Freemasonry, plutocracy, and careers open to talent regardless of social origin. All this was so contrary to what Europeans raised in traditional Catholic homes had been taught. Moreover, antipathy toward British society was encouraged in the classrooms of the École navale and in the wardrooms of the fleet. Books by French admirals on strategy warned of the Anglo-Saxon threat, and from a boy's first day in the navy, he learned to seek restitution for what the English had done to France over the years at sea and in the colonies.[49]

Many French naval officers of the 1920s and 1930s remembered the battle of Trafalgar of 1805 with a sense of "permanent torment," as though they had participated in the great maritime tragedy themselves. As one of these officers said, the word *Trafalgar* "still sounded awful to our ears." Admiral Darlan felt personally in-

47. Admiral Antoine Schwerer, "Armée et marine," *Action française*, March 25, 1928; Edward R. Tannenbaum, *The Action Française: Die-Hard Reactionaries in Twentieth Century France* (New York, 1960), 225.

48. Tuchman, *Guns of August*, 25–26; Judith Hughes, *To the Maginot Line: The Politics of French Military Preparation in the 1920's* (Cambridge, Mass., 1971), 112–13; Richard D. Challener, *The French Theory of the Nation in Arms, 1866–1939* (New York, 1952), 139–40.

49. Abrial to parents, November 11, 1898, February 18, 1899, both in Jean Abrial Papers; Admiral Paul Auphan, *La Marine dans l'histoire de France* (Paris, 1955), 213; "Armée et marine," *Action française*, August 25, 1932, April 30, 1934; Godechot Interview; Loïc Abrial Interview.

sulted when the 1930 London Naval Conference convened in the Trafalgar Room of Saint James Palace. "Charming," was his only comment as he viewed the murals and the captured memorabilia of the battle, convinced of what the British disarmament officials had in store for France.[50]

The French officers could hardly resist the temptation to better the English in almost any situation. Even little symbolic victories were worth a long wait. As captain of a new cruiser on a goodwill mission, Jean Abrial wrote home with glee when a small British warship went unnoticed next to his in a South American port. "For once France has outdone England," he said in a letter to his family. "I am surprised to have withstood the shock." Another officer seriously believed a legend about British sailors infesting Martinique with poisonous snakes.[51] Even those few who were not anglophobic had ongoing difficulties working with their Royal Navy counterparts because of entrenched feelings in both services that went back many generations. Personal beliefs easily spilled over into the realm of official activities. Until 1904, French naval war plans considered Britain as the most likely adversary. Even into the 1930s, naval planners continued to view the English as the opponent they preferred to engage long after they were dropped from the Quai d'Orsay's list of hostile peoples.[52]

A journalist friend of the French navy, Jean Gautreau, wrote one of the few regular columns about naval matters in the domestic press. He published under the pen name of Captain John Frog, posing as a retired French officer living in London. Frog's monthly column reached an annual climax on Trafalgar Day when it sounded more like an emotional obituary than a normal editorial. He explained the mutual feeling of distrust between the two navies as a

50. Darlan quoted in Commander Jacques Bodin, Interview, November 24, 1977, and in Débat, *Marine oblige,* 73; Alain Darlan, *L'Amiral Darlan parle* (Paris, 1953), 32.

51. Abrial to family, May 24, 1929, in Jean Abrial Papers; Admiral Antoine Schwerer, *Souvenirs de ma vie maritime, 1878–1914* (Paris, 1933), 34.

52. ONI, Naval Attaché Report, London (Sample of British naval opinion on France), January 19, 1932, C-9-e, 19447-B, NA; Theodore Ropp, "Continental Doctrines of Sea Power," in Edward Mead Earle (ed.), *Makers of Modern Strategy: Military Thought from Machiavelli to Hitler* (Princeton, 1971), 448–50; French naval war plans, September, 1920, April 29, 1921, both in Sér. Ca, Car. 27, September 10, 1930, in Sér. FMF-SE, Car. 14, all in Archives de la marine; Violette to wife, March 10, 1930, in Violette Papers.

natural phenomenon that could not be altered. Although his column focused on British attitudes, it says just as much about French sentiments of the day. "In short, John Bull wishes to live with his eyes fixed on the sea. Across his path , he first sees the Frenchman, John Toad [Jean Crapaud], who has erred by living where he does in Europe, as he has also done in Africa and Asia as well. . . . It is not Germany but France which in the naval and diplomatic circles [of Great Britain] remains Enemy Number One; neither detested nor scorned but instead the preferred and classic enemy as if the Lord God had made France into a target or a punching bag for Albion."[53] Years before, when naval officers worried about England at the time of the Entente Cordiale, a French officer wrote an anonymous book warning about Latin vulnerability to Anglo-Saxon pressure. He begged his countrymen "to defend themselves against English policy and the universal tendency of the Anglo-Saxons to ignore the rights of all peoples, those in France in particular."[54] French naval opinion seemed immovable.

Animosity toward the Anglo-Saxon rarely included unfriendly views about the United States, however. Memories of having jointly defeated the English at Yorktown provided a foundation for friendship that was augmented by romanticized dreams of America as a land of cowboys and gangsters where fortunes grew on trees. The Franco-American connection remained a strong, if occasionally strained tie for naval officers in both countries to build upon.

Today, on a wall in the chateau of Compiègne, far from the sea, hangs an allegorical painting by a seventeenth-century court artist, Pierre Mignard. Entitled *Neptune Offering the Empire of the Sea to Louis XIV*, it portrays the timeless image held by French naval officers of their service's relationship to the state. Through many changes of regime and maritime technology, the representation of this relationship is as valid today as it was for Colbert's corsairs and for Admiral Darlan's officers too. The enormous canvas done in grand baroque style shows all the creatures of the sea rising up to greet the Sun King who appears as a sunburst on a royal banner car-

---

53. John Frog, "Armée et marine," *Action française*, November 10, 1932, August 25, 1935. Identity of the journalist provided by Bernard Paquet, Interview, June 30, 1975.
54. Lieutenant X, *La Guerre avec Angleterre*, viii–ix.

Hands Across the Sea: Franco-American Naval Friendship
A French naval officer cordially greets the American naval attaché. This
special Franco-American friendship survived the interwar years in spite of
French worries about the "Anglo-Saxon" naval powers. *National Archives
Photo*

ried by angels and cherubs. In the center stands Neptune on his
chariot made of a giant conch shell and drawn by sea horses and
mermaids. This god of the sea offers his coral crown and trident,
symbols of the maritime empire, to France. Cherubs bear the fleur-
de-lys and angels play royal fanfares while Colbert's fleet lies at anchor on the horizon, adding to the splendor of this magnificent
occasion.

Nothing better portrays the image officers had of themselves
both as Neptune's agents in this world and as representatives of the
French state on the seas. Yet, French naval officers of the 1930s and
of more recent times are disturbed by what Mignard put on the canvas. For them, the real question raised by the artist is whether or
not France would ever accept these gifts so graciously offered by

Neptune offrant à Louis XIV l'empire de la mer
Pierre Mignard captured the timeless image French naval officers have
of themselves in their relationship to the state. *Musee national de
Compiegne*

Neptune. Alas, to the French naval officer, the sea is something to which he must devote body and soul, painfully separated from his family and often left to carry on without any support from political superiors who rarely understand the sea. Like the majority of Frenchmen, governments from King Louis' to President Loubet's looked upon the oceans of the world as "exotic lands," to be dreamed of but never owned. Meanwhile, the less-deserving English saw the seas as their "own native soil."[55] The French naval officer also believes that Mignard caught that glorious moment just before Louis said *non* to Neptune and ran off to make further conquests with his victorious army on the continent. They knew that the final scene of Mignard's allegory would have showed Neptune giving the empire of the sea to Britannia after the Sun King refused it. Naturally, a French court artist could not paint that final tragic moment. That was left to a nineteenth-century English painter commissioned by Queen Victoria.

All these customs and ideas have their foundation in the intellectual formation and bias within the *grand corps* and, to a lesser degree, in the various *petits corps*. Though not accepted by all the officers, these images of friend and foe, of good and evil, are a distillation of their values during those two decades between the world wars. A stringent moral code, offering very little room for interpretation, channeled these men in their professional behavior. Dissent within the technical branches was tolerated because it offered no threat, but few in the *grand corps* succeeded in marching to other than the official tune. A cleavage between those who treated the *grand corps* as a quasi-religious order and those few who did not dates at least from the turn of this century. At that time, the Dreyfus affair and the separation of church and state permanently influenced the future of the civil-military balance in France.[56] France's naval officers did not escape these controversies without acquiring a new taste for politics and the affairs of state in the last decades of the Third Republic.

55. Bodin Interview; Commander André Sauvage, Interview, September 10, 1977.
56. Decoux, *Adieu marine*, 10–11; Auphan, *Marine dans l'histoire*, 215; ONI, Naval Attaché Report, Paris, March 1, 1907, E-5-c, 4542, May 21, 1908, E-5-b, 692-a, both NA; Charles Braibant, *Un bourgeois sous trois républiques* (Paris, 1961), 340 *et passim*.

PART III

The Officer Corps Engagé

Il y avait en France un pouvoir légitime et stabilisé depuis plus de mille ans. C'était la monarchie qui avait fait la France. Elle a été renversée par des moyens tout à fait illégitimes; et aujourd'hui le régime que nous subissons est le régime judéo-maçonnique qui veut détruire à la fois la famille, la patrie, et la religion. . . . J'ai la conviction absolue que la République nous mène à une nouvelle guerre qui fera encore couler des flots de sang, qu'elle nous conduit au morcellement de notre patrie, qu'elle démoralise et déchristianise la France.

VICE ADMIRAL ANTOINE SCHWERER, *Action française*, May 3, 1928

CHAPTER 5
Temptations from the Right

In November, 1918, many naval officers, along with other Europeans, believed that the armistice would restore the life of the *belle époque*. They were shocked to return home and find, on the contrary, how much conditions had changed and how different the navy now was from the rest of France. For the first time since the founding of the Third Republic, the Ministry of Marine placed greater strategic emphasis on Europe than on the colonies or other distant concerns. Surely the days of colonial conquest and exploration were over; there remained only the tasks of administering and policing the empire. Some felt rejected by the country when the Parliament failed to mention the navy in a postwar address of thanks to the armed services. In the following months, there quickly spread throughout the officer corps a sense of bitterness and isolation, which the Naval General Staff recognized but felt powerless to correct.[1]

Hopes remained high that funds would be provided to rebuild the fleet. The pitiful condition of the ships after four years of neglect could no longer be ignored. There were barely enough seaworthy vessels for the 1920 Black Sea campaign in support of the White Russian forces against the Bolsheviks.[2] There the poor state of readiness and the general lack of preparation for the Russian campaign doomed the French cause almost from the start. Moreover,

1. Commander Stanislas de David-Beauregard, Personnel Report, March 20, 1921, p. 35, in Série. Ca, Carton 34, Archives de la marine.
2. Admiral Paul Auphan and Jacques Mordal, *The French Navy in World War II*, trans. A. C. J. Sabalot (Annapolis, 1959), 8; Espagnac du Ravay [Louis de La Monneraye], *Vingt ans de politique navale, 1919–1939* (Grenoble, 1941), 51; Admiral Paul Auphan, Interview, June 5, 1974.

widespread demoralization among the French sailors, tired of war, led to sit-down strikes and demonstrations in support of the Soviet cause. The officers were appalled; they sincerely believed that these sailors would bring home the ideas for a Marxist revolution. This first contact with militant communism had an enduring effect on the attitudes of many French naval officers.[3]

For those who returned from overseas in 1918 and from Russia in 1921, the most difficult thing to comprehend was how different life would be for the foreseeable future. The postwar inflation in Paris and the port cities was particularly shocking to those who remembered the stable prices of the years before the war. As it became clear that naval salaries would not rise accordingly, many realized that their pay would no longer support their traditional standard of living and some faced financial ruin. Some complaints about pay may have been self-serving or exaggerated, but the sense of slipping behind that pervaded the officer corps was very real to people accustomed to bourgeois comforts.[4]

The regressive system of taxation hurt the younger officers more than their superiors. One estimate by the Association amicale des anciens élèves de l'École navale found that ensigns fell about ten thousand francs short annually trying to meet the rising costs of food, shelter, and clothing. The same study found that captains were better off, averaging a shortfall of only three thousand francs each year. These figures were based on necessities alone; they did not include the cost of nonessentials, such as private education, which naval families preferred. In 1927 the annual tuition for a private or parochial school ranged from eight thousand to sixteen thousand francs per year, depending on geographical location and a student's age.[5]

3. General Lester Dessez to the author, April 26, 1973; Paul Masson, "La Politique navale française: les mutineries dans les grandes marines" (MS in preparation for publication).

4. David-Beauregard, Report, March 20, 1921, pp. 29–32; Paul Marie de La Gorce, *La République et son armée* (Paris, 1963), 241–46; Ministère du Travail, *Bulletin de la statistique général de la France*, IX (October–December, 1929), 62–63, XXI (October–December, 1931), 42–43.

5. "Rapport sur la 'situation matérielle' de l'officier de marine," *Bulletin de l'Association amicale des anciens élèves de l'École navale*, XXVII (January, 1927), 9–10, hereinafter cited as *Bulletin de AEN*.

This and other studies warned that the existing economic conditions were forcing naval families to practice family planning. The authors warned against the dangers of the "declining birthrate of the elite" and predicted that the sons of officers would avoid careers in the navy. Certainly, the cost of the preparatory courses leading to the École navale would now pose a significant burden on officers whose children were interested in the navy.

It was a new situation for the elite to have to quibble over money, and it infuriated Admiral Schwerer, the inspector general of naval personnel. Although he believed in good wages for the officers, he deplored the "mercenary spirit" of those who asked for better pay and living conditions. He invited those who complained either to silence themselves or to resign from the navy. Yet the seriousness of these economic predicaments was enough to gain the attention of the American naval attaché. He noted with amazement that only the very rich enjoyed many basic conveniences and that an enormous gap was growing between officers with supplemental private incomes and those living only on their salaries. The comment which a petty officer made that "there was no longer honor or money in the Navy" captured the imagination of many in the 1920s.[6]

The search for solutions to these career frustrations produced no easy answers nor did any leaders show the way out of the quagmire. Prospects for a dismal future contributed to the anxieties of officers in the early postwar years. Claims of elite status no longer made sense when families could not afford to maintain their traditional social position.[7] At the same time, the future of the navy itself was at stake, adding to anxieties about the future. Funds for new warships were not forthcoming until 1922, leaving many to wonder if Parliament had any serious interest in the navy and the colonial empire. The officers who viewed the future with little hope for im-

6. *Ibid.*, 10; David-Beauregard, Report, March 20, 1921, p. 15; Captain Charles Berthelot, Personnel Report, December 31, 1920, in Sér. Ca, Car. 34, Admiral Antoine Schwerer, Reports, April 2, 1920, December 30, 1920, December, 1920, in Cars. 34 and 36, all in Archives de la marine.

7. On status anxieties, see Martin Trow, "Small Business, Political Tolerance, and Support for McCarthy," in Lewis A. Coser (ed.), *Political Sociology* (New York, 1967), 198–99.

provement became living examples of Maurice Barrès' uprooted Frenchmen. The bitter mood that spread throughout the Navy would fade very slowly.

As men of habit and tradition, many officers were inclined to revive customs and thoughts from better years gone by. They sought ways to reconstruct the life and excitement of the years before 1914. Some looked for a renewed effort in the colonies, where the navy had large responsibilities. Others took up old disputes about naval strategy that had their foundations in the early years of the Third Republic. A few officers even engaged in the ideological debate over the legislation separating church and state as it was applied to the navy. In the journals and in private discussions, these men pursued their ideas with the fervor of converts, believing that their personal energy would somehow produce a stronger navy and a better way of life for its personnel. Generally, the officers split into two groups, paralleling the division in France between progressive and conservative factions.

Although an officer could pass freely from one bloc to the other, the issues each faction supported remained unreconcilable. So long as no one group of men dominated the navy, there would be a seesaw competition for domination at the higher ranks. The 1920s turned out to be just that. These were years of groping for restored naval power and prestige after a long decline. With the lifetime of every government uncertain, the power of the Naval General Staff to formulate policy was all the more enhanced.

The progressive and conservative factions within the naval officer corps can be traced directly to the mid-1870s when lines were first drawn over ways to modernize the fleet. The two opposing cliques split further during the Dreyfus affair when each rallied behind a banner of ideological, religious, and political slogans. Those who sought some technical and social change in the navy usually found themselves in the minority. In the 1880s, these officers tended to be young and less influenced by tradition than their military superiors. Admiral Théophile Aube, a spokesman for this reformist movement who served as naval chief of staff in the mid-1880s, set modernization of the fleet as his prime objective. In addition to new technology, he and his followers also sought a number of social changes during the following decade. By the turn of the century, reform-minded officers became the protégés of the new Radical party leaders under the Dupuy, Waldeck-Rousseau, and Combes governments.[8]

Naturally, this progressive wing of the naval officer corps met resistance from others in the navy who believed in preserving the *status quo.* Each side usually had an unofficial senior spokesman who attracted the following of younger officers seeking kindred souls and protection for their ideas. In the 1920s Admirals Henri Salaün and Hector Violette wore the mantle of their predecessor, Admiral Aube. During the interwar years, conservatives served as naval chief of staff from 1918 until 1924.Their tenure was briefly interrupted in 1920 when Admiral Salaün held office for a few months. He soon lost his job when Admirals Antoine Schwerer and Lucien Lacaze complained that, as a former official in the Combes government, he was a political liability to the navy. In 1924 Salaün was reappointed naval chief of staff for a full term, and in 1928 Admiral Violette succeeded him for the next four-year term. The 1932–1936 term went to a conservative, who was succeeded by Admiral François Darlan. He was the leader of a small group of officers who emerged during World War I but exerted no independent power until Darlan became chief of staff. These men identified themselves with efficiency and good management techniques and allied themselves with whatever political or uniformed leader offered strong, centralized guidance to the minister of marine. It was only in the last few months before World War II that this technocratic group emerged on top, espousing a specific political cause. Until then, these men served under both progressive and conservative leaders without any apparent ideological conflict. Meanwhile, the two larger groups of naval officers competed for influence at the cabinet level where the minister of marine retained an admiral as personal aide and confidant. When one faction got their man appointed as naval chief of staff, the other sought to maintain a balance by having one of theirs appointed aide to the minister.[9]

8. Theodore Ropp, "Continental Doctrines of Sea Power," in Edward Mead Earle (ed.), *Makers of Modern Strategy: Military Thought from Machiavelli to Hitler* (Princeton, 1971), 446–49; Theodore Ropp, *War in the Modern World* (Rev. ed.; New York, 1962), 208–209.

9. Captain Renan to Admiral Hector Violette, January 28, 1921, Admiral Georges Mouget to Violette, July 17, 1929, both in Admiral Hector Violette Papers, Private

The Salaün-Violette Staff
Admirals Henri Salaün, *front right,* and Hector Violette, *front center,*
brought together the progressive elements in the naval officer corps.
Violette was the only Freemason to reach top rank in the navy between
the world wars. *Violette Family Photo*

Officers who sought technological reforms in the 1880s took up
the name Jeune École, a title implying both their youth and the
new thought that characterized these men. At first, they only sought
to expand the use of the steam engine as a substitute for sails. By
the 1880s, marine engineering had advanced only far enough to
make steam practical on small vessels. Later on, Jeune École theo-
rists tried to adapt commerce raiding and ironclads to French use.
Eventually, these officers began a campaign to convert the entire
French navy into a force of light coastal defense ships and fast com-

Collection; Admiral Raoul Castex, *Questions d'état-major: principes, organisation, fonctionnement* (2 vols.; Paris, 1923–24), I, 366; Captain Charles Ferrand, *Programme naval, études maritimes* (Paris, 1908), 206–208.

merce raiders. With these two weapons, the members of the Jeune École believed that France could dominate the western Mediterranean and, if necessary, destroy any unsuspecting European fleet in a sneak attack. These men also believed that this new strategy would provide the best possible colonial defense at the lowest possible cost. They knew that the war debt to Germany after 1871 and the need to rebuild the French army after Sedan would favor a national strategy that called for an inexpensive navy.[10] But this kind of fleet based on the latest technology would require new kinds of sailors whose mechanical skills were more important than either seamanship or navigation. This led the Jeune École to seek a broader pattern of recruitment, beyond the traditional source of Breton fishermen and merchant sailors.

Debates over the merits of this new kind of navy started in the Parliament and the leading journals in the late 1870s and continued for the next half century. Leading naval officers and political figures often joined in heated discussions over the merits of the Jeune École's proposals. Although opposing factions in this debate declared a truce during World War I, they fell out again in the 1920s over the same unresolved issues. This time, technological breakthroughs and political considerations modified the positions of the two factions in the navy.[11] Engineers were capable of building steam engines that could power even the largest warships at great speeds, and this innovation narrowed the advantage that smaller warships held up to that time.

In 1918 as in 1871 the French government was on the verge of bankruptcy. Once again, the Parliament found it easy to accept any argument for a less expensive fleet. Moreover, the political Left of the 1920s found Jeune École doctrines congenial to their own be-

---

10. Ropp, "Continental Doctrines of Sea Power," 448.

11. *Journal officiel de la République Française. Chambre des députés. Projet de loi, propositions et rapports.* November 21, 1878, Annexe 926, pp. 125–29; ibid., *Débats parlementaires,* December 5, 1891, p. 710; Gabriel Charmes, "La Réforme de la marine," *Revue des deux mondes,* LXVI (December 15, 1884), 872–906; Jean La Bruyère, "Revue des questions navales et maritimes," *Revue politique et parlementaire,* CXXX (January, 1927), 141; "Chronique des marines française et étrangères," *Revue maritime,* CLXXV (July, 1934), 93–94; Commandant Z [Paul Fontin], "Chronique maritime," *Nouvelle revue,* LIV (September, 1888), to LXXII (September, 1891), an ongoing column supporting Admiral Aube.

liefs. Beyond the economic argument that small ships cost less, these politicians believed that a fleet without battleships was most appropriate for a democratic nation seeking self-defense rather than imperial conquest.[12] This view was the naval equivalent of Jean Jaurès' appeal for a conscript army. As his army of short-term conscripts would theoretically provide the best defense of French territory, so too would the fleet of small warships that had only short range and little offensive power. Thus tied to the *métropole*, the navy could not have an imperial role.[13]

Political support for Jaurès' conscript army and the navy's Jeune École doctrine arose at the same time. From 1895 until 1905, three men from the Radical party dominated the Ministry of Marine. They sponsored programs for small, fast warships, and they favored the progressive officers who wanted them as parts of a parallel effort to modernize the fleet and to democratize the officer corps by opening the doors to a diversity of young men. These politicians also sought to implement the separation of church and state in this strongly religious institution.[14]

The first of these radical ministers, Edouard Lockroy, pushed through a series of institutional reforms after witnessing the poor response of the navy in the Fashoda crisis of 1898. He was succeeded by Jean de Lanessan, a natural historian and fervent social Darwinist who taught evolution theory at the Faculté de médecine in Paris. His ideas about evolution and social progress were at the heart of his efforts to reform the naval officer corps. The masonic lodge, Grand Orient, named him a mason of the thirty-third order when he terminated compulsory religious ceremonies aboard French warships. These services had been very important to many officers, especially on Good Friday when the vessels were draped in black, the crew dressed in mourning, and the flag flown at half mast. De Lanessan saw democracy, social progress, and colonial ex-

12. *Journal Officiel. Députés. Débats*, December 5, 1924, pp. 4190–92, April 24, 1925, pp. 2213–14, December 9, 1929, pp. 4488–4508; du Ravay, *Vingt ans*, 171–72.
13. Richard D. Challener, *The French Theory of the Nation in Arms, 1866–1939* (New York, 1952), 71–74.
14. Jean Jolly (ed.), *Dictionnaire des parlementaires français: notices biographiques sur les ministres, députés, et sénateurs français de 1889 à 1940* (8 vols.; Paris, 1960–77), VI, 2120–21, 2288–89, VII, 2637–38.

pansion all tied together as three pillars of human evolution. He and his supporters believed all Frenchmen fell into one of two categories: agricultural men, who belonged to an "outdated society," and all others, whom de Lanessan saw as "modern believers in intense civilization."[15]

Although de Lanessan irritated many conservative officers, he appeared mild by comparison with the man who followed him, Camille Pelletan. As minister of marine in Emile Combes' government, Pelletan pushed anticlerical reforms even further than either of his predecessors and believed in the "democratic" value of a fleet limited to small warships. Poor administrative practices plagued his ministry, adding to the already tense relations between him and a large number of naval officers.[16]

His counterpart at the Ministry of War was General Louis André, whose attempts to democratize the army officer corps finally toppled the government in the *affaire des fiches*. André was accused of using information about the political beliefs of his officers, which he obtained from the Masonic lodges, against them. On his staff was the energetic young naval officer Lieutenant Hector Violette, who had become a Mason while on duty in Tunis. There, in a small closely knit French colony, the local bishop introduced Violette to the president of the local lodge. The three men shared a common desire for social reform in France at a time when the lodges sponsored this cause and attracted a significant military following. True to the hereditary traditions in the navy, Violette's son became a career naval officer and a Mason and married the niece of General André.[17]

15. *Ibid.*; Office of Naval Intelligence, Naval Attaché Report, Paris, July 22, 1897, June 30, 1899, February 8, 1902, all E-5-c, 4794, in National Archives; Jean-Louis de Lanessan, *La Lutte pour l'existence et l'évolution des sociétés* (Paris, 1903), 9, 274; David Shapiro (ed.), *The Right in France, 1890–1919: Three Studies* (Carbondale, Ill., 1962), 121; Louis V. Méjan, *La Séparation des églises et de l'état* (Paris, 1959), 55; Admiral Paul Reveillère, "France et marine," *Nouvelle revue*, LXXVII (August 15, 1892), 682–92.

16. Jolly (ed.), *Dictionnaire des parlementaires*, VII, 2637–38; ONI, Naval Attaché Report, Paris (Discussion of Gabriel Bonhomme and Pelletan), December 15, 1904, E-5-c, 4794, NA; Gabriel Bonhomme, *Trois ans rue Royale; moeurs ministérielles, 1901–1904* (Paris, 1904), Chap. 1.

17. Madame Jean Violette, Interview, July 18, 1975; Pierre Chevalier, *La Maçonnerie: église de la république, 1877–1944* (Paris, 1975), 95, Vol. III of *Histoire de la*

Another young naval officer, Henri Salaün, served as a junior aide to Camille Pelletan. It was during their two and a half years in the Combes government that Violette and Salaün met and formed a lifetime friendship. Other officers close to them who also became admirals were Louis Le D'O and Michel Le Vavasseur, who were well respected in the navy as seagoing officers. Another follower was the strategist Admiral Raoul Castex. Louis de La Monneraye and François Darlan were also close to Salaün and Violette but outside the progressive movement; they too would eventually reach the top rank.[18]

Violette and Salaün tried to alleviate some of the more blatant inequalities within the officer corps by opening admissions to more qualified men. Both frequently appeared at the interwar disarmament conferences, where they supported mutual, balanced naval arms reductions. Naturally, they favored Aristide Briand's diplomatic efforts, to the dismay of their conservative opponents in the navy, who believed he was sacrificing French strength without sufficient concessions from rival powers. Like Briand, Violette and Salaün tended to be anglophile in their foreign policy outlook, though they were disappointed with British intransigence during these disarmament conferences.

By 1924, Violette and Salaün had generated such hostility in the officer corps that only the return to power of Edouard Herriot, the famous prewar Radical, saved the two from early retirement. One usually friendly journalist was moved to warn the officers against this political antagonism, reminding them that "they had other cats to skin."[19] Violette and Salaün, though condemned for their political affiliations, were universally respected for their professional talents, however. Violette's technical knowledge of optics and gunnery and Salaün's skill as a strategic planner were unsur-

---

franc-maçonnerie française, 3 vols.; General Louis André to Commander Jean Violette, April 14, 1950, in Hector Violette Papers.

18. Admiral Louis Le D'O to Hector Violette, February 5, 1930, Admiral Raoul Castex to Hector Violette, June 28, 1904, January 8, 1929, all in Hector Violette Papers; Admiral Louis de La Monneraye, Interview, July 23, 1975.

19. ONI, Naval Attaché Report, Paris, July 29, 1924, E-5-c, 4794-B, NA; Jean La Bruyère, "Questions navales et maritimes," *Revue politique et parlementaire*, CXX (August, 1924), 311.

passed in the French navy. Violette often sat in for the minister of marine at defense planning conferences, where his detailed knowledge of agenda items boosted the navy's position during the bureaucratic infighting for money.[20] In the end, these two men retained a small following within the navy and gained the respect of political leaders from the Center as well as the Left. Georges Leygues, an old opportunist republican who frequently served as minister of marine from 1917 to 1933, became one of Violette's leading supporters.

The progressive movement lost its last major spokesman within the officer corps when Violette retired in 1932. Both he and Salaün warned about the motives of the new regimes in Germany and Italy from retirement, as did Admiral Louis Jaurès, younger brother of the famous Jean, who had retired in 1924 and came to serve as deputy of the Socialist party.[21] Violette was among the last of several prominent officers commissioned in the 1880s and early 1890s who did not conform to the traditional mold of the *grand corps*. The cause of naval reform sponsored by men like Aube and Violette had always attracted a disproportionately large number of officers from atypical homes and nontraditional preparatory schools leading to the École navale. The impetus for change, therefore, had a strong foundation among those officers who did not fit the more elitist mold of the *grand corps*. After Violette's retirement, such men no longer rose to the top.[22]

In the years after 1918 the greatest obstacles to naval officers like Salaün, Violette, and Jaurès were their ties with the political Left and anticlerical groups. Aggressive officers who had at first favored

---

20. Georges Leygues to Hector Violette, April 11, 1929, March 3, May 2, 1931, all in Hector Violette Papers; La Monneraye Interview.

21. Admiral Henri Salaün, *La Marine française* (Paris, 1934), 388–89, 399, 421, 425, 441–57; Hector Violette to his wife, March 31, 1930, in Hector Violette Papers. Violette wrote articles for three regional newspapers: *La République*, *Le Petit Var*, and *Le Socialiste Cote d'Orien*, from his retirement in 1932 until his death in 1950.

22. Madame Jean Violette Interview; Commander Loïc Abrial, Interview, July 28, 1975; La Monneraye Interview; President of the Toulon Lodge of the Grand Orient, Interview, June 29, 1975; Mouget to Hector Violette, April 23, 1929, in Hector Violette Papers; Henri Salaün to Minister of Marine, Memoranda, August 15, 1920, in Sér. 1BB2¹, Car. 86, August 13, 1920, in Sér. Ca, Car. 36, both in Archives de la marine; "Le Nouveau Chef de l'état–major général de la marine," *Action française*, February 10, 1928, p. 3; Jolly (ed.), *Dictionnaire des parlementaires*, VI, 2017.

the strategic benefits of the Jeune École later went on to support other kinds of change within the navy. The Dreyfus affair, the separation of church and state, and finally the naval disarmament talks all attracted these officers, who cultivated friendships with like-minded politicians. Without a senior officer to push along new ideas, however, the progressive movement within the navy largely ceased to exist as an alternative point of view on maritime affairs. If the number of articles published on naval reforms is any indication of the strength of this group, the progressive element within the navy shrank from just under one-half of the *grand corps* in the early 1880s to less than one-tenth of this same group in the late 1920s. Naval officers with Masonic affiliations, characteristic of this progressive group, almost vanished after World War I. This trend is consistent with the flocking of young conservative boys to the French armed forces under the Third Republic. Those who entered in the 1890s had reached the top by the 1930s.[23]

The conservatives took control of the naval officer corps in 1932 with the appointment of Georges Durand-Viel as naval chief of staff. Married to the daughter of the shipbuilding magnate August Le Normand, Durand-Viel was an avid supporter of the elitist tradition within the *grand corps*. He followed in the footsteps of earlier admirals who treated a naval commission more as a deed to a piece of property than as a certificate of professional qualification. Under the Third Republic, the first in a long line of naval traditionalists had been Admiral Jurien de La Gravière, whose history books on ancient and early modern naval campaigns earned him membership in the Académie française and whose position in the Parisian aristocracy of the *belle époque* was noted even by Proust.[24] Among his fellow spokesmen for the conservative cause within the navy were Admirals Lucien Lacaze, Antoine Schwerer, and Jean Decoux.

23. These estimates are based on articles on naval subjects appearing in *Revue maritime, Revue nautique, Revue politique et parlementaire, Revue des deux mondes, Nouvelle revue, Revue hebdomadaire, Revue universelle, Revue de Paris, La Vie des peuples, L'Almanach de l'Action française,* and *Revue politique et littéraire* during the era 1871–1940. These were the most important journals covering naval matters under the Third Republic. On social composition of the officer corps, see La Gorce, *La République,* Chap. 2.

24. Marcel Proust, *A la recherche du temps perdu* (3 vols.; Paris, 1947), I, 340–41 (*Le Côté de Guermantes II*); Madame Roger Houzel (née Durand-Viel), Interview, June 24, 1974, July 10, 1975.

By the early 1930s, the conservative officers were in a clear majority. Although they had never formally organized themselves, they banded together to oppose the appointment of men like Salaün and Violette and their proposals. By sheer weight of numbers, they came to dominate existing naval institutions such as the Association amicale des anciens élèves de l'École navale, which assisted in preserving the elitist social composition of the *grand corps*. In the days of Admiral Aube, conservative officers wished to retain the big, slow-moving battleships as queens of the fleet. They continued to believe that only these large warships could win decisive battles at sea. They also resisted the move of the École navale ashore in Brest, and they saw little need to expand the curriculum there to include more science and engineering. They blamed Admiral Violette for the reforms of the school, which they viewed as desecration.[25]

Schwerer and others also worried about the problems in the shipyards. Although they needed them to build and repair ships, these officers feared the growth of syndicalism among shipyard workers would have a harmful effect on naval personnel. Consequently, there was a strong conservative effort in the Parliament to turn all shipyards over to the private sector through the 1920s. Sponsors of this idea wished to keep the navy as far from organized labor as possible. One deputy genuinely believed that "the naval shipyards were the place for the next Bolshevik revolution." To reduce contact between civilians and sailors to an absolute minimum, Admiral Schwerer recommended that the fleet remain permanently at sea except for brief port calls to refuel and replenish.[26]

At the heart of this conservatism was the desire to preserve the naval officer corps as a special caste within French society. From the 1880s through the 1920s, opinions on this were quite consis-

---

25. *Journal officiel. Sénat. Débats*, March 27, 1888, p. 536; Vice Admiral Siméon Bourgeois, "La Guerre de course–la guerre et les torpilles," Pt. 1, *Nouvelle revue*, XLI (July 15, 1886), 273–307; Admiral Jurien de La Gravière, "La Marine d'aujourd'hui," *Revue des deux mondes*, XCIV (August 15, 1871), 689–717; Commandant Z [Paul Fontin], "Le Péril maritime," *Nouvelle revue*, LII (June 15, 1888), 821–46; du Ravay, *Vingt ans*, 240–42; La Monneraye Interview; Captain Aubert du Parc, "Dégénérescence de notre marine de guerre," *Action française*, April 17, 1921, p. 3.

26. Comte de Fels, "Les Richesses de l'état française: notre établissement naval," *Revue de Paris*, XX (October, 1925), 725; Albert Thomas, "Les Problèmes de la marine de guerre," *Action française*, January 23, 1921, p. 2.

tent. Senior officers sponsored the careers of young men who would be groomed as the next generation of naval leaders. This plan went hand in hand with the selection of midshipmen for the École navale and the continued dominance of the *grand corps* over the rest of the naval officers. Even the promotion system became an extension of the preferential treatment for a select few. At one time, an officer was promoted less on his performance than on sociological data showing the number of children he had, the kind of family he came from, the type and location of his home, and any honors he might have received. Note was also made of his "morality," though the means of evaluation remain unclear.[27]

Officers of the *grand corps* and their wives developed an entire vocabulary of snobbish terms to describe their *petits corps* subordinates. Petty bickering also persisted among the wives, reaching its worst level in the decades prior to the First World War. The two-tiered system in the officer corps survived the war and became official in 1922 when Admiral Maurice Grasset pushed through new regulations formalizing the split between the *grand* and the *petit corps*. Admiral Salaün and a few in the navy's Premier bureau (personnel) warned of future problems if the two-class system in the officer corps, pitting officer against officer, were continued. But Admiral Grasset won the support of the École navale alumni society, by arguing that the same dangers would arise if the officer corps were opened to all on the basis of talent alone. Evidently the alumni society, conservator of the prestige and honor of the *grand corps*, held the majority view. As in the past, the line officers of the navy would continue to be "the elite of the nation."[28]

27. Rear Admiral Louis Mandet, "La Loi des cadres de la marine," *Nouvelle revue*, XLVI (June 1, 1887), 510, 516; Commandant Z [Paul Fontin], "L'Amiral Aube," *Nouvelle revue*, LXVIII (February 1, 1891); 613, 620; Salaün to Minister of Marine, memorandum, August 13, 1920, in Sér. Ca, Car. 36, Archives de la marine; Mouget to Hector Violette, April 23, 1929, in Hector Violette Papers; Un ancien officier de la marine, "L'Avancement dans la marine," *Nouvelle revue*, XVI (June 1, 1882), 481–517.

28. Lieutenant François de Mury, "Nos officiers de marine," and "Un dernier mot," both in *Revue politique et littéraire*, XVII (February, 1902), 132–36 (March, 1902), 265–66; Salaün, *Marine française*, 384–85; Salaün to Minister of Marine, memorandum, August 15, 1920, in Sér. 1BB2¹, Car. 86, Archives de la marine; G. G., "La Question des cadres," *Nouvelle revue*, LII (June 15, 1888), 800; Lieutenant Raymond de Villaine to École navale alumni, October 18, 1920, Program for the AEN ball, Admiral Le Bris, open letter, February 14, 1935, all in Archives de AEN.

Elitism in the navy went hand in hand with attitudes toward race and religion that the Dreyfus affair brought into public view. This crisis involving an army captain of Jewish parentage did more than anything else to divide naval officers into two permanently hostile camps. Officials at the Ministry of Marine had contact with France's leading anti-Semite, Edouard Drumont. They attempted to expose a Jewish conspiracy within the ministry, showing that "beyond a doubt, the Jews are our masters." The officer making these claims could not back his findings with facts but assumed he could identify Jews merely by their work habits and secretive life-styles.[29] A less virulent form of anti-Semitism, common in the French bourgeoisie and aristocracy of the day, also pervaded the naval officer corps. Conservative Catholic officers believed that Jews exerted a strong influence over the École polytechnique and the *corps de génie maritime*. The American naval attaché at the time of the Dreyfus affair, Lieutenant W. S. Sims, found "the treatment of the Jews shameful" during his tenure in France. Even as late as the 1930s, naval officers remained anti-Semitic in outlook. Admiral Castex saw in the Stalinist regime a "Judeo-Slavic" plot to dominate the rest of Europe. Admiral Durand-Viel was very sensitive to remarks that he looked "a little bit Jewish."[30] If there was any trend, those officers with the strongest ties to Catholicism, like Admirals Schwerer and Decoux, tended to be most anti-Semitic.

One of the most vocal anti-Semitic naval officers, Admiral Schwerer, called the French government "a Jewish-Masonic regime which sought to destroy the family, the country, and religion all together . . . by de-Christianizing France." He condemned communists, socialists, radicals, liberals, and even Christian Democrats for trying to destroy essential French values. Probably the toughest decision for Schwerer and others who supported the *Action française* came in 1928 when the Vatican placed the neomonarchist

---

29. Paul Masson, *Le Juif dans la marine: étude de moeurs administratives* (Paris, 1891), 171.

30. W. S. Sims to his mother, January 24, 1898, in Box 4, Admiral W. S. Sims Papers, Naval Historical Foundation Section, Manuscript Collection, Library of Congress; Admiral Raoul Castex, *De Gengis-Khan à Staline; ou, les vicissitudes d'une maneuvre stratégique, 1205–1935* (Paris, 1935), 43; Bernard Paquet, Interview, June 30, 1975.

daily newspaper of Charles Maurras on the papal *Index*. Naval officers, like all other French readers, could choose between excommunication and subscribing to other similar newspapers that were not banned by the Church.[31]

Potential rival nations disturbed conservative naval officers even more than the Vatican and the papal *Index*. Although progressives from Aube through Violette had all favored good relations with Britain, conservative officers remained confirmed anglophobes. Memories of naval campaigns lost to the English, and the burning desire to seek revenge were too strong to overcome in many French naval circles. Traditionalists led the campaign for the Latin alliance and a concentration of naval might in the Mediterranean, stressing the ties with the empire in North Africa. A journalist and friend of naval conservatives spoke of this diplomatic dream as the start of a "United States of Europe" and as a bulwark against communism. Throughout the 1920s, however, little was done to piece this alliance together, for the official mood remained anglophile under Salaün and Violette.[32]

From the start, efforts toward naval disarmament raised the ire of many conservative officers. At the Washington Naval Conference of 1921–1922, many believed that Britain had duped the French government, and they maintained this attitude throughout the interwar years. Many officers believed that the two Latin powers, France and Italy, had been sacrificed to meet the security needs of the three larger naval powers, Britain, the United States, and Japan. Even moderates in the French delegation at Washington expressed dismay at the outcome.

> From our side, we Frenchmen have the impression of finding ourselves here in the presence of an Anglo-American alliance in which England sacrificed Japan so that the United States would help her ally in finally doing away with the remainder of the European navies. Possibly this is not so but such is the impression of a large majority of Frenchmen. We cannot avoid being upset when we hear Lord Lee [head of the British delegation] declare that England must have three times more capital

31. Admiral Antoine Schwerer, "Un correspondance de l'Amiral Schwerer avec Cardinal Binet," *Action française*, May 3, 1928, pp. 1–2; Hélène de David-Beauregard, *Souvenirs de famille* (Toulon, 1970), 179.

32. Du Ravay, *Vingt ans*, 74–75, 81–92; René La Bruyère, "Revue des questions navales et maritimes," *Revue politique et parlementaire*, CXLVII (April, 1931), 18.

ships than France whereas the [British] Admiralty found it sufficient to have two capital ships against every one German. This does not endanger our material independence but it does our diplomatic independence and we cannot understand the motives which made America join her efforts to those of England, placing France in this inferior position.[33]

Admiral William S. Sims, the American recipient of this letter, had no explanation for his French friend of many years. The author captured the spirit of French naval opinion, which became a rallying point for many conservative officers throughout the interwar period. Far to the Right, Léon Daudet went even further in condemning the Washington Naval Treaty as "a new Trafalgar" for France.[34] With the French and Italian fleets pegged at the same size by this treaty, officers in both navies saw their mutual security assured only as close allies in the Mediterranean.

For the time being, budgetary constraints in France kept naval construction within the ceiling imposed at Washington. This created a situation in which progressive and conservative officers together endorsed a plan for a new fleet of small warships like the one advocated by the Jeune École. This accord between Right and Left in the navy was only a temporary alliance of convenience, which ended in 1933 with the end of centrist domination of the Ministry of Marine. The same year also marked the virtual end of constructive efforts to reach consensus on European disarmament. The rise of the Nazi party in Germany and the trend toward confrontation in diplomacy encouraged the Naval General Staff to seek new alternatives for French security. At the same time, officers turned more to extremist politics such as the Action Française, which now had widespread support among the bourgeoisie and within the military in particular.

Prior to 1914, the Action Française had been the political home of the French aristocracy, who saw in Charles Maurras a flicker of hope for their own political future. In those years, the aristocratic families were economically strained, and they had little hope for a

---

33. Captain Joseph Frochot to Sims, December 29, 1921, in Sims Papers.
34. Sims to Admiral Ferdinand de Bon, December 28, 1921, *ibid.*; de Bon, notes, November 18, 1921, February 18, 1922, both in Sér. Ca, Car. 50, Archives de la marine; ONI, Naval Attaché Report (Press reports), Paris, July 30, 1922, C-10-L, 14811-D, NA; Léon Daudet, "Briand, naufrageur de la marine française," *Action française,* March 26, 1922, p. 1.

return of the Bourbon monarchy. The Count de Chambord's refusal to compromise with the Orléanist heir over the issue of the French flag split the royalist cause badly and ended its chances to achieve political ascendancy. During the first fifty years of the Third Republic, the bourgeoisie lived comparatively well in a nation with very little inflation and hardly any organized labor to cut into business profits. By 1920, however, these bourgeois families faced many of the same problems that the aristocracy had known for years. The end of economic stability and the growing labor movement changed the balance that the bourgeoisie had relied upon before 1914.

The military services remained a special haven for sons of the aristocracy and those bourgeois families in search of secure employment or just familiar company. In the armed forces, the sons of impoverished or economically strained homes could find the kind of prestige, dignity, and good pension available nowhere else. Moreover, the officer corps became a melting pot where families from the old second and third estates could mix and intermarry. Every fifth wedding of an École navale alumnus between the world wars involved at least one spouse from a noble family. One-eighth of the admirals came from the aristocracy as well. Two-thirds of all men entering the École navale came from elitist preparatory schools where either wealth or prominent social status were prerequisites for admission. It was natural that these two classes, which now also faced hard economic times together, would search for joint solutions to their common frustrations.[35]

In the gloomy days of the early 1920s, the Action Française became a very important institution for naval officers from aristocratic and bourgeois homes alike. Their growing interest in the theories of Charles Maurras coincided with a nationwide growth in his following. By the early 1930s, approximately one-sixth of all Action Française supporters willing to identify themselves claimed the military as their occupation. Neomonarchism exerted its strongest influence upon young professional men, including junior naval officers.[36]

35. Pierre Chalmin, L'Officier français de 1815 à 1870 (Paris, 1957), 149–93, and Chap. 2, Tables 4–7.
36. Eugen Weber, Action Française: Royalism and Reaction in Twentieth Cen-

Naval ties with the Action Française certainly predate 1918. From 1905 on, naval officers and even a former minister of marine joined in public support of Charles Maurras. Commander and Madame Stanislas David-Beauregard were both introduced to French royalism as children, and they in turn indoctrinated their own sons and daughters in the same political tradition. The biggest single influx of naval followers to neomonarchism and the Action Française came in 1924 when Admiral Schwerer retired from the navy to join Maurras' editorial board. He brought with him other former naval officers who set out to expand the coverage of maritime affairs from an occasional article to a major topic of interest. The tone of their columns obviously satisfied some of the frustrations that naval readers had experienced but had been reluctant to discuss openly. Schwerer's pessimism about France's future also attracted officers who had a difficult time understanding how a victorious nation could be in such distress after the war.[37]

Military and naval interests in the daily *Action française* supported the expansion of armed forces coverage to a biweekly full page entitled, "Armée et marine." Writers focused on veterans' rights, deficiencies in pay, and the importance of military honor. Additionally, Jacques Bainville devoted a great deal of attention in his front-page columns to the naval disarmament conferences.[38]

Naval officers placed a great deal of emphasis on the written style of their newspapers and literature. The sophisticated flair of the *Action française* appealed to many who read only that material they considered "well written." Moreover, if Commander David-Beauregard's feelings are at all representative of those of other naval readers, then the officers found intellectual comfort in the strongly

tury France (Stanford, 1962), 267, 420, and Chap. 8; Samuel M. Osgood, *French Royalism under the Third and Fourth Republics* (The Hague, 1960), 113; Edward R. Tannenbaum, *The Action Française: Die-hard Reactionaries in Twentieth Century France* (New York, 1960), 134.

37. Tannenbaum, *Action Française*, 34, 254; David-Beauregard, *Souvenirs*, 36; Admiral Antoine Schwerer, "Armée et marine" (Obituary of J. Monlau), *Action française*, November 25, 1931; Commander Georges Débat, Interview, June 22, 1976; Paquet Interview.

38. Bainville's articles on the naval conferences appeared in *Action française*, October 29, 1921, June 22, 1927, February 14, November 15, 1929, almost daily from January 10 to March 30, 1930, and March 24, 1932.

nationalist tone of the articles by Admiral Schwerer, Charles Maurras, and several others. Additional political and literary reading material likely to be found in ships' wardrooms in the 1920s were *Revue des deux mondes, Journal des débats, Revue de Paris,* and *Revue universelle.* All shared a conservative political outlook; some even employed writers who also worked for the *Action française.* Naval leaders identified closely with Marcel Proust's interpretation of the French aristocracy, and few officers expressed any interest in non-French or non-Latin writers.[39]

One naval officer who bore the requisite marks of the elite in his birth, education, and tastes was Commander René Guilbaud, a naval aviator who captured the fancy of his fellow officers by his romantic dash before losing his life in an airplane accident. Guilbaud was born into a rural landed family in the Vendée, traditional home of the French aristocracy. He attended the École navale, where he demonstrated a preference for romantic literature and foreign languages over the applied sciences. He turned to the *Action française* prior to World War I because of the newspaper's style and political outlook. He spent his off-duty hours reading the works of Gide, Rimbaud, and Baudelaire, while espousing an intellectual preference for neomonarchism. Admirals Lucien Lacaze and Jean de Laborde, both affiliated with royalist politics, sponsored the young pilot throughout his short career. Commander Guilbaud became one of many officers to see the neomonarchist cause as a great public supporter of the navy and its elitist *grand corps.*[40]

Conservatives began to fear that they were no longer in the mainstream of French society and that they would need to work very hard to preserve what remained of their former status. The Action Française attracted many of these officers, who found postwar conditions too confusing or threatening. Georges Débat was shocked to find that the École navale had become a special haven for Maurrasism, which had taken hold in the officer corps just when, he believed, caution and moderation were the most needed.

39. Weber, *Action Française,* 188–93, 266; Charles Peyrucq, Interview, June 8, 1974; Loïc Abrial Interview; Paquet Interview; Admiral René Godfroy, Interview, July 2, 1975.

40. Roger Coindreau, "La Vie héroique de René Guilbaud, 1890–1929," *Revue de Bas-Poitou,* n.v. (November, 1958), 1–33; Osgood, *French Royalism,* 100.

Débat evidently believed that self-pity had overcome critical judgment within the navy. "Under the sentimental reaction, efforts to analyze [problems] died before they hatched. Moreover, in a profession like ours, a sort of instinct drove us toward order, military discipline and repression, the unacknowledged prelude to fascism."[41]

The *Action française* staff shared the same authoritarian instincts that Débat recognized in his classmates. Former naval engineer Bernard Paquet considered it "a law of nature" that French naval officers should turn to the Action Française in the 1920s. Even the papal interdict against the newspaper in 1926 did little to dissuade officers and their families from the doctrines preached by Charles Maurras. Those who chose to obey Rome did so only in a technical sense by turning to other newspapers like *Gringoire* and *Candide* that shared the outlook and even some of the same journalists with the *Action française*. Many families simply defied the ban in the belief that the French clergy would look the other way rather than enforce canon law.[42]

As time passed, officers began questioning the legitimacy of national institutions more seriously. Such crises of legitimacy tend to occur whenever a group sees change threatening institutions it depends upon or when the group loses power and prestige to other interests in the society. In the case of the French naval officers, they turned to the *Action française* in a desperate attempt to preserve their elite status. Neomonarchism seemed a sturdy beacon of hope when nothing else provided any stability. It offered a chance for a return to "the good old days" when everything had been just fine.[43] At first, right-wing ideology seemed a sort of pastime; officers read it along with their romantic fiction and poetry. It seemed to require no action. Gradually, however, the dilettantish preference for nationalistic prose by authors like Barrès became serious political reading with the *Action française*. Maurrasism became the backbone that many of them felt France had lost after 1918. The officers

41. Georges Débat, *Marine oblige* (Paris, 1974), 13–14, 19.

42. Paquet Interview; David-Beauregard, *Souvenirs*, 183; Jacques Godechot, Interview, June 25, 1975.

43. On the concept of legitimacy, see Seymour Martin Lipset, *Political Man: The Social Bases of Politics* (New York, 1960), 64–65; Loïc Abrial Interview; Débat Interview.

came to need this cause to help bring back the life they had known before the war.

Although moderate and conservative naval officers did not agree in detail, they traveled in the same direction, seeking a confrontation with the parliamentary process. For the time being, few had the courage to challenge the constituted authorities directly. They simply set about to test the limits of their ability to speak out on political matters that interested them. Blatant protest remained muffled. If officers wished to demonstrate their feelings in public, they did so by marching in the Joan of Arc Day parades at which government figures and Action Française leaders appeared together. In more private surroundings, naval officers sought other outlets for their frustrations with a system they no longer trusted. Midshipmen eyed the bust of Admiral de Rigny, minister of marine to the last Bourbon king in 1830. Situated in the main corridor of the École navale, the bust "represented without any doubt 'La Royale,' faithful no matter what to his military duty and to the crown."[44]

The 1920s were a terribly difficult period of adjustment from wartime to a period of peace without the anticipated fruits of victory. The expectations of many that the armistice would restore prewar conditions were thwarted. Officers returned home only to encounter the same shortages and miseries that they had experienced during the war. This decade was also a period of confusion for many in the navy who sought answers to their economic and professional dilemmas. They simply could not find a satisfactory balance between existing conditions and their own aspirations.

Although 1932 probably did not seem like a threshold to them, it was a serious turning point for the French navy. As progressivism faded away and the centrist parliamentary influence over the Ministry of Marine ended, the competition for influence at rue Royale ceased. From that year on, a single voice rose to dominate the naval officer corps, which in political terms expressed itself through the Action Française. Although these officers had historical leanings toward conservative politics, before 1930 no one ever dared to speak as though the entire group supported royalism. The 1920s, how-

44. Photographs of the Fête de Jeanne d'Arc, *Action française*, May 17, 1932, p. 1; Débat, *Marine oblige*, 14.

ever, were the vital years when these men groped for a new direction for their profession and when they tested the political system to see how far they could go without causing a public outcry. By 1933, many who had earlier hesitated to speak out on national politics no longer feared to do so.

A few considerations remained unresolved. There was little doubt that there would be fewer leaders like Salaün and Violette at the top, but there was less assurance about the influence of future ministers of marine. These politicians could come from any political party and could alter existing naval programs, a fact that greatly disturbed officers who wanted to have the final say themselves. No one could yet see that a new technocratic faction within the *grand corps* was gaining power under the already well known Admiral François Darlan. The future of Europe, where the navy had its greatest interests, also remained unclear, although in 1932 many officers saw diplomatic instability and the failure of naval disarmament as warning signals. Certainly, all of this played a part in the outlook of influential officers who pondered the future in the tranquil setting of their wardrooms.

CHAPTER 6
What Do We Do with the Legislature?

While the admirals focused much of their attention on internal factional disputes, the Parliament spent unprecedented sums of money on the navy, completely renovating the fleet in short order. From 1922 until 1940, the legislature spent more on the navy than it had to that date under the Third Republic. A broad range of political interests singled out the navy from the other armed forces as a military institution worthy of generous and continued financial support. Throughout the two decades between the world wars, the Parliament set out to rebuild the entire battle fleet in a single coordinated program, something that had last taken place in France during the Seven Years' War. Of all the political parties, only the Communists voted as a bloc against naval funding during the interwar years. And when Léon Blum came to power in 1936, he even reversed the Communist stand and got record numbers of deputies to vote in favor of the navy's arms requests. His Popular Front government doubled the construction of warships after the failure of the naval disarmament talks and the repudiation of the Washington Naval Treaty in 1935. From 1936 until the armistice of 1940, not one senator or deputy cast a single vote against the annual naval appropriation bill.[1] Most casual observers of these events would conclude that French civil-naval relations were a model of how the Parliament and bureaucracy could strike an accord along professional and generally nonpartisan lines. Under the surface, however,

1. *Journal officiel de la République Française. Chambre des députés. Débats parlementaires*, and *Sénat. Débats parlementaires*, January 11, 1881–July 9, 1940, annual naval debates. See the tables in Admiral Raymond de Belot and André Reussner, *De 1919 à 1939* (Paris, 1971), 217–18, Vol. III of Andre Reussner (ed.), *La Puissance navale dans l'histoire*, 3 vols.

an intense and apparently incurable antiparliamentary sentiment survived in the officer corps throughout these years of nautical plenty.

Crucial to the navy's efforts in modernizing the fleet was the elderly statesman Georges Leygues. He began his parliamentary career in 1885 as a deputy from the remote southwestern town of Villeneuve-sur-Lot, which he represented without interruption until his death in 1933. He also rose to the leadership of the relatively unknown centrist party, Républicains de Gauche. Although the French political center had lost much of its previous strength by the 1920s, it still controlled enough votes in the Parliament to make or break coalitions on both the Left and Right. As an old republican of the opportunist school, Georges Leygues believed in political solutions through negotiation and compromise, an attitude that served him well as premier and during his twenty-one terms as cabinet minister, including minister of marine, in thirteen governments. His years at rue Royale attested to his durability as a politician in an era of revolving-door cabinets, spanning the political spectrum from Aristide Briand on the Left to André Tardieu on the Right. Leygues also enjoyed that rare sort of popular support from within the French naval officer corps that Winston Churchill won from the British navy when he served as first lord of the admiralty. At rue Royale headquarters, men on his staff called him "Père Leygues," a gesture of personal respect that they extended to no other politician between the world wars. He earned his reputation as an efficient organizer by orchestrating the Parliament's efforts to rebuild the fleet after 1918. Leygues also initiated an innovative public relations campaign that targeted nontraditional regions of the country where the navy had never recruited before.[2]

Leygues did not try to use the navy as a stepping stone to higher office. Even when he served as premier in 1920, he did so as a sort of caretaker for his predecessor, Alexandre Millerand, who became

2. Jean Jolly (ed.), *Dictionnaire des parlementaires français: notices biographiques sur les ministres, députés, et sénateurs français de 1889 à 1940* (8 vols.; Paris, 1960–77), VI, 2275–78; René Rémond, *La Droite en France de 1815 à nos jours* (Paris, 1954), 223, 269; Admiral Paul Auphan, Interview, June 5, 1974; Admiral René Godfroy, Interview, July 23, 1975; Jacques Raphaël-Leygues, "De Georges Leygues à la marine d'aujourd'hui et de demain," *Revue des deux mondes*, IX (September, 1972), 575–86.

Georges Leygues
Taking the navy as his special field of interest, Georges Leygues served as minister of marine in eleven governments from 1917 to 1933 and presided over the rebuilding of the fleet. He was one of the few politicians whom the officers liked. *National Archives Photo*

president. His public and private comments attest to Leygues' long-term interest in restoring French sea power as quickly as possible. Even during years of great fiscal austerity, Leygues always managed to obtain the necessary support for his naval programs from virtually the entire Parliament in spite of the fierce competition for money. During the lengthy parliamentary debates, he presented the navy as a nonpolitical institution, which every member of the Chamber of Deputies and the Senate could vote for without ideological qualms or guilt feelings. When the the rhetoric mounted to fever pitch and tied up his proposals in partisan squabbles, Leygues had an uncanny way of moving discussions along to a successful vote. His soothing comments during the 1926 naval budget debates demonstrate how he could intervene at precisely the right moment to convince his embattled colleagues that everyone stood to gain from his programs. "I thank the spokesmen who have given homage to my Ministry and those who have criticized it. . . . We shall gain much profit from these speeches for they all have been inspired by a unique concern to correct the errors, to destroy the abuses, to stimulate innovation and to give the country the naval forces which it is worthy of and which are indispensable to it."[3] This speech, like so many others of his, ended a lengthy fight between the Left and Right and carried the program through to a successful vote.

3. Georges Leygues, Speech during annual budget debate, in *Journal officiel. Députés. Débats*, December 12, 1925, p. 4263.

Georges Leygues' death came at a very untimely moment in 1933 while he was serving once again as minister of marine. Naval Chief of Staff Hector Violette had recently retired and the budget debates for that year had not opened. The loss of both the minister and his senior uniformed assistant created a temporary power vacuum at rue Royale. Violette was the last of the progressive admirals to serve as naval chief of staff, and Leygues' death meant an end to the centrist political control of the navy. Fortunately, the long-term program for modernizing the fleet that Leygues had devised survived as the centerpiece of all future naval appropriations through 1939. Moreover, the tradition of multiparty support for the navy also continued even though ministers of marine who succeeded Leygues were ideologically committed men of either the Left or the Right.

The newfound support for the ministry of marine, which by the 1920s allowed renovation of the navy to begin, by 1936 included a majority of the senators and deputies from all political groups and from all regions of the country. In both houses of Parliament, the naval committees, or *commissions de marine*, prepared and sponsored all legislation for rue Royale. All funding originated in the lower house where the deputies served four-year terms, elected directly by the voting public. On the various committees, however, the legislators served only one-year terms and were selected by their party leaders each year according to the rule of proportional representation. As with many of the more specialized committees, the two *commissions de marine* attracted men with special interests in supporting the navy.[4]

A majority serving on these two standing committees always came from the naval, maritime, or colonial constituencies where the navy played a major part in the local life and economy. Although these coastal towns and departments made up less than one-third of the entire Chamber of Deputies, they supplied more than two-thirds of the members of the naval committee in the lower house. Thus, even though each political party was represented only according to its strength on each of the committees,

4. R. K. Gooch, *The French Parliamentary Committee System* (New York, 1935), 165, Chap. 4.

special interest groups had twice their commensurate power on the *commission de la marine*. In the Senate, this also meant that the fishing and merchant marine interests enjoyed the same inflated power, for in the upper house the *commission de la marine* oversaw all maritime affairs. Each legislator normally served on two different standing committees and those who worked on the *commission de la marine* gravitated toward the colonial, army, and military pension committees, reflecting the natural affinity for these various interests.[5]

In the Chamber of Deputies, about one member in five on the naval committee came to politics after a career in the navy or the merchant marine or from a traditional seafaring household, a common background that favorably influenced them toward the Ministry of Marine. The committee's leadership came from among those legislators who managed to get reappointed year after year to work on naval affairs. At the committee level, tenure and a pronavy bias meant a good deal more than party affiliation. During each of the five interwar legislatures, a majority of the Chamber's naval committee had at least three years' service on that body. Moreover, these two committees groomed a number of senators and deputies for the marine portfolio. Energetic and promising young politicians frequently obtained their working knowledge of naval affairs while serving on a *commission de la marine*. Many earned reputations as naval experts while successfully defending the Ministry of Marine's budget as its *rapporteur* before the entire house.[6]

The navy and the two naval committees developed a kind of close political alliance rare between ministries and their parliamentary counterparts during the later years of the Third Republic. On roll call votes, members of the Chamber's *commission de la marine* were twice as friendly toward the navy as was the lower house as a whole. Naval committee members supported the Ministry of Marine 80 percent of the time in formal roll call votes. Seven of the

5. *Journal officiel. Députés. Bulletin des commissions* (Paris, 1928–39). These annual volumes listed members and office holders on each committee and summarized the weekly highlights of all forty-four standing committees. These were used in conjunction with the biographical sketches in Jolly (ed.), *Dictionnaire des parlementaires*.

6. *Journal officiel. Députés. Bulletin des commissions*.

Table 7. Partisan Success with Naval Legislation, 1920–1935

Party	Number of Bills Sponsored	Percentage Passed
Joint proposals	2	100
Republican Independent	1	100
Socialist	7	14
Communist	14	7
Conservatives	1	0

SOURCES: *Journal officiel. Députés. Bulletin des commissions, Journal officiel. Députés. Débats*, and *Sénat. Débats*, scrutins: 136 of June 23, 1920, 670–71 of December 18, 1922, 1120 of April 8, 1924, 69–70 of December 6–8, 1924, 264 of April 24, 1925, 661–62 of July 6, 1926, 702–703 of November 13, 1926, 1006–16 of November 21–22, 1927, 480 of February 18, 1931, and 723–24 of March 25, 1935.
NOTE: The *Journal officiel* lists sponsors of *scrutins* by name and party.

twenty-five votes on naval funding between the world wars can be regarded as symbolic demonstrations by the Communist party that had no realistic chance for success. On all the remaining eighteen roll call votes, the navy still managed to obtain the support of a comfortable two-thirds majority. In the upper house, the senators tended to rubber-stamp whatever the Chamber of Deputies proposed for the navy, and there they never brought the naval budget to a roll call vote between the world wars. The Senate's naval committee spent most of its time on the problems of a faltering merchant marine and an antiquated fishing industry.[7]

Fifteen of the twenty-five roll call votes in the Chamber of Deputies on the naval budgets produced more money than the minister of marine originally requested. None of the ten votes to slow down work or to reduce personnel ever succeeded. The closest two challenges came from the Socialist party in 1926, when 37 percent of the Chamber voted against the navy on these two funding issues. This represented the high mark of antinaval sentiment between the two world wars. The minister of marine generally received what-

7. *Ibid.* Statistics taken from *Journal officiel. Députés. Débats*, and *Sénat. Débats*, scrutins: 136 of June 23, 1920, 670–71 of December 18, 1922, 1120 of April 8, 1924, 69–70 of December 6–8, 1924, 264 of April 24, 1925, 661–62 of July 6, 1926, 702–703 of November 13, 1926, 1006–16 of November 21–22, 1927, 480 of February 18, 1931, and 723–24 of March 25, 1935.

Table 8. **Party Solidarity on Naval Legislation, 1920–1935**

	Legislature			
Party	12th	13th	14th	15th
Communist	1.0	1.0	1.0	1.0
Socialist	.4	.23	.5	.25
Radical-Socialist	.77	.87	.63	.94
Centrist parties	.88	.97	.97	.96
Rightist parties	.92	1.0	1.0	1.0
Independents	1.0	1.0	.68	.67

NOTES: The index of cohesion formula used,

$$C = \frac{\text{yeas} - \text{nays}}{\text{total membership}},$$

was taken from Charles M. Dollar and Richard J. Jensen, *Historian's Guide to Statistics: Quantitative Analysis and Historical Research* (New York, 1971), 107–108. Complete party unity is shown as a score of 1, and total disunity is shown as a score of 0. After 1935 there were no roll call votes on naval budgets.

Table 9. **Voting Similarity on Naval Legislation, 1920–1935**

Issues	Socialist and Radical-Socialist Similarity	Socialist and Communist Similarity
Four major budget votes *	.53	.73
All twenty-five budget votes	.47	.81

NOTE: Dollar and Jensen, *Historian's Guide to Statistics*, 107–108, provided the equation for likeness:

$$L = 1 - \left(\frac{a}{a+c} - \frac{d}{d+f} \right).$$

It is designed to measure the similarity of voting patterns between two political groups on roll call votes. Identical voting records of two groups would produce a score of 1, and disagreement on all votes would produce a score of 0.

* The four *scrutins* used are 136 of June 23, 1920, 662 of July 6, 1926, 480 of February 18, 1931, and 723 of March 25, 1935.

ever he formally requested in the way of money for expansion or modernization of the fleet. On the other hand, only one of ten proposals to raise wages for naval workers ever passed in the Chamber. Legislators gave modernization of the fleet top priority, and human needs came in a poor second.[8]

8. *Ibid.*

The parliamentary favor showered upon the navy in the 1920s and 1930s marked a distinct change in the traditional support of army programs to the detriment of the Ministry of Marine. But this support did not come automatically. Bills sponsored by coalition groups or by Georges Leygues' centrist followers stood the greatest chance of passage. Budget amendments with strong ideological overtones from either the Left or Right continually failed passage although many were intended largely as votes of protest by hopelessly outnumbered minorities.

The parties of the extreme Left and Right maintained excellent integrity in spite of the remote chances of success. In the Center, however, and among independent deputies as well, there was less party cohesion, resulting in crossover voting on naval legislation. The Socialist parties, including the parent Section française de l'international ouvrière (SFIO) and the tiny Republican Socialist, were the most divided of all political blocs, with the Radical-Socialists not far behind. A slim majority of Socialists went on record against naval budgets prior to 1935, but a slightly larger proportion of the Radical-Socialist vote favored these same funds. Overall, this meant that the Socialist parties' voting record on these naval programs was closer to the Communist than to the Radical-Socialist record.

The split in the Socialist vote reflected the dilemma this bloc faced on all arms legislation. Many Socialist deputies believed in international disarmament and thought that France should set the example by taking unilateral action against the military credits. Other Socialists, coming largely from the maritime constituencies, voted in favor of naval arms legislation because of personal or constituent interests.[9] Socialist deputy Admiral Louis Jaurès sponsored one of the bills to provide supplemental money for new warships in 1926. Two other members of his party, colleagues on the naval committee, Vincent Auriol and Jules Moch, in 1935 cosponsored a bill to provide the navy with additional last-minute funds.[10] They brought this proposal to roll call vote in order to demonstrate party solidarity behind an expanded naval program after the failure of the

9. Nathanael Greene, *Crisis and Decline: The French Socialist Party in the Popular Front Era* (Ithaca, 1969), 68, 179–80.
10. Jaurès sponsored *scrutin* 662 on July 6, 1926; Auriol and Moch cosponsored *scrutins* 723–24 on March 25, 1935.

naval disarmament treaties during the same year. This was to be the last roll call vote on naval matters under the Third Republic.

Socialists from the colonial delegation also believed in a strong fleet to protect the vital link with the *métropole*. The heavy dependence on French exports to the colonies and the vulnerability of the overseas possessions may have encouraged these deputies to vote for a strong navy and against the narrow Socialist majority. Émile Morinaud, an SFIO representative from Algeria, considered a big navy "a question of life or death" for his homeland. The transcript for the day shows that the Chamber applauded his speech to which the minister of marine added that a large navy was equally "a question of life or death for France." Another Socialist deputy and former naval officer demanded a strong fleet to protect France "from any nation where the democratic spirit had not yet swept away crass nationalism and imperialism." Émile Goude, a former shipyard worker and leader of the Chamber's naval committee, encouraged fellow Socialists to rally behind the non-Socialist minister of marine without demanding his adherence to the SFIO platform on other issues. Goude also sought to build up the fleet as quickly as possible by endorsing construction of many small, inexpensive warships rather than a few large ones.[11] Though a majority of the Socialist bloc voted against naval programs until 1935, they reversed their stand when Stalin asked French Communists to spend money on arms against the Nazi menace.[12]

For twenty years, the Chamber's voting record on the navy shows how differently each region felt about money spent for warships. The colonial delegation stood most consistently behind the Ministry of Marine. Close behind were the representatives from Brittany, which had the highest concentration of naval employees anywhere in France. Deputies from the Southwest, in the area around Bordeaux, also voted for naval expansion as part of their generally con-

11. *Journal officiel. Députés. Débats.* All these arguments appeared in the budget debate of December 5–8, 1924, pp. 4168–246. On colonial trade, see Herbert I. Priestly, *France Overseas: A Study of Modern Imperialism* (New York, 1939), Chap. 18, Tables I, V, VI, pp. 437, 442–45.

12. Édouard Bonnefous, *La République en danger: des ligues au front populaire, 1930–1936* (2nd ed., Paris, 1973), 331–32, Vol. V of *Histoire de la Troisième République*, 7 vols.

Table 10. **Regional Cohesion on Naval Legislation, 1919–1935**

Region	Average	Naval Departments in the Same Region	Average
North, Northeast, and East	.58	Manche	.92
Paris	.48		
Southwest	.64		
Brittany	.75	Finistère	.64
		Loire-Atlantique	.84
		Morbihan	.69
Midi	.42	Var	.35
Colonies	.84		

NOTES: The index of cohesion formula used,

$$C = \frac{\text{yeas} - \text{nays}}{\text{total membership}},$$

was taken from Dollar and Jensen, *Historian's Guide to Statistics*, 107–108. Complete unity is shown as a score of 1, and total disunity is shown as a score of 0.

servative position on national defense. Well behind these regions, however, were the deputies from the Northeast, the East, Paris, and the Midi, who either had very little vested interest in the navy or came from areas traditionally opposed to military expenditures.

Among the five departments with the greatest concentration of naval bases, all but one supported the navy and had a voting record similar to its parent region. Only Manche, containing the port city of Cherbourg, differed from the other departments in the northern and eastern parts of France. Finistère, Morbihan, Loire-Atlantique, and Var had slightly better voting records on naval projects than their parent regions but not by a margin of more than 10 percent. Overall, the public attitude toward naval spending had broad general support that extended beyond those special communities dependent on the navy for economic survival.

In general, the navy could appeal to a far larger group of legislators than the army could because the Ministry of Marine had something to offer virtually everyone. Even before the Communist party switched its votes in favor of the navy, the Parliament had supported every financial request by rue Royale. Elderly Radical deputies identified with the navy after winning a series of parliamentary battles for social reform in the fleet. This same party also represented several of the colonial regions, which relied heavily on the navy and merchant marine for protection and economic survival. Further to the Left, many of the Socialists voted for these same credits because these men had spent careers as sailors or shipyard workers and now represented towns that depended on the navy payroll. On the Right, former naval officers like royalist Jean Le Cour Grandmaison had equally strong feelings about the Ministry of Marine. For him and other retired officers in the Parliament, a large navy symbolized the kind of national strength and prestige that they believed the regime sorely lacked.[13]

Moreover, the French navy performed a number of administrative and humanitarian duties that had no political overtones. The navy maintained the ports and patrolled the coastline at home and in the colonies. Warships accompanied the fishing fleets on their long voyages, providing medical and postal services in addition to arbitrating international fishing rights with other nations. In exchange, of course, the navy relied heavily on the merchant and fishing communities as the major sources of enlisted manpower for the fleet. Throughout the country, the lighthouses, some lifesaving services, and even the fire department in Marseilles fell under the jurisdiction of the minister of marine. This was all in addition to the routine naval duties of maintaining the fleet and building warships. All of these various duties had been organized by Colbert in the seventeenth century and survived virtually unchanged into the mid-twentieth century. In most other countries, one or more civilian agencies had evolved to oversee the noncombatant naval tasks, but in France these remained as much a part of the Ministry of Marine as the main battle fleet. Few citizens outside the small maritime enclaves of Brittany, Normandy, and the Midi knew of the navy's involvement in everyday life there. In some of the colonies, naval jurisdiction extended even further to include the police, military, coast guard, prefectoral, civil engineer, and even gubernatorial

13. Ronald Chalmers Hood III, "The Crisis of Civil-Naval Relations in France, 1924–1939" (M.A. thesis, University of Maine, 1972), 28–29, 38–43; Jolly (ed.), *Dictionnaire des parlementaires*, VI, 2196–97 *et passim*.

responsibilities. In a sense, the Ministry of Marine survived overseas as a small government within a government, which many small and diverse groups of Frenchmen had a vested interest in maintaining. This consolidation of maritime duties was very efficient in a country with a limited budget and a small seagoing population. As for the navy, it had no desire to lose any of these traditional functions since they guaranteed such broad support for the annual budget.[14]

In contrast to the navy's successful modernization efforts, the French army's legislation remained tied up in countless debates over the proper length of conscripted service and the correct strategic plans for national defense. And the air force budget also ran afoul of parliamentary debates over the purchase of foreign aircraft and the modernization of the French aviation industry.[15] By 1939, only the navy's plans for modernization were complete, thanks largely to two decades of unparalleled support from the Parliament. Neither of the other two armed forces enjoyed the broad political backing that the Ministry of Marine had in both the Chamber of Deputies and the Senate under virtually every interwar government. The army budget came to roll call vote twice as often as the navy's. Moreover, the government's survival was challenged eighty-eight times in interpellations of questionable army programs, whereas the navy's budget never became the subject of a vote of no confidence.[16] In those years, the French army remained at the center of public debates on disarmament, manpower shortages, and overall national defense policy. Conversely, the Parliament always agreed with the navy's stands on these same issues after 1922, when they saw the disappointing results of the Washington Naval Conference. The legislators also supported the two-century-old belief in an all-volunteer navy, unique among France's otherwise conscripted

14. Espagnac du Ravay [Louis de La Monneraye], *Vingt ans de politique navale, 1919–1939* (Grenoble, 1941), 203–205, 210–11.

15. Philip Bankwitz, *Maxime Weygand and Civil-Military Relations in Modern France* (Cambridge, Mass., 1967), Chaps. 2, 3; Judith Hughs, *To the Maginot Line: The Politics of French Military Preparation in the 1920's* (Cambridge, Mass., 1971), Chap. 5; Pierre Cot, *Le Procès de la république* (New York, 1944), Chaps. 8–10.

16. *Journal officiel. Députés. Tables analytiques et tables nominatives* (Paris, 1919–39), *passim*.

armed forces. And while the two houses tied up army moderniza-tion for years as they pondered the Maginot Line, they continued to support both offensive and defensive naval plans along with the warships required to implement them.[17]

The air force, which became an independent service under a sep-arate minister of air in 1928, remained the victim of an inefficient bureaucracy and of a backward aircraft industry. Political leaders also had problems deciding between an offensive and defensive air strategy. Parliamentary indecision added to the delays in producing suitable weapons and led to battles over the suspected wasting of public funds by the minister of air and over the poor state of readi-ness for war. Eventually, the political leadership accepted the reali-ties of an antiquated air industry and purchased foreign planes during the mid-1930s to make up for existing shortages. Unfortu-nately, these machines arrived too late to alter the outcome of the war in 1939 and 1940.[18]

While the public started to question the need for large military forces after 1918, the navy escaped most of the criticism leveled at the other two services. Although the army received widespread thanks for the victory in World War I, it remained an institution that many Frenchmen had never trusted. Ever since the Georges Boulanger affair, or even the coup that brought Louis Napoleon to the throne, public opinion had cast a jaundiced eye on the French army during peacetime. These concerns grew during the Dreyfus scandal and reached a very delicate point during World War I. After 1918, parliamentary debates on the army turned to Jean Jaurès' prewar proposal for an all-volunteer force. The fears he and many other Frenchmen shared of generals leading coups against the re-public, however, did not spill over into their feelings about the navy. Sailors had not fought against other French citizens since Adolphe Thiers had led them during the Commune. Thus, any bit-terness toward the navy was long forgotten by the same public that

17. Bankwitz, *Maxime Weygand*, Chaps. 2, 3; Hughes, *To the Maginot Line*, Chap. 5.
18. Cot, *Le Procès*, Chaps. 8–10; Alexander Werth, *The Twilight of France, 1933–1940* (New York, 1942), 272–75; Colonel von X, "Les Armées françaises de-vant le Parlement: rapport d'un attaché militaire étranger en mission à Paris," *Revue politique et parlementaire*, CLXXII (September, 1937), 467–77.

had very ambivalent feelings toward its army. No one of significance believed that the navy posed any threat to democratic institutions in France, and therefore, the navy escaped serious public
scrutiny of its leaders and their work. Undoubtedly, this freedom
of action pleased the admirals, but it also left a void in the civil-
military balances.

Overall, the navy presented an image of loyalty and stability to
the public. Moreover, since the admirals were so few and spent so
little time in the *métropole*, the average man in the street did not
have the occasion to view them as he did the army officers stationed throughout the country. For the most part, only the residents and the newspapers in the half dozen naval towns and in the
colonies followed the navy's activities with any real interest. Until
the 1920s, these remote locations were relatively inaccessible and
were of interest primarily to the Ministries of Marine and the Colonies. Meanwhile, the vast majority of Frenchmen worried far more
about the military situation that they could see developing close at
hand. They were far more concerned about the German threat
along the Rhine than about the remote Atlantic coast and the empire overseas. News from the colonies or about foreign trade or
about problems with the fishing fleet rarely made front-page head-
lines in Paris even if they appeared in New York or London.[19]

For decades—some might say since Trafalgar—the absence of
good publicity went hand in hand with parliamentary neglect of the
navy. The depressing state of the fleet at the end of World War I indicated to many naval officers that there was not much hope for the
future. The situation changed dramatically, however, when the legislature approved funds to build 33 warships in 1922. From then until 1935, the minister of marine received money to build 172 ships
of all classes. On an average, this amounted to over thirty thousand
tons of vessels every year. Only once, just after Georges Leygues'
death in 1933, did Parliament fail to provide for new shipping in the
annual budget. After 1935, the navy's appropriation nearly doubled,
making these the most productive of the interwar years. Between

19. Jacques Godechot, Interview, June 25, 1975; Mattéo Connet, Interview, July
10, 1974; Jean-Michel Renaitour, Interview, July 13, 1974. The first Paris daily newspaper to cover the French navy on a regular basis was the *Action française.*

1919 and 1939, the fleet was entirely rebuilt. Except for five renovated battleships, the oldest ship in 1939 was only seventeen years old, and the French navy was the most modern in the world. In terms of matériel, this fleet was the fourth largest in the world and second only to Britain in European waters.[20]

During the interwar years, the Parliament never placed the navy's modernization program effort in jeopardy. In 1927, the Chamber of Deputies slowed down approval of the naval budget in a preelection debate that tied up the appropriations of several government agencies for a number of days. Even then, the navy's budget passed easily in both houses, and the Ministry of Marine won all eleven roll call challenges to its programs by a margin of two to one or better.[21] Of the twenty-five times the navy's budget came to roll call vote in twenty years, fifteen came during election-year debates, and no government in power lost one of these votes to the opposition.[22]

By any measure of comparison, Admiral Darlan's fleet of 1939 was far better prepared for war than either the army or the air force. Presumably, the French naval officers would have seen this and would have enjoyed healthy and constructive relations with the legislators and the two naval committees that orchestrated the annual budgets. Oddly, however, no such close civil-naval relationship ever existed between the world wars. Actually, the distance between the naval leaders and the public they served had never been greater.

Naval officers began to express their doubts about the French political system in the early 1900s. Although stated openly, these attitudes had little political significance until 1920 when the level of personal frustration within the officer corps increased dramatically. Budgetary constraints immediately following the 1918 armistice and the outcome of the Washington Naval Conference started the

20. De Belot and Reussner, *De 1919 à 1939*, 207–18; du Ravay, *Vingt ans*, 178–86; Francis E. McMurtie (ed.), *Janes Fighting Ships, 1939* (London, 1939), v–vi, 169–216.

21. Édouard Bonnefous, *Cartel des gauches et union nationale, 1924–1929* (2nd ed.; Paris, 1973), 229, Vol. IV of *Histoire de la Troisième République*, 7 vols.; *Journal officiel. Députés. Débats*, November 21–22, 1927, pp. 1006–16.

22. *Journal officiel. Députés. Débats*, and *Sénat. Débats*, scrutins: 136 of June 23, 1920, 670–71 of December 18, 1922, 1120 of April 8, 1924, 69–70 of December 6–8, 1924, 264 of April 24, 1925, 661–62 of July 6, 1926, 702–703 of November 13, 1926, 1006–16 of November 21–22, 1927, 480 of February 18, 1931, 723–24 of March 25, 1935.

rapid downward trend in this relationship. Many officers simply could not understand why the Parliament refused to approve the twenty-year program that the admirals proposed in 1924. In fact, had Parliament approved the proposed document, it would have surrendered its right of oversight and review of the navy's modernization and shipbuilding programs for two decades. After this defeat, although the French navy became the second largest in Europe, naval officers in France continued to lament the fiscal constraints placed upon their ambitions for expansion of their service. Even middle-of-the-road officers with no apparent ax to grind started to question the viability of fundamental Republican institutions. One of the relatively moderate voices within the *grand corps* was Admiral Raoul Castex whose books and articles on maritime strategy attracted a worldwide following. By the mid-1920s, even he began to examine authoritarian solutions to frustrating political dilemmas that only extremists like Admiral Schwerer had spoken about before.

> What do we do with the legislature? Grave question. Obviously, it would be desirable for it to be on vacation at this time. This would conform to the program of reinforcing the executive. But one cannot do it in our times because of the problems with public opinion. What is more, if the executive shows both character of decision and a certain understanding of things in this patriotic crisis, it will do what it wishes with the Parliament. It is up to it [the executive] to conquer the independence and freedom of [the legislature's] action, as Bonaparte conquered those representatives sent to control him through charm and enchantment.[23]

Castex published his disturbing views on the parliamentary system in a multivolume study of French naval policy, which appeared in 1924 just as the Chamber of Deputies approved new funds for a major shipbuilding program. Throughout the interwar period, other official and unofficial spokesmen in the naval officer corps continued to voice these same opinions even after this new funding effort reached fruition in the navy. Darlan complained about Parliament during 1931 just as the Chamber of Deputies approved the

---

23. Admiral Raoul Castex, *Questions d'état-major: principes, organisation, fonctionnement* (2 vols.; Paris, 1924), I, 290–91.

construction of eleven new warships. Two years later, Admiral Degouy called in a speech for a new Napoleon or a Frederick the Great to take over the combined functions of the legislative and executive branches of French government, thereby eliminating the competition between them that he found counterproductive and a waste of valuable time. Darlan's executive assistant, Admiral Louis de La Monneraye, recalled the "routine indifference of the legislators" in 1940 and the distasteful necessity of soliciting public support for various naval programs. Even after World War II, other admirals who had been in high offices during the 1930s had similar recollections and sentiments about the Parliament.[24] Memory and the legislative record, particularly the record after 1935, did not match on these points. Officers who felt compelled to attack the legislature's failure to rebuild the fleet appear to have been influenced by reasons which had nothing to do with naval politics. Coming from frustrated army or air force officers, comments like those uttered by Castex and Degouy would have been more understandable, given the poor legislative records of those two services.

The strong antiparliamentary tone in naval thought, which blossomed during the 1920s, actually dated from a quarter century earlier but lay dormant until the end of World War I. For the most part, French naval officers did not possess a liberal political heritage based on either democratic or pragmatic ideals. At the highest ranks and to a lesser degree at the junior-officer level, many of these men came from homes that withheld their support from the Third Republic and its institutions. This detachment from the mainstream of French society went unnoticed by outsiders until the Dreyfus affair and the legal separation of church and state hardened the positions of the political Left and Right. Admirals Auphan, Abrial, and Decoux all recalled how the Dreyfus affair had been an ideological watershed for them and their families and how the secularization of the navy in 1905 had caused irreparable damage to

24. François Darlan to Admiral Hector Violette, November 24, 1931, in Admiral Hector Violette Papers, Private Collection; Admiral Jean Degouy, "Les Flottes européennes et leurs champs d'action," *Revue politique et parlementaire*, CLVII (December, 1933), 530; du Ravay, *Vingt ans*, 180, 261; Admiral Paul Auphan and Jacques Mordal, *The French Navy in World War II*, trans. A. C. J. Sabalot (Annapolis, 1959), 11; Admiral Jean Decoux, *Adieu marine* (Paris, 1957), 332–33.

civil-naval relations. Those who had privately been skeptical of the republic's viability became emotionally involved in an open search for political alternatives. Family suspicions about the regime evolved into criticism of the Parliament, which symbolized all that was wrong with the French political system. Moreover, the Parliament, no matter that it now singled out the navy for long-term modernization, had earned naval enmity by destroying that fleet during World War I. The officers' attitudes were much like those to be found in the United States Navy among southern officers. Although these Americans welcomed Theodore Roosevelt's expansion of the navy, they denied him their vote on the grounds that his party had ruined their homeland following the Civil War.[25] In the same way, during the years that his American peers developed such contempt for the Republican party, young Antoine Schwerer rejected the new French republic in favor of royalism.[26] Finally, the growth of the Socialist and Communist parties after World War I further alienated many naval officers from the parliamentary regime, regardless of how individual legislators voted on the navy's budget.[27]

Officers who spoke out either condemned the legislature outright, as did Decoux and Schwerer, or, like Castex and de La Monneraye, maligned it for not approving even larger naval credits. French admirals did not invent this style of complaining about insufficient parliamentary backing for the armed forces. They did,

25. This was the position expressed by Admiral John Hood, USN, to his brother at the time of Roosevelt's campaign of 1904. Hood's stand was typical of southern naval officers and of the reaction throughout the American South against Roosevelt and his party. On southern origins in the U.S. Navy, see Peter Karsten, *The Naval Aristocracy: The Golden Age of Annapolis and the Emergence of Modern American Navalism* (New York, 1972), Chap. 1. Information on the voting habits of American naval officers at that time comes from discussions with John A. Gamble, director of the Theodore Roosevelt Association, Oyster Bay, N.Y., and Patrick J. Abbazia, author of "Theodore Roosevelt and the U.S. Navy" (MS in preparation for publication).

26. Admiral Antoine Schwerer, *Souvenirs de ma vie maritime, 1878–1914* (Paris, 1933), 167–69.

27. Connet Interview; Bernard Paquet, Interview, June 30, 1975; Commander Georges Débat, Interview, June 22, 1976. See also Hélène de David-Beauregard, *Souvenirs de famille* (Toulon, 1970), 177–85; Charles Braibant, *Un bourgeois sous trois républiques* (Paris, 1961), 342; Commander Loïc Abrial, Interview, July 28, 1975; Admiral Jean Abrial to his parents, April 18, 1900, in Admiral Jean Abrial Papers, Private Collection; Admiral Paul Auphan, *Mensonges et vérité: essai sur la France* (Paris, 1949), 20; Decoux, *Adieu marine,* 9–11, 292.

however, carry this behavior to an extreme in the 1930s when the two houses were giving the navy more money than it asked for. The effect of these political opinions on the naval officer corps as a whole was dramatic. In a strictly hierarchical institution like the French navy, a few spokesmen set the tone and behavior patterns that subordinates emulated. Leaders sought intellectual conformity in the navy beyond that normally required in military organizations. Darlan and de La Monneraye spoke of the need to create a semiofficial ideology, while Schwerer addressed the need to purge officers who could not agree with existing opinions of the Naval General Staff. Georges Débat explained how this kind of pressure influenced the behavior of midshipmen and junior officers at the École navale and in the fleet. In his opinion, an officer could not survive either professionally or socially if he did not fit the well-defined intellectual mold established for the naval officers. The ship wardrooms served as informal classrooms where the officer corps could "create in its bosom a strong unity of opinion."[28]

French military officers, however, could not use the democratic system to express their viewpoint. They were forced to remain outside the political process by the law of July 29, 1872, which denied all uniformed personnel the right to vote. The intent of this law was to keep the armed forces ideologically neutral and above partisan politics, but without this means of expressing their needs and desires, the French officers were driven to seek other ways to voice their opinions. The Action Française and other extreme right-wing organizations gave military men the outlet they needed, and they were therefore very popular in the armed forces.

Between the world wars, French civilian leaders failed to grasp the importance of the poor relationship between themselves and the professional military caste. Public efforts to reconcile the career officers with the regime came too late to accomplish meaningful results. Civilians viewed the military fascination with the Action Française as an amusing idiosyncrasy but no cause for alarm. Since the navy had no tradition of plotting coups against the

28. Morris Janowitz, *The Professional Soldier: A Social and Political Portrait* (New York, 1960), 220; du Ravay, *Vingt ans*, xi–xii, 172; Admiral Antoine Schwerer, Study of officer pay, December 1920, in Série Ca, Carton 36, Archives de la marine; Georges Débat, *Marine oblige* (Paris, 1974), 14.

Republic, no one in a position of authority believed that the admirals would do anything to destabilize the regime. Officers who read the royalist and antirepublican press were labeled "platonic monarchists," as though they were quaint but harmless museum pieces. Yet in the eyes of the royalist naval officers, the republic depended on vacillating and superficial public opinion and the shifting political alliances of the middle and lower classes. The officers considered these to be far inferior to the reliance on blood ties and the Catholic church that they saw as the foundations of French civilization.[29]

Stories from the navy's *petite histoire* revealed the symptoms if not the cures of the growing distance between the professional naval officer corps and the political leadership embodied in the Parliament. In 1935 the navy's civilian archivist, Charles Braibant, went on a short cruise aboard a French warship. He described his journey in an article that he submitted to *La Revue maritime*, the navy's official mouthpiece on maritime affairs. The journal's editor, Commander Pierre de Loÿs, rejected the original manuscript because he objected to Braibant's favorable depiction of the playing of *La Marseillaise* by a Norwegian band. De Loÿs explained to his friend Braibant that as a monarchist he would not print a story about the singing of a song that he found unpatriotic. Although these two men were close professional associates and respected each other, they remained poles apart. Braibant was an agnostic and a member of the Socialist party; de Loÿs was a staunch Catholic and supporter of the Action Française. When he finally accepted a modified version of Braibant's article, de Loÿs told his archivist friend, "you are beautiful fruit. Too bad there is a worm in you."[30] At that time, no one saw the danger signals in comments like these or worried about an unhealthy trend developing in civil-naval relations. In those final years of the Third Republic, tradition prevailed and the compartmentalized elements of the society continued to do business as usual in self-imposed isolation.

29. Bankwitz, *Maxime Weygand*, 289; Godechot Interview; Paquet Interview; Colonel Raymond Abrial, Interview, June 27, 1975. See also Admiral Schwerer's column, *Action française*, May 3, 1928, 1–2.
30. Braibant, *Un bourgeois*, 342–47.

CHAPTER 7
La Politique d'Abord

When moderate influence waned in the navy during 1932, constraints on the naval officers diminished quickly. What had been only one of several currents of opinion within the service during the 1920s now became the dominant body of professional opinion well into and beyond World War II. On every issue that had divided officer opinion, from promotions to politics, the navy presented a coherent and unwavering body of opinion in the 1930s. Among the most obvious changes was the expanded interest in the Action Française.

Widespread open involvement in the Action Française was a fairly recent phenomenon. Of course, many had subscribed to the newspaper for years, and individually many had followed the writings of Charles Maurras and other royalist authors with a great personal interest. Nevertheless, it was the trauma of readjustment after World War I that led many officers to express their political frustrations more openly. During the interwar years, Maurras' doctrine of *politique d'abord* became the rallying cry for Frenchmen who no longer felt the need to hide their ideological preferences. This venting of frustrations spread throughout the fleet and the École navale where newspapers kept everyone abreast of the latest gossip at the rue de Rome where Maurras had his headquarters.

In 1934 a new journalist came to the staff of the newspaper as the fourth naval writer, after Jacques Bainville, Antoine Schwerer, and John Frog. Unlike his predecessors, Pierre Varillon turned to Maurrasism because of a strong nationalism rather than the religious or royalist sentiments that attracted the others. Varillon was actually an agnostic as a result of unfortunate experiences in a parochial school. His first articles appeared on the "Armée et marine" page early in 1934 when he wrote of his experiences aboard the destroyer *Simoun*. That cruise and others that followed on the cruiser *Tourville* were all arranged by the minister of marine, François Piétri, who sought friendly press coverage of the navy. Varillon's articles eventually supplanted most others on naval affairs. He had an uncanny ability to gain the confidence of the usually reticent naval officers, many of whom remained close to him for many years. What they explained to him in their personal letters became the subject of future articles in the *Action française*, and this personal touch attracted readers.[1]

In this process of making friends with the officers, Varillon also became the political mentor of some influential men. Admiral Auphan, for example, gave Varillon the credit for teaching him that the Washington Naval Treaty was actually a plan to guarantee Anglo-American naval supremacy at the expense of France and Italy.[2] Pierre Varillon's most influential friend in the navy was Admiral Jean Fernet, a rising star in the *grand corps* who had several family ties with the Action Française directorate. Fernet went on to become the secretary general to the Senior War Council for National Defense and later commanded the Far Eastern Fleet. He spent the Vichy years as secretary general to Marshal Pétain. Both Fernet and another friend, Captain Boulat, relayed information to Varillon about political attitudes and daily life within the officer corps. Boulat even asked Varillon to obtain autographed copies of Maurras' books for use as lottery prizes at the annual ball held by the Association amicale des anciens élèves de l'École navale.[3]

With the passage of time, the political views of the Action Française spread through the naval officer corps. As personal frustrations remained unresolved and professional conditions appeared to worsen, officers who might otherwise have supported republican institutions turned to Maurrasism. Georges Débat explained this process, which he encountered aboard ship.

1. Madame Pierre Varillon, Interview, July 27, 1975.
2. Admiral Paul Auphan, Interview, June 5, 1974.
3. Captain Louis Boulat to Pierre Varillon, March 22, July 19, 1935, August 6, [1935?], November 9, 1938, all in Pierre Varillon Papers, Private Collection; Eugen

Even those of my friends who did not believe this doctrine were se-
duced without realizing it. Some who thought of themselves as republicans admitted privately that the military way of life, as followed in our
own careers, could be applied to the civilians as well. . . . Minds more
adept at mathematics than the humanities, and for whom growing up
was often a narrow experience, took up this dogma for the sake of conformity. They also leaped upon it with the zeal of neophytes and an ob-
session untempered by critical thought. Thus, later, they were to be led
to accept totalitarian doctrines which Maurras certainly never intended
but which nevertheless permeated his arguments. The liberal minority,
often Protestants, rejected the form and the royalist temptations but the
positivist element of Maurras made them admit the conclusions if not
the methods of this school.

In the 1920s, Débat found, midshipmen who resisted peer pressure
to accept this ideology had little chance of survival at the École
navale. Professor Jacques Godechot reached the same conclusion
while teaching there from 1935 through 1939. He believed that the
boys entering Navale differed little from their contemporaries going on to the universities. The pressure and isolation unique to the
midshipmen, however, "distorted their thinking," making career
officers "more and more peculiar" with each year they spent in the
navy cut off from the public.[4]

In this artificial environment, antirepublican fever thrived. A favorite play on words at that time was, "La Marine, c'est une chose
Royale," making reference to the Ministry of Marine located on rue
Royale in Paris as well as the growing royalist support among the
officers.[5] A photograph of Pierre Varillon seated on the shoulders of
the junior officers aboard the *Tourville* symbolized the carefree relationship between the Action Française and the young men of the
grand corps. Some felt that an isolated home life and a narrow education prevented many of these officers from understanding the implications of their political commitment. For many of them, it was
a simple extension of the wardroom camaraderie. In off-duty hours,
they got together to sing royalist songs and to speak romantically of

Weber, *Action Française: Royalism and Reaction in Twentieth Century France*
(Stanford, 1962), 444.

4. Georges Débat, *Marine oblige* (Paris, 1974), 18–19, 14; Jacques Godechot, Interview, June 25, 1975.

5. Bernard Paquet, Interview, June 30, 1975.

Pierre Varillon Aboard the *Tourville*
Aboard the cruiser *Tourville*, Pierre Varillon, of the *Action francaise* staff,
posed for a snapshot with his friends. Such young naval officers were
among the strongest supporters of Charles Maurras and neomonarchism
within the French navy. *Pierre Varillon Photo*

"the good old days" when they imagined life must have been far
better. Those who supported this ideology even reached the point
in the 1930s of questioning the legitimacy of the republic. Slowly
and, in many cases, unwittingly, the naval officer corps exchanged
its traditionally neutral role of *la grande muette* for that of a possible enemy of the existing political system.[6]

Ashore, the Action Française attracted officers to its ranks while
circumventing the law banning military personnel from political
activity. Active-duty military personnel could not join Admiral

6. Débat, *Marine oblige*, 20; photographs in Varillon Papers; Admiral Louis de La
Monneraye, Interview, July 23, 1975; Godechot Interview; Commander Loïc Abrial,
Interview, July 28, 1975.

Schwerer's Ligue de l'Action Française, but they could become members of a sister organization called Alliance de l'Action Française. Membership in the ligue required proof of French citizenship at birth, dues, and a sworn oath of loyalty to the neomonarchist cause. For an allié, however, the financial pledge was optional and the oath was not formalized. One simply had to be an avowed supporter of the movement and had to accept the opportunity to make voluntary contributions to the cause. In exchange for this backing, alliés received membership cards that entitled them to all benefits of a ligueur.[7] To dodge the law it was necessary to forego the oath but nothing else. In reality, an allié was a member of the ligue in all but name.

Among the more enterprising local chapters of the ligue were the branches in Paris and in the departments of Finistère and Var, including the port cities of Brest and Toulon. Active-duty and retired naval officers dominated the Toulon branch, where after 1933 the branch president, Commander François Ollivier, was himself a former naval officer. He managed the ligue's local affairs and even contributed to the Paris daily on regional activities. Ollivier socialized with his followers every afternoon at the Grand Hotel on the place de la Liberté. There, ligueurs and alliés met from five to seven o'clock for cocktails and to discuss the world they believed was crumbling about their feet. Bernard Paquet recalled that about half of those in attendance were active-duty officers, while the remainder were either retired officers or civilian members of the ligue.[8]

Overall, the atmosphere at these social events was rather elegant, open, and relaxed, as one might expect of a group dedicated to the preservation of aristocratic values. The Grand Hotel had the highest Michelin rating of any dining establishment in Toulon. Alliés and liguers were allowed to bring friends from outside the organization to the cocktail hour, in contrast to the formal, secret gatherings of the military Masonic lodges, which had been popular

7. *Almanach de l'Action Française* (Paris, 1930), 472; Débat, *Marine oblige*, 19.
8. Weber, *Action Française*, 179–80, 365; Samuel M. Osgood, *French Royalism Under the Third and Fourth Republics* (2nd ed.; The Hague, 1970), 152; Paquet Interview; Ollivier's contributions to the *Almanach de l'Action Française* (1931), 433–37.

only thirty years earlier but had virtually disappeared by the 1930s. The ligue, like those lodges, provided a forum for discussion among naval officers outside the confines of military authority, though in most other respects, of course, the two causes had nothing in common.[9]

In keeping with their social elitism, naval officers in the ligue and the alliance avoided violent political activities. While some had children or friends who became Camelots du roi, street hawkers of the *Action française,* most naval officers left the violent side of right-wing politics to groups such as the Croix de feu and the Parti populaire français of Jacques Doriot. Nevertheless, officers shared many of the political goals if not the methods of the more violent groups. Naval personnel were on the fringes of the Corvignolles and the Cagoule, organized in the 1930s to ferret out suspected Communists from the military and other walks of life. The leader of the Cagoule was Eugène Deloncle, who had been a naval officer in the *corps de génie maritime.* Unlike most of his fellow graduates of the École polytechnique, whose students tended to be less committed to extremist politics than were their contemporaries at the École navale, Deloncle was a radical rightist. He found the Action Française too passive and intellectual for his tastes.[10]

Conservative and neomonarchist attitudes became intertwined with official naval policy under Admiral Georges Durand-Viel. A classic supporter of the navy's conservative causes, he promoted a program to build large warships, an officer corps of elitists, and a pro-Latin foreign policy favoring Italy and Spain. As his leading policy formulator and day-to-day planner for the Naval General Staff, Durand-Viel chose Admiral Jean Decoux as head of the Section d'études.[11]

9. Paquet Interview; President of the Toulon Lodge of the Grand Orient, Discussion, July 1, 1975.

10. Georges Loustaunau-Lacau, *Mémoirs d'un français rébelle* (Paris, 1948), 112; Jacques Szaluta, "Marshal Pétain Between Two World Wars, 1918–1940: The Interplay of Personality and Circumstance" (Ph.D. dissertation, Columbia University, 1969), 211; Paul Marie de La Gorce, *La République et son armée* (Paris, 1963), 316–17; Department of State, Documents on the Internal Affairs of France, December 30, 1937, 851.00/1765, in Record Group 59, National Archives.

11. Vice Admiral Georges Durand-Viel, "L'Esprit de la marine," *Revue des deux mondes,* XLVI (January, 1939), 143–53; "La Communauté maritime," *Revue maritime,* LXIV (August, 1951), 1007–26; Madame Roger Houzel (née Durand-Viel), Interviews, June 24, 1974, July 10, 1975.

This new office took over some of the responsibilities formerly handled by the Deuxième bureau (Intelligence) and the Troisième bureau (Operations). As a spiritual heir to Admiral Schwerer, Decoux used his new office as a vehicle to convert his political ideas into active naval policy. At first under the direct supervision of the naval chief of staff, the Section d'études soon enjoyed a broad range of powers and Durand-Viel's full backing. During his four-year tenure, Decoux prepared the navy's positions on disarmament, relations with other naval powers, and a host of lesser issues. Decoux's dislike of the League of Nations, Great Britain, Jews, and Freemasonry became the foundation of Naval General Staff policy from 1932 through 1936. Decoux also sought somewhat less successfully to arrange for a formal alliance of Latin powers in the Mediterranean.[12] While Admiral Durand-Viel tried to persuade the foreign minister, through Alexis Léger, of the merits of a pro-Italian policy, Decoux worked in secret through French naval attachés abroad to push the French navy's plan in overseas capitals.[13]

The desire for this alliance affected even the daily life of the common French sailor. Joint Franco-Italian fleet maneuvers became an annual training highlight for the two navies. Afterward, there would be social interaction when sailors from both fleets mixed freely in parties held ashore. Adulation of Mussolini impressed French visitors to Italian warships. There, in sailors' wall lockers where snapshots of nudes or loved ones usually hung, were pictures of Il Duce, whom the Italians appeared to idolize. Some of the French sailors, however, felt that this personal commitment to fascism went too far.[14]

12. Admiral Jean Decoux, Adieu marine (Paris, 1957), 281, 285, and Chap. 22; Houzel Interview, June 24, 1974; Paquet Interview; Admiral René Godfroy, Interview, July 2, 1975; Admiral Henri Salaün, Strategic appraisals, September, 1920, April 29, 1921, in Série Ca, Carton 27, Archives de la marine; Admiral Henri Salaün, La Marine française (Paris, 1934), 339, 421, 441–57; Admiral Hector Violette to his wife, March 31, 1930, in Admiral Hector Violette Papers, Private Collection.

13. Charles Bloch, "Great Britain, German Rearmament, and the Naval Agreement of 1935," in Hans W. Gatzke (ed.), European Diplomacy Between Two World Wars, 1919–1939 (Chicago, 1972), 128–29; Admiral Jean Decoux to French naval attachés, letters of instruction, September, 1933–September 1935, in Sér. FMF-SE, Car. 20, Archives de la marine. All further references to these archives in this chapter are to Série FMF-SE.

14. Débat, Marine oblige, 27–29; Malcolm Anderson, Conservative Politics in France (London, 1974), 61.

Friendship with Italy also became a favorite project of the navy's Deuxième bureau. Working closely with the Section d'études, the navy's intelligence officers produced a strategic analysis of Italy in 1932 that urged strong backing of Mussolini. The authors of this document, Admirals Fernet and de Laborde, saw Il Duce as a modern-day Julius Caesar, pursuing legitimate expansionist goals in Africa and the eastern Mediterranean. The study also justified a Franco-Italian rapprochement for reasons of racial solidarity in a world French officers perceived as distinctly anti-Latin. "Everything," they wrote, "that can be attempted for a close union between Italy and France, between the Latin nations in general, is worth encouragement and praise. We will never reach open discord. No vital question divides us. The Franco-Italian entente is necessary for the continued peace and salvation of the Latin World. If the Latin peoples do not unify, our civilization is lost."[15]

This document set the diplomatic tone on the Naval General Staff for several years. Over in the Section d'études, Admiral Decoux used friendly persuasion to secure this alliance, which he compared to "a fragile plant which stays alive only through constant care."[16] He frequently preceded his letters to the French naval attachés with reminders that the contents were either secret or of a personal nature, for he knew his efforts ran counter to those of the quai d'Orsay. To reinforce his arguments, he frequently enclosed clippings or entire issues of right-wing newspapers such as *Candide*, *Gringoire*, or *Action française*, which were all pro-Italian. Decoux's urgent pleas during the Ethiopian War included suggestions that the French government offer troops and use of the railroad from Djibouti in support of Mussolini. French help was justified, Decoux said, because "Italy defended the cause of Civilization in that area."[17]

Years later, Decoux blamed his country's failure to support Italy on the combined efforts of "the French Left, the Communists, and [masonic] lodges, international Jewry and the fifth column, the

15. Deuxième bureau, Reports on Franco-Italian relations, November 8, 1932, June 23, 1934, both in Car. 15, Archives de la marine.
16. Decoux to French naval attaché, Rome, January 19, 1935, *ibid.*, Car. 20.
17. Decoux to French naval attaché, Rome, December 20, 28, 1933, June 29, 1934, March 30, June 8, 1935, all *ibid.*

[British] Intelligence Service."[18] Communism frightened him so much that he did not find German aggression in Europe sufficient justification for a Franco-Russian alliance. His racial, religious, and political views epitomized the conservative French naval officer after 1918.

Even after Decoux's replacement as head of the Section d'études in 1936, the pro-Italian tone in French naval affairs prevailed, though in a more discrete form. The Section d'études wanted greater political leverage, the kind of power that the German General Staff had exercised during World War I.[19] Even with Decoux gone, the Naval General Staff continued to identify closely with right-wing and neomonarchist politics on both private and official levels. The Anglo-German accord of 1935 confirmed Darlan's belief in the hostility of the Anglo-Saxon powers toward their Latin neighbors. Like Charles Maurras, he believed that "La France seule" stood alone against all adversaries. Darlan's anglophobic opinions date at least from the London Naval Conference of 1930 when he perceived British attempts to dominate all the European navies.[20] Yet his close family ties with political moderates were sufficiently strong that he appeared to be a progressive and was appointed by Léon Blum as his naval chief of staff in 1936. Perhaps the political leaders considered Darlan the most likely of all the admirals to support the government's social reforms within the navy. Darlan did endorse these programs throughout the fleet in widely publicized meetings designed to enlighten his subordinates on the benefits of social reform. Darlan also openly supported Blum's prorepublican stand in the Spanish Civil War.[21]

18. Decoux, *Adieu marine*, 328.

19. Gordon A. Craig, *The Politics of the Prussian Army, 1640-1945* (New York, 1972), Chap. 8; Hans Spier, "Ludendorff: The German Concept of Total War," in Edward Mead Earle (ed.), *Makers of Modern Strategy: Military Thought from Machiavelli to Hitler* (Princeton, 1971), Chap. 8; Fritz Fischer, *Germany's Aims in the First World War* (New York, 1967), Chaps. 16, 23.

20. Bloch, "Naval Agreement of 1935," 144–45; Admiral François Darlan, Naval policy objectives, September 10, 1930, in Car. 14, Archives de la marine; Admiral Jules Théophile Docteur, *Darlan, amiral de la flotte* (Paris, 1949), 39–40; Office of Naval Intelligence, Naval Attaché Report, Paris (Interview of Admiral Darlan by the American attaché), December 11, 1931, C-10-L, 14811-L, NA.

21. Memorandum on Franco-British cooperation in the Spanish Civil War, August 5, 1936, in Car. 35, Archives de la marine; ONI, Naval Attaché Report, Paris, April, 1937, E-4-c, 22100, NA.

By endorsing the cabinet's interest in social reform, Darlan gained widespread support from the government in his own campaign for bureaucratic changes within the navy. He appeared with the minister of marine at a seminar for senior officers at which the government explained the new positions on labor unions, the forty-hour work week, and the rights of government employees. Darlan's subordinates believed he was the only admiral who could get what he wanted from the Popular Front while sheltering the navy from unwanted socialist influences.[22]

Darlan offers the most confusing image of all the interwar naval chiefs of staff. He fit neither the conservative nor the progressive mold, though he had solid connections with officers in both groups. His father had been a leading Freemason and a Radical deputy from Lot-et-Garonne in southwest France. Georges Leygues was a friend of the family who became the admiral's godfather. As a young officer, Darlan added to his formidable political connections by marrying the cousin of Alphonse Gasnier-Duparc, an influential Radical-Socialist and mayor of Saint-Malo. Blum took Gasnier-Duparc from his Breton city hall to be his minister of marine. He was a compromise candidate, for the government feared the naval officers would have balked had a Socialist been given that portfolio. It was Gasnier-Duparc who in turn selected Darlan as naval chief of staff.[23]

In spite of close family ties with anticlerical politics, Darlan met little resistance from his very Catholic officers in pursuing a new reform policy. Leygues had groomed him over many years, and so his appointment came as no surprise. Moreover, Darlan "knew how to pick his subordinates," said a civilian aide to Gasnier-Duparc, balancing all factions within the officer corps to support his long-term plans. With the image of one who always got the job done and one who was comfortable in political circles, Darlan worked with the full backing of the *grand corps*. He was the first naval chief of

22. ONI, Naval Attaché Report, Paris, April, 1937, E-4-c, 22100, NA; Decoux, *Adieu Marine*, 237; Godechot Interview; Mattéo Connet, Interview, July 10, 1974; Godfroy Interview.

23. Jean Jolly (ed.), *Dictionnaire des parlementaires français: notice biographiques sur les ministres, députés, et sénateurs français de 1889 à 1940* (8 vols.; Paris, 1960–77), V, 1786–87; Connet Interview; Admiral Paul Auphan and Jacques Mordal, *The French Navy in World War II*, trans. A. C. J. Sabalot (Annapolis, 1959), 10; Godfroy Interview.

Admiral Darlan with President Lebrun
Admiral François Darlan escorted the president of France from the
deathbed of Georges Leygues. Son of a deputy and godson of Leygues,
Darlan was envied by other naval officers as the one "with the greatest
backing." *National Archives Photo*

staff to gain the support of both conservative and progressive factions within the navy in modern times. He cleverly used this support to centralize power in his own hands. In the process, he created
a dedicated following of officers popularly known as the "ADD" or
amis de Darlan. To rise to the top under him, an officer had to be
part of this inner circle of friends.[24] Darlan's ability both to control
his officers and to work in the political arena was not usually seen
among French naval officers. He represented the new breed of civil
and military public servants who focused on power and efficiency
rather than old family alliances and cliques. Appearing in the mid-
1930s, these men who possessed the new technocratic mentality

24. Connet Interview.

strengthened the bureaucracy at the expense of political control, which was already weak because of constantly changing governments. Darlan's ambitions went beyond the reach of most admirals, however, and he dropped hints that one day he would like to become president of France after serving his tenure in the navy. No one knew if his comments were serious or only in jest.[25]

Within six months of his appointment as naval chief of staff, Darlan published a major policy document entitled Order Number One. In it he presented his decision to completely revamp the naval bureaucracy and to centralize power in his own hands. Unlike earlier chiefs of staff who decentralized decision making by providing several paths of access to the minister of marine, Darlan sought to be the focal point for everything. Even the powerful Section d'études, the personal staff of the minister, and the Senior Naval Council fell under Darlan's personal supervision. The Section d'études, which had formulated most of the navy's policy, now became the mouthpiece for Darlan's own thoughts on naval affairs.[26] The admiral followed this reshuffling of his staff with a proposal that he personally write the efficiency reports on all the navy's captains. Inasmuch as these annual documents were the principal records used in promoting officers, his plan would allow him to control the choice of all future admirals. It was the cornerstone of his design to surround himself only with those he trusted and liked.[27]

These changes within the navy produced mixed results. A certain amount of lethargy within the General Staff vanished when Darlan took over. He achieved centralization, however, only at the expense of cutting off loyal opposition and any but his own views about the conduct of naval affairs. He also succeeded in isolating the minister of marine from the rest of the officer corps. In the end, Darlan became the only effective voice on policy matters, a satisfactory arrangement as long as the minister of marine and the naval chief of staff worked well together and had full confidence in each

25. Ministère de la Marine, *Annuaire de la Marine* (Paris, 1924, 1927, 1937), sections showing the reorganization of the naval bureaucracy. On the centralization of power and the "amis de Darlan," Connet Interview; La Monneraye Interview; Godfroy Interview; Godechot Interview; Madame Jean Violette, Interview, July 18, 1975.
26. Order Number One, March 20, 1937, in Car. 32, Archives de la marine; ONI, Naval Attaché Report, Paris, April, 1938, E-5-c, 4794, NA.
27. Darlan, Memorandum, December 19, 1938, in Car. 33, Archives de la marine.

other's opinions. This was the case with Gasnier-Duparc, but when César Campinchi succeeded him in June, 1937, suspicions and barriers arose between the officers and the civilian leadership. Officers who spoke out too independently of Darlan or whom he perceived as a threat were retired or sent as far away as possible.[28]

Darlan intended his reforms to improve performance and end internal bickering, but he was unable to solve the problem of his officers' personal involvement in politics. Although Blum gave the navy its largest budgets to date, the officers never saw the Popular Front as a friend.[29] Yet, Darlan did not seriously try to halt political activity even when it went beyond the line of normally accepted conduct for uniformed personnel. So long as the officers remained personally loyal to Darlan, he did not chastise them for their political conduct. As for himself, Darlan used his office as a vehicle to enhance his own power in the political world beyond the realm of naval matters. He spoke openly of how he saw political and military leaders as interchangeable men at the top echelons of government. To him, politics and strategy could not be divided into separate areas of responsibility.[30]

Darlan also harbored the kinds of antiparliamentary and authoritarian sentiments that a strong-willed technocrat might easily hold when frustrated by his political superiors. He believed the navy could survive only by fighting on five fronts simultaneously. These were, "London, Rome, the Quai d'Orsay the rue de Rivoli [Ministry of Finance] and the Palais Bourbon, the last three being more difficult to sustain than the first two."[31] With time, his apprehensions about the Third Republic grew. He was appalled by the February, 1934, riots on the place de la Concorde and complained that Gaston Doumergue failed to take these disturbances as a pretext "to use the vacuum cleaner" to sweep a weak cabinet aside.[32] Darlan

---

28. Connet Interview; Godfroy Interview; Godechot Interview; Darlan Diary, November 14–16, 20, 1939, in Car. 14, Archives de la marine; Auphan and Mordal, *French Navy*, 154.

29. Espagnac du Ravay [Louis de La Monneraye], *Vingt ans de politique navale, 1919–1939* (Grenoble, 1941), 180–86.

30. Alain Darlan, *L'Amiral Darlan parle* (Paris, 1953), 19–20.

31. Admiral François Darlan to Hector Violette, November 24, 1931, in Heçtor Violette Papers.

32. Docteur, *Darlan*, 30, 44.

also recalled how his father, who had strong republican feelings, always taught his children "the many weaknesses of the French political regime" and that only a fundamental change would produce "new strength and public sanity." In this respect, Admiral Darlan's views differed little from those of his monarchist subordinates in the *grand corps* who wanted to rebuild the French government from the bottom up.[33] Technocrats and monarchists had a common interest in strengthening the central power of government.

The navy's passive acceptance of the Popular Front government came to an abrupt halt during the Spanish Civil War, which provided one of the most important ideological issues of the interwar years. The French naval officers saw that the symbolic value of the conflict far exceeded the practical importance of Spain as an ally. Darlan's administrative assistant, Admiral Louis de La Monneraye, was among many in the navy who considered Franco the savior of cherished Catholic values. La Monneraye cited José Antonio Primo de Rivera to explain the failure of parliamentary regimes in Europe. "The masses today, having no guide, throw themselves upon the most convenient distraction while governments remain content in following their routine chores."[34] Some French officers boasted that they had refused to participate in the shipment of French arms to the Spanish republic and expressed reservations about joining the maritime patrols designed to keep foreign weapons out of the war. Admiral Fernet told Pierre Varillon of the *Action française* about the distastefulness of the patrols, which French naval officers "did begrudgingly." Professor Godechot asked his officer friends at the École navale what they did on patrol when they saw a ship loaded with arms on its way to Franco's troops. One replied, "we imitated Nelson at Copenhagen," recalling the way that the British admiral had avoided a signal to cease fire by holding up a telescope to his blind eye.[35]

Attacks on the Popular Front increased during the war in Spain.

33. Darlan, *Amiral Darlan parle*, 23; Hélène de David-Beauregard, *Souvenirs de famille* (Toulon, 1970), 170; Decoux, *Adieu marine*, 292; Decoux to French naval attaché, London, September 23, 1935, in Car. 20, Archives de la marine.

34. Du Ravay, *Vingt ans*, 41–42.

35. Auphan and Mordal, *French Navy*, 14; Admiral Jean Fernet to Varillon, December 27, 1937, in Varillon Papers; Godechot Interview.

Pierre Varillon published a book in which he warned that the government was ruining the navy, and he suggested in his newspaper column that the navy take a stand against the Spanish republic in order to force the Blum cabinet to change its Iberian policy.[36] From September, 1937, until December, 1938, articles on the "Armée and marine" page of the *Action française* condemned the application of the forty-hour work week to the naval shipyards. The Section d'études retained a copy of a French general's report following his visit to Franco's army. The Frenchman was obviously impressed by the Spanish campaign to defend Catholicism, nationalism, and the traditional domestic role for future generations of Spanish women.[37] Meanwhile, at the École navale, Jacques Godechot encountered only one French naval officer sympathetic to the cause of the Spanish republic. Witnessing the slow collapse of the Barcelona regime, French naval officers patrolling the coastline imagined that the same thing might happen next at home. Moreover, said Georges Débat, belief in the values of discipline and order made fascist ideology appealing to officers who wanted a quick solution to France's problems.[38]

The American naval attaché in Paris developed an interest in the political behavior of French naval personnel. He questioned career enlisted men on their reactions to the Spanish Civil War and how they might have reacted had a similar crisis reached France. Answers to these questions led the attaché to question the loyalty of French naval personnel to the Popular Front government of Léon Blum.

> Q. There is a possibility, even though improbable, that France could be faced with a similar condition of civil war as has occurred in Spain. Should such an unfortunate state of affairs arrive, what would be the attitude and choice of French naval personnel?
>
> A. *Officers*—No need for discussion as all officers, by tradition as well as religious beliefs, would immediately go "RIGHT." That is they

36. Pierre Varillon, *Sacrifiera-t-on la marine française?* (Paris, 1937), 38; Varillon, "La Concentration navale allemande dans les eaux espagnols?" *Action française,* August 15, 1936, p. 1.

37. General Camille Walch, Report on his visit to Franco's headquarters, April 30–May 13, 1938, in Car. 35, Archives de la marine.

38. Godechot Interview; Débat, *Marine oblige*, 33.

would swing to the side which in Spain is represented by General Franco—this, of course, providing the movement in France was of sufficient strength to carry its cause.

Enlisted Men—All *career* men, which represents seventy-five percent of the entire Navy, would follow the officers. The "conscripts," doing obligatory military service, because of the fact that they would come largely from close industrial centers, would probably go "LEFT," unless the enthusiasm of their comrades carried them with the gang.

. . . .

Q. What would be the attitude of the large Army contingents, large garrisons being stationed in all military ports, in such an event?

A. *Officers*—No doubt they would follow the lead of naval officers for similar reasons. Army officers are drawn from the same elite personnel. The enthusiasm and cooperation might not be the same in the Army as in the Navy because of the many staff corps, etc., which have civilian "leanings" because of closer contact with the people and industry.

. . . .

Note: (by Naval Attaché): The above view of enlisted personnel is considered an index to which way the wind is blowing. There was never any doubt as to which way the officers would turn in a real showdown between the Right and Left forces. One need only have read the editorials appearing in the Royalist newspaper *Action française* by Admiral Schwerer . . . proving by forceful arguments that naval officers "were" and "must necessarily be Rightists" if not "royalists."[39]

These interviews, conducted during the spring of 1937, confirmed the attaché's suspicions about political involvement in the French navy. Perhaps the most significant finding in the report was the opportunist approach officers would take when tossing their hats in with a coup. Unlike the more violent groups in right-wing politics, the naval officers still had little interest in street fighting even to defend their own class. Moreover, they would verify the strength of the movement before committing themselves to overthrowing the government. Admiral Jean Fernet, who was the image of the aristocratic naval officer, explained his frustration in a letter to his friend and confidant, Pierre Varillon. After explaining the self-destructive qualities of French society, Fernet cited a passage from a favorite book, Daniel Halévy's *La République des ducs*,

39. ONI, Naval Attaché Report, Paris, September 24, 1937, E-5-a, 17281, NA.

in which the author analyzed flaws in the national character, concluding with a greeting to the spiritual father of the Action Française:

"One fault spoils everything. These people have little ambition and are foolish, priggish and even roguish. Stirred up by these [values], they surrender themselves without limit to countless follies. Thus, the most beautiful country in the world becomes the world's greatest and worst kept mad house." [40]

Fernet then suggests that Frenchmen hadn't changed since that passage was written in 1873. He closes with a warm farewell to Charles Maurras, who was also godfather to Varillon's son.

Fernet made his remarks on the French political process when antirepublican sentiments were at their height in the navy. Although no officer on active duty led a coordinated attack on national institutions, more and more of them found consolation in the heated ideological atmosphere of the fleet's wardrooms. Widespread negativism unified these men in their attacks upon the foundations of the Third Republic. They found it easier to agree on what they disliked than on what they wished to see as replacements for existing institutions. This destructive thought also typified the mood at the *Action française*. Naval officers speaking out on politics posed a far greater potential threat to stability than the more frequent comments in the civilian sector. The conscription law of 1872 denied active-duty personnel both the vote and the right to join in partisan politics. Unfortunately, neither the realities of a newly expanded fleet nor the promises of improved wages alleviated the naval officers' disgust with French politics and their sense of impending personal ruin. An officer's wife spoke for many in her position when she explained in 1937 that the new minister of marine "was not qualified by breeding or experience to take his place at dinner with ladies and gentlemen." Her arrogance and contempt are indicative of how far things had gone.[41]

Comments of this sort also show how insensitive some in the navy were to the impact of their political views. In spite of this kind of inflammatory rhetoric, many officers genuinely believed

---

40. Fernet to Varillon, December 27, 1937, in Varillon Papers, citing a passage from Daniel Halévy, *La Fin des notables* (Livre de poche ed.; Paris, 1937), 113–14.
41. ONI, Naval Attaché Report, Paris, June 23, 1936, C-10-j, 20921, NA.

themselves to be nonpolitical servants of the state, whose duty it was to speak out whenever the navy faced some foreign or even a domestic threat. They did not wish to be caught off guard as their fathers had been in the Fashoda crisis and the First World War. The history lessons at the École navale and the École de guerre navale played an important role in the political awakening during the 1930s when the officers saw cabinets inadequately preparing for yet another conflict. Though Marc Bloch had not yet written his *L'Étrange défaite*, the spirit of alienation he discovered in the army was already widespread in the navy by 1936.

The only evidence uncovered that attempted to measure the strength of the navy's antirepublican leanings was gathered by American naval attachés. One focused on this key problem in 1936, and he pursued his analysis through the summer of 1939. The attaché had to measure this behavior through indirect evidence, for military personnel had no public voting record, and their affiliations with the Action Française were clandestine. He began with a look at the 11 percent of the *grand corps* having the *particule* "de" in their family names, indicating an aristocratic or quasi-aristocratic lineage. These men, he presumed, were the most likely adherents to the royalist cause. Knowing the political climate within the French navy in general and seeing which leading officers favored neomonarchism, he concluded that "were it possible to define accurately 'Right and Royalist,' the table [of figures he provided] would show a high increase in favor of this caste."[42]

Officers demonstrated their political convictions in many ways. The right-wing press was prominent in the wardrooms throughout the fleet. Some officers complained about the custom of naming French warships after heroes and virtues of the Republic such as *Clemenceau, Rousseau, Voltaire, République,* and *Démocratie.* One royalist shipbuilder balked after winning a contract for one of these ships simply because of its republican name.[43] More recently, the last heir of Admiral Trogoff to bear his name recounted how her ancestor turned over Toulon to the English in 1792 without firing a shot. She explained her ancestor's act from the esplanade of her

---

42. *Ibid.*, August, 14, 1936, E-5-a, 20257, NA.
43. Captain John Frog, "Armée et marine," *Action française*, August 1, 1934; Paquet Interview.

villa overlooking the port Trogoff had relinquished nearly two centuries before. Faced with a republican regime at home, she said, the least he could do was to side with an enemy serving a king. For the admiral, she said with a wave of her hand, "there was no choice."[44]

Immersed in a society imbued with such attitudes, it was only a matter of time before the naval officers developed general reservations about the institutions they were sworn to defend. But they were not alone in their doubts. The same problem arose in the other military services and to a lesser degree in the civil service as well.[45] A biographer of General Maxime Weygand explained that army officers during the 1930s saw themselves as the best judges of the national interests. Their view derived from the separation they perceived between the "legal" France, made up of elected officials, and the "real" France, symbolized by the army. Because men from all parts of the country and from all walks of life served as soldiers, the army officers believed they were a better sounding board for the national will than the governments, which changed frequently and unpredictably. Army officers assumed that somehow they had an unwritten veto power over the direction of national affairs, which they exercised normally through the General Staff's participation in policy formulation. Though the *pays légal* might have been the Third Republic, the more important *pays réel* was the French nation, encompassing its land, its traditions, its people and all symbolized by its army.[46]

But the naval officers, presiding over a small volunteer rather than a conscript institution, could not set themselves above the political system for the same reasons as their army counterparts. Instead, they believed in tradition, their elitist social status, and isolation from the rest of the nation, and they viewed France first as a colonial empire rather than a European power. Anything that threatened these values, even if it was the people through a duly elected government, was unacceptable.

Rallying behind so many causes including the Catholic church,

44. Paquet Interview; Madame Eynaud de Fey (née Trogoff), Interview, June 30, 1975; Alfred Cobban, *A History of Modern France* (3 vols.; Baltimore, 1963), I, 224.
45. David Thomson, *Democracy in France Since 1870* (5th ed.; London, 1969), 62.
46. Philip Bankwitz, *Maxime Weygand and Civil-Military Relations in Modern France* (Cambridge, Mass., 1967), Chap. 6.

neomonarchist and racist leaders, and even the nationalist causes in Italy and Germany, the French naval officer corps was difficult for any outsider to understand or explain. One American made a good attempt, however, after a stimulating evening of conversation with a French naval couple. His account is preserved in an official report, recalling many a passage from *A la recherche du temps perdu.*

On the occasion of an impromptu and very informal dinner, where our two wives were the only other persons present, a French officer made several interesting remarks. My informant is a lieutenant and occupies an important position in the Ministry [of Marine]. His name does not begin with the "de" indicating title, he seems to be very highly regarded by his associates, possesses unquestioned intelligence and good balance, and information informally obtained from him in the past had proved correct in every instance.

In the course of the conversation the "Cagoulards" were lightly mentioned and my friend said that this matter was no joke as two of his friends were in prison. He followed this by the remark, "We are sick of the present mess; what will you bet that within two years there will be a King of France?" When I expressed my incredulity he added, "Ninety-five percent of the officers of the Navy are for it." We then added, "But how about the Army officers, how do they feel?" To this he replied rather sadly, "No, they are not all like us," to which his wife interjected, "The Cavalry," and he added, "Oh yes, the Cavalry officers all feel as we do." When asked what the Royal family were like he stated, "Very good, he [the heir] is serious and able and all the family are attractive."

While the writer feels that in this case, "the wish is father to the thought," and does not for a moment share the view that the restoration is near, it was interesting to hear an officer in a key position express such views. From the way the wife suggested, "The Cavalry," I feel sure that what was said reflected the honest convictions of this couple. Certainly, it could not have been an act staged for our benefit, for the dinner invitation was entirely impromptu and we all came straight from the cocktail party.

From this point the conversation drifted into a discussion of the Navy commissioned personnel. My informant made the following observations: the Navy line, *officiers de marine,* is a *corps élite,* a distinction shared with the Cavalry. While nothing derogatory was said it was inferred that the rest of the Army was average and the Air Army beyond the pale. He stated that there was "*not one single Jew in the line [grand corps].*"

As regards the staff corps [*petits corps*], it was stated that doctors and supply officers were accepted or not depending entirely upon the individual. Engineers were under no circumstance accepted and my informant explained with great warmth that "*the only thing* they had in common with the line was that upon entering the service candidates from both had to be 1.60 meters tall." This was the only point of similarity as in all other respects—birth, education and training—they were poles apart.[47]

In this conversation, all the frustrations that had simmered for two decades in the naval homes came to a boil. The diffused worries about the future of the naval officer corps, the threats to French society from the Left, the return of the Bourbon monarchy, and nostalgia for better times all blended together. As in many right-wing speeches of the day, this French officer's comments contained a mixture of accuracy and falsehood, reality and fantasy, with enough truth to make it all believable. Men like this lieutenant, raised to have more *élan* than objectivity, could easily believe these fantastic explanations of all that was wrong with their country.

When this officer cited 95 percent of his comrades as fellow royalists, he probably overestimated their strength. Of course, no two ships or staffs were identical nor will exact figures ever be found, for no statistics were recorded. Nevertheless, an estimate is possible, based on comments by men who were there or by their relatives and on information obtained in biographical material. Other helpful sources are the published membership lists of the Ligue and the Alliance de l'Action Française which appeared in the daily newspapers. Probably as many as three-quarters of the *grand corps* were sympathetic to the Action Française or some other affiliated group seeking to end the parliamentary regime and to replace it with some kind of authoritarian model.

Support for these causes reached their height between 1936 and 1939. Among the *petits corps*, that is among the naval officers in the specialized fields who did not attend the École navale, those who favored a new regime probably never exceeded 50 percent of the members. Among them, royalism had its greatest following in the *corps de santé*, which, from a social point of view, was closest to the *grand corps*. Like the student body at Navale, those attending the École de santé navale in Bordeaux had a strong monarchist

47. ONI, Naval Attaché Report, Paris, December 6, 1937, E-5-a, 17281, NA.

tradition. Support for the less common Bonapartist and genuinely fascist ideologies came more often from the *commissariat* and the *corps de génie maritime* but in relatively small numbers. The offices in the lesser *petits corps* retained the opinions of the social circles they came from. In some cases, these men received their commissions directly from the enlisted ranks; others came from vocational schools or universities. According to opinions of officers on the scene, the *petits corps* aboard ship tended to moderate the more fanatical in the *grand corps* when ideological and political disputes flared up. Unfortunately, no statistical information has been uncovered to measure this interplay between the two unequal halves of the naval officer corps.[48]

Even Darlan, who had dismissed the seriousness of his officers' involvement in politics, finally became concerned very briefly in 1938. Earlier, he had tried to calm the minister of marine when figures on the widespread support for the Action Française first appeared. Later, however, Darlan ordered his subordinates to correct the situation, but he did nothing to follow his order through to a successful conclusion. No examples were set by official reprimands or courts martial.[49] The lack of continued official interest in the political activities of the naval officers probably contributed to the failure of any reform. Although most observers knew the Action Française had a large following in the navy, those who could have done something about it in the early stages chose not to interfere. Civilian leaders and many admirals believed that the officers were merely dabbling in harmless "platonic monarchism," and they feared that an overreaction would create unnecessarily bad feelings in the fleet. Parliament and the public devoted much attention to the army's threats to republican stability, but no one felt the navy had a realistic chance of harming the civil-military balance in

48. These estimates are based on the figures cited in: ONI, Naval Attaché Reports, Paris, series August 14, 1936–December 6, 1937, E-5-a, NA; membership and contribution lists of Liguers and Alliés in the *Action française*, 1924–1939; opinions provided in Godechot Interview; Paquet Interview; Connet Interview; Godfroy Interview; Madame Varillon Interview; La Monneraye Interview; Commander Georges Débat, Interview, June 22, 1976; Admiral Jean Nielly, Interview, July 26, 1975.

49. Bulletin de Haut, Commandement, November, 1938, in Car. 2, Archives de la marine; Docteur, *Darlan*, 27; Godechot Interview.

France. Politicians appear to have accepted the navy's widely publicized claim of political neutrality at face value.[50] It was simply impossible for them to believe that the admirals could lead a coup.

In the final three years before World War II, when ideological unrest reached its peak in the navy, the Commission de la marine militaire of the Chamber of Deputies never touched this problem at all. Instead, it devoted its energies to bolstering the pace of naval arms production and backing Darlan's requests for added personal power. The committee even gave him full control over all operational and intelligence matters, free of any direct supervision by the minister of marine. Naturally, the threat of war encouraged the Parliament to prepare for armed conflict and to set aside what appeared to be petty thoughts expressed by bored officers in peacetime. The Parliament appears to have viewed the officers' political activity as trivia that would fade away once the navy mobilized for war.[51]

In the last few years of peace, the junior officers, the admirals, and the naval writers on the *Action française* staff all reached a general consensus of opinion on the navy's future. Anglophobia and defeatism were frequent points of official and unofficial discussions. While these three groups believed in Britain's support of the French army's role in Europe, they also knew that a French navy frightened London very much. The same officers and journalists also expected the close cultural and racial ties between Britain and Germany to produce a stronger bond than the one between Britain and France. French naval writers had even less hope for an Anglo-French accord after the Munich crisis. Even the normally anglophile minister of marine, César Campinchi, wondered if Britain were not purposely ignoring German naval rearmament in 1939. Darlan's longtime distrust of Great Britain also grew in the last months of peace. In joint staff talks with the Royal Navy, he did all he could to avoid making any firm commitments by keeping discussions on a

50. Godechot Interview; Connet Interview.
51. Chambre des députés, "Procès-verbaux de la Commission de la marine militaire," February 20, 1919–December 2, 1939. Social and political problems within the navy came up only twice and only tangentially in these committee debates between the two world wars, first on November 24, 1922, and later on December 11, 1928. The final meeting endorsed the separation of operational matters from the direct supervision of the minister of marine.

"nonofficial" basis. He also feared British intentions to withdraw precipitously from the Mediterranean, leaving French interests particularly vulnerable in an important area of the world.[52]

One French naval officer wrote to his friend, the American naval attaché, in April, 1939, blaming the "'newly-arrived' bourgeoisie" in the government for a feeble foreign policy. "In a word," he said, "we are so completely enmeshed in the parliamentary tangle that we cannot react with the speed and rapidity that events demand."[53] Two months later, Darlan went so far as to suggest that democratic powers simply did not have the wherewithal to stand up to the tougher fascist states. He told Admiral Jules Docteur that he had little faith in the French army's leadership and that he found civil-military relations at a new low in 1939. Darlan and others expressed some threads of hope in official and private correspondence, but these themes were lost in the overwhelming spirit of worry and despair. Years of prejudice and bad experiences simply could not be eliminated with the stroke of a minister's pen.[54]

While normal preparations for war went on uninterrupted, the reservations officers felt about it grew as an important undercurrent of opinion. By September, 1939, the French navy consisted of a fleet totally rebuilt since 1918 but led by men whose ideas and habits dated from an earlier period. Certainly, the fleet went off to fight in the fall of 1939 more like the optimistic French army of 1914 than the demoralized army of 1939. For the first eight months of fighting, discussions about pyrrhic victories temporarily disappeared in the navy if not in the army. But the war was not the sure remedy many hoped it would be for the political discontent in the naval officer corps. Combat in the Mediterranean and in the Atlantic temporarily distracted them from their peacetime involvement

52. Policy memorandum, February 17, 1937, in Car. 14, Archives de la marine; "Armée et marine," *Action française*, November 15, 25, 1937, November 10, 1938; César Campinchi, Memorandum, January 9, 1939, in Car. 12, Darlan, Memoranda, July, 1939, in Car. 22, August 3, 1939, in Car. 14, all in Sér. FMF-SE, Archives de la marine.
53. ONI, Naval Attaché Report, Paris, April 15, 1939, C-10-j, 15373-H, NA.
54. Darlan, Memorandum, June, 1939, in Car. 15, Archives de la marine; "Armée et marine," *Action française*, January 25, 1939, with the same conclusions as in Darlan's memorandum; Docteur, *Darlan*, 55, 57; Darlan, Memoranda, November, 1937, in Car. 14, September 26, 1938, in Car. 15, all in Sér. FMF-SE, Archives de la marine.

in right-wing politics and journalism.[55] Nevertheless, the officers remained content with the political process only so long as they believed that victory would come and that the government had the ability to manage the wartime emergency. When chances for a quick end to the fighting dimmed, the cracks in the wall reappeared, and old hatreds surfaced once again.

55. Admiral Raymond de Belot and André Reussner, *De 1919 à 1939* (Paris, 1971), 217, Vol. III of André Reussner (ed.), *La Puissance navale dans l'histoire*, 3 vols.; Auphan and Mordal, *French Navy*, 17–18.

CHAPTER 8
Denouement
Vichy and Beyond

The history of the French naval officers at Vichy has been dealt with at length by historians and participants in that tragic interlude. What needs emphasis here is the reason why this group, almost to a man, disavowed the republic. Also of great interest are the differences between the ways naval officers and other groups reacted to the extended crisis in French politics from 1939 to 1962. A full career lasted forty years, which meant that officers who entered the navy in the early 1920s went through the interwar era, World War II, and two colonial wars, while witnessing three changes of regime. Throughout all this, these officers were expected to manage naval affairs in a routine fashion.

For the navy, the opening of hostilities in 1939 caused the kind of exuberance that the army had experienced in 1914 but certainly not twenty-five years later. The army, however, had declined in strength and readiness between the world wars, while the navy experienced the kind of growth that the army had last known fifty years earlier. In addition, the naval officer corps preserved its pre-1914 social composition, which the army had lost by the 1930s. Naval officers remembered the lean years at the turn of the century when the fleet was reduced to a shambles, and they vowed it would never happen again. Today, an enormous mural of the fleet at anchor in 1939 covers an entire wall in the officers' mess at Brest. That fleet symbolizes the restoration of French naval power. Those days were the *bon vieux temps* of which so many would speak about in years to follow.

The euphoria that the officers felt on the eve of the war, however, vanished in the summer of 1940 when they saw the army collapse in a matter of weeks. When victory no longer seemed a realistic possibility, many of the senior naval officers turned to the political world and sought scapegoats for the impending defeat or alternatives to existing policies. Admiral Darlan became pessimistic during the winter of 1939–1940, well before a French military defeat was dreamed of. He kept a diary during those months, noting on several occasions his growing displeasure with the military and political leadership running the war effort. He commented often on the poor state of military readiness on land and returned to his chronic anglophobic worries about British reliability as an ally. On December 14, 1939, he concluded that the French government was incapable of coping with the wartime crisis. He believed success would follow only if the government were completely reorganized and geared toward the elimination of communism, which he saw as the greatest threat to French security. "We must," he wrote, "have a government which governs and I can hardly see that except with a smaller war cabinet with full powers, not only until the end of hostilities but also until the country regains its stability."[1] In January 1940, eighteen months before Hitler opened his Eastern Front Campaign, Darlan even suggested that France declare war on the Soviet Union.[2]

No voice in the officer corps spoke out against Darlan's proposals. Independent spokesmen did not exist. Even Admiral Castex, the only published strategist among the admirals, had no voice in policy matters, being relegated to a secondary coastal command from which he retired late in 1939. Darlan's chief subordinates, Admiral Jean de Laborde who commanded the Atlantic fleet, and Admiral Jean-Pierre Estéva who commanded the Mediterranean fleet, had no interest in policy matters. Rather, they were reputed to be strong taskmasters who preferred to be at sea and were not the sort to deviate from established procedures.[3]

In Paris, Darlan increased his influence over war policy when he

---

1. Admiral François Darlan, Diary, August 22–December 14, 1939, June 17–September 5, 1940, in Série FMF-SE, Carton 14, Archives de la marine. All citations of these archives in this chapter are to Série FMF-SE.

2. Darlan, "Current Situation" (MS, January 22, 1940, *ibid.*).

3. William L. Langer, *Our Vichy Gamble* (New York, 1966), 167; Jacques Godechot, Interview, June 25, 1975; Admiral Paul Auphan, Interview, June 5, 1974.

obtained parliamentary support for a major reorganization of the naval hierarchy. He managed to completely sever the minister of marine from all operational matters. This permitted him to run his part of the war from an isolated bunker in Maintenon, with little oversight by either the minister or the Parliament.[4] Until Darlan's assassination in December, 1942, the navy's *grand corps* remained tightly knit even when disaster struck. His careful selection of subordinates in the years prior to the war paid off well in terms of zealous personal loyalty under the most trying conditions.

Darlan also had the ability to detect the faintest breeze of political change before it happened, making him enormously successful at surviving in a very unstable environment. Frenchmen have called this a highly refined sense of opportunist politics. On May 5, 1940, five days before the German invasion of Belgium and ten days before the French defeat on the Meuse, Darlan hosted Marshal Pétain during a secret visit to naval headquarters at Maintenon. The marshal was still ambassador to Spain and would not be recalled to a cabinet post for a fortnight. Yet his visit to Darlan gives every indication that Pétain was already testing the political climate within the armed forces. He asked Darlan for open-ended recommendations on how best to restructure the government for the war effort.[5] All this preceded any hint of a French military collapse. Darlan's reply was a formal expression of his resentment against coping with a parliamentary regime while trying to conduct a war. The admiral suggested that the day-to-day operations be relegated to a very few ministers, the chief of staff for national defense, the chiefs of staff for the three armed forces, and Marshal Pétain himself. Darlan also included the marshal's name on an even smaller list of suggested members of a war policy committee, the so-called Conseil supérieure de la défense nationale, responsible for overall war planning. That list did not include any of the three civilian ministers of war, marine, or air, presumably because they were not in the chain of operational decision-making. Darlan concluded his recom-

4. Chambre des députés, "Procès-verbal de la Commission de la marine militaire, December 2, 1939; Admiral Paul Auphan and Jacques Mordal, *The French Navy in World War II*, trans. A. C. J. Sabalot (Annapolis, 1959), 24–25.
5. Adrienne Doris Hytier, *Two Years of French Foreign Policy, 1940–1942* (Geneva, 1958), 45–49.

mendations to Pétain with a contemptuous evaluation of the civilian government in power and his personal endorsement for the marshal's inclusion in a government of national unity.[6] We can only presume this is what Pétain wanted to hear.

Turning next to his admirals, Darlan circulated several memoranda concerning various naval contingency plans on which he sought advice. Included were plans on what to do in the event of a military collapse in Europe. These documents offered a wide range of options from continuing the war effort abroad to keeping the fleet out of German hands in the event of a national disaster. The exploratory and nondirective nature of these documents, which were circulated to the navy's senior commanders at sea and ashore show that Darlan was perhaps testing the climate of opinion before committing himself. Certainly he did not usually seek a collective decision. Normally, he concocted his plans in total secrecy before issuing an abrupt command to his subordinates, providing no time for feedback or discussion. It is likely, therefore, that Darlan either suspected or knew that something was afoot, though he made sure to cover his tracks, for the available documentation is not conclusive. The gun is only warm, not smoking.[7]

Although he had been a lifetime critic of the French army, Darlan reversed himself, to everyone's surprise, on June 16, 1940. On that day, his arch-rival General Maxime Weygand resigned, and Darlan decided to support his refusal to continue the war from North Africa in the event German troops overran France. Although such a colonial defense would have been perfectly in line with the navy's historical claim as the ultimate defender of the empire, Darlan chose to support the army's refusal to leave the *métropole*.[8] In choosing between a last-ditch battle followed by a punitive occupation, as happened in Poland, or an armistice that would preserve some residual powers for a French government, Darlan embraced the latter course of action. He even used Weygand's traditional argu-

6. Darlan, Notes, June, 1939, in Car. 15, Archives de la marine. These match a letter cited in Alain Darlan, *L'Amiral Darlan parle* (Paris, 1953), 50–52.

7. Notice to Amiral Le Luc, May 28, 1940, Additional notes and memoranda, all in Car. 14, Archives de la marine.

8. Robert Aron, *The Vichy Regime* (Boston, 1969), 25; Philip Bankwitz, *Maxime Weygand and Civil-Military Relations in Modern France* (Cambridge, Mass., 1967), 310–12.

ment that the conscript army was inseparably linked to the soil of the *patrie*. Darlan added that the immediate laying down of arms would preserve some national independence, which might serve as a stage for a comeback one day. In practical terms, an armistice would avoid destruction of the army and possible massive loss of civilian lives. Yet none of this had much direct impact on the navy, which did not face the German navy and was doing quite well against the Italians in the Mediterranean.[9]

Darlan's position was totally contrary to the timeless justification for the French navy, which Colbert had first used—namely, to protect the colonies overseas. Presumably, this point did not go unnoticed among the leaders of 1940 when they asked Darlan and the other chiefs of staff if they would continue the war from North Africa. By rights the navy should have leaped at President Lebrun's plea. In such an event, the navy would have been in charge, and the war would have continued essentially as a naval or amphibious campaign. Until that moment, Darlan had claimed the empire and maritime trade as the navy's chief strategic concerns.[10] Moreover, the Armée Coloniale and the Armée d'Afrique, though less well equipped than the Armée Métropolitaine, had the capacity to fight on provided supplies came from some external source, as Churchill offered in a last-ditch effort to keep France in the war. But Darlan also rejected the idea of integrating the French and British forces, explaining that "it was simply a question of honor" for France to stand alone. For one who took pride in his far-reaching views within the naval officer corps, this grasping at chivalrous justifications was highly unusual. He told his admirals in July and again in September, 1940, that the fleet had to survive intact "to justify its utility" and to assure the navy's "freedom of action." He went on to explain how the armistice benefited Frenchmen everywhere, "It is for us Frenchmen to profit from their [Germany's] hopes and, if we play the game with enough finesse, it is possible that we will come out of this adventure in good shape."[11]

9. Aron, *Vichy Regime*, 328; Darlan, Memorandum, July 16, 1940, in Car. 14, Archives de la marine; Darlan, *Amiral Darlan parle*, 84; Auphan and Mordal, *French Navy*, Chap. 10.

10. Darlan, *Amiral Darlan parle*, 47; Darlan Diary, October 7–12, 1939.

11. Darlan, *Amiral Darlan parle*, 67, 84; Memorandum, July 16, 1940, Darlan Diary, September 5, 1940, both in Car. 14, Archives de la marine.

Withdrawing from the Anglo-French alliance and cooperating with the Germans must have been easier for the anglophobic naval officer corps than for their army counterparts. Darlan frequently complained about Britain's shortcomings in the war, and when Churchill ordered the Royal Navy's raid on the French squadron at Mers-el-Kébir on July 3, 1940, he rekindled the dormant flame of virulent anglophobic sentiment. Lifetime suspicions about British intentions were confirmed in this act and in later efforts to seize parts of the French empire. Darlan sought retaliation in talks with his Italian counterparts after the armistice of 1940, when he encouraged a raid on the British squadron at Alexandria, Egypt.[12]

Darlan's change of heart on June 16 assured that France would collapse rather than stumble in 1940. For years, sailors had complained that on the eve of victory, the nation had always let the navy down. For once in French history, the tables were turned. Had more officers challenged this decision, Darlan might not have made it so easily, but habits are difficult to change. The rigid obedience to authority and the chivalric code prevalent in the naval officer corps encouraged a rallying together in the face of external danger, which many saw not in the Germans but in France's own civilian leadership. Certainly the political system left a great deal to be desired, for Lebrun either could not or would not force a continued resistance overseas. The navy showed how well it had groomed its men for the test. In the postarmistice purge of 135 Freemasons from the armed forces, only one naval officer lost his commission.[13] Evidently, years of selective recruiting had assured a unified corps for war and for moments like these.

A few young officers were surprised to see how passively their shipmates accepted the armistice. Reactions to the cease-fire varied from resignation to joyous celebration. On one ship, the junior officers broke out champagne to toast the news. Aboard another ship, Ensign Roger Barberot chastised his comrades who welcomed the end of hostilities. "'We must continue,' I said. No one answered.

---

12. Darlan Diary, December 14, 1939, July 6, 1940; Robert O. Paxton, *Parades and Politics at Vichy: The French Officer Corps Under Marshal Pétain* (Princeton, 1966), 73–74.

13. Paxton, *Parades and Politics*, 31–32, 58–59, 176.

The spirit of all these men appeared broken in a single stroke. From the start, the defeat was accepted. No anger, no disobedience. Simply resignation and languor. The junior officers' mess was full of light and gaiety. Champagne bottles circulated around. I remained for a few embarrassing seconds like someone who came for a funeral and stumbled upon a wedding."[14]

Georges Débat encountered the same response on his ship when Pétain announced the armistice over the radio. The news shocked Débat, for in remote Alexandria, Egypt, he had no inkling that an end to the fighting was in sight. "Anger took hold of me and I cried out, 'Do not listen to that old fool!' I recall my words perfectly. Immediately, someone asked me to be quiet and I felt embarrassed at having lost control of myself again. Then I listened to the rest with the others. Silence followed. Only two or three officers spoke, 'Since the Marshal said it. . . .' Already 'The Marshal,' as though one said, 'The King.'"[15] Several of the ships' chaplains began praying for Pétain, some asking the officers to obey him and others comparing him to Joan of Arc.

A few of the officers who chose not to obey the cease-fire had more pragmatic goals than either Débat or Barberot. Admiral Émile Muselier headed for England; he was one of a very few who reached Great Britain and remained. His irascible temper, which contributed to his fight with Darlan and discharge from the navy in 1939, eventually led to a showdown with de Gaulle too.[16] De Gaulle promoted two other officers to admiral. Thierry d'Argenlieu was better remembered as the Carmelite priest, Louis de la Trinité, who often celebrated the memorial masses for the Association amicale des anciens élèves de l'École navale, of which he was also a member. Captain Philippe Auboyneau resigned from his position with the French squadron in Alexandria, explaining his intentions in a letter to his commander, Admiral Godfroy. So long as there was a chance to resist from abroad, he could not accept demands for "blind obedience" to Pétain. He admitted that, as a bachelor, his

---

14. Roger Barberot, *A bras le coeur* (Paris, 1972), 13–14.
15. Georges Débat, *Marine oblige* (Paris, 1974), 84–85.
16. Brian Crozier, *De Gaulle* (New York, 1973), 137–38, 141–42, confirms the information in Darlan's diary and in Auphan and Mordal, *French Navy*, 154.

decision to fight on was far easier than for most naval officers whose families were vulnerable to German reprisals.[17]

Barberot, Débat, d'Argenlieu, and Auboyneau did not form a homogeneous group, though all were graduates of École navale. The decision to continue the fight crossed religious, ideological, and family backgrounds. What they all shared, finally, was a curious sense of intellectual independence that placed them in the minority, perhaps even made them outcasts in their profession during those years.

Both d'Argenlieu and Auboyneau remained close to de Gaulle throughout the war and well after 1945, when they served prominently in Indochina and Algeria. Other than Muselier, they were the only admirals in the resistance prior to the liberation of North Africa in November, 1942. The attack on Mers-el-Kébir swayed many others who were still uncommitted.[18]

When Admiral de Laborde ordered the scuttling of the fleet at Toulon in 1942 to avoid capture by the Germans, chivalric ideas of honor played a large part in his decision not to sail for North Africa instead. Swearing not to let the fleet fall into any foreign hands, de Laborde and Auphan saw the destruction of the ships as the only way to live up to their oath and their personal commitment to the armistice with the Germans. Even the pragmatic Darlan appealed to his officers' sense of honor when he reminded them "not to forget that we have been defeated and that all defeats must be paid for."[19]

Darlan rewarded his followers by giving them political assignments in the Vichy government, where ten admirals served at the cabinet or subcabinet level. Two became ministers of the colonies; another served as secretary general to Pétain; four were governors general of colonies; another ran the police; and one served as secretary general for family affairs. Darlan took for himself at various times the vice-presidency of the council, second only to Pétain, and the portfolios of national defense, marine, foreign affairs, interior, and information. He converted his Section d'études navales into

17. Philippe Auboyneau to Admiral René Godfroy, August [?], 1940, in Car. 10, Archives de la marine.
18. René Jouan, *Histoire de la marine française* (Paris, 1950), 309.
19. Auphan and Mordal, *French Navy*, 271; Aron, *Vichy Regime*, 421–22; Darlan, Message, September 12, 1940, in Car. 34, Archives de la marine.

Pétain and Darlan at Vichy
This improbable alliance began with Marshal Pétain's secret visit to naval
headquarters in May, 1940, and lasted until Darlan switched to the Anglo-
American forces in November, 1942. Some called the Vichy regime "the
government of the admirals" because of the numbers of senior naval
officers holding political jobs. *U.S. Naval Institute Photo*

the Section d'études générales when its scope of work expanded
from purely naval to the full range of political issues.[20] Though the
fleet was tied up or lost, the navy was at the pinnacle of power in

20. Paxton, *Parades and Politics*, 147–52; *Les Annuaires des temps nouveaux*
(Paris, 1942), 2–15.

France for the first time. The public appropriately labeled the Vichy government the "Society for the Protection of the Admirals."[21] When so many institutions had fallen apart, Darlan provided a loyal and dedicated group of intelligent professional administrators who could run the state bureaucracy. But these wartime assignments soon proved more than their education or profession had prepared the officers to handle. Trained in an environment that never encouraged a sense of compromise or an understanding of public needs, the naval officers had few of the intellectual tools required to survive in the political world. Some reacted naïvely, as though the collapse of everything about them provided them with carte blanche to correct all the ills they perceived in French society. As for Darlan, he treated the occasion as a chance to realize his political ambitions.

The German authorities under Ambassador Otto Abetz identified Darlan as one of the few French leaders capable of managing an anticommunist campaign while pursuing what the Germans called a "modern policy."[22] The navy's support of the terms of the armistice with the Third Reich was the cornerstone of the entire Franco-German relationship through 1942. While Darlan and his followers saw cooperation as a path to success, other government servants gained the name of *napthalinards*, so called for their uniforms packed in moth balls while they waited out the war at home. To the admirals, France seemed like the yolk of an egg for which the navy was the protective shell, warding off outside dangers. With hindsight, it is easy to see that the values many of the officers had acquired at home and in school prepared them well for their work at Vichy, where the government focused on a return to an agrarian, preindustrial form of society.

It was precisely the elitism of the admirals and others of the technocracy that was condemned in the postwar trials, and naval officers stood out among the defendants who had been Vichy officials. Among the 108 men prosecuted by the Haute Cour de Justice, 11 were naval officers and 2 others were civilians affiliated

21. Alexander Werth, *France, 1940–1955* (Boston, 1966), 92.
22. *Documents on German Foreign Policy, 1918–1945*, Series D (1937–1945) (London and Washington, 1958), XI, Documents 531, 588.

with the navy. A twelfth officer, Admiral Fernet, was initially charged with the rest, but the charges were dropped prior to his trial. Apart from professional politicians, who were a very diverse group, the naval officers made up the largest single bloc of defendants, representing 12 percent of all tried by the Haute Cour. One of them received the death penalty, which was later commuted; two got life imprisonment; five got sentences of between five and ten years; three were not tried; two died before their trials; and one had the charges dropped. As for the two civilian naval officials, Minister of Marine François Piétri received degradation *in absentia*, and strategic advisor to the Naval General Staff, Henri Moysset, died before appearing in court. These trials took a heavier toll on the navy's leaders than on those of any other group, including army officers, educators, lawyers, prefects, and even private citizens. The ensuing bitterness carried over into the postwar years, when the naval officers sought exoneration for friends and professional associates.[23]

Even after the trauma of the war and its distasteful aftermath, the new Fourth Republic continued old habits in the management of the navy. Somehow, the flaws exposed during the war and the trials afterward were not immediately evident to the new government. Unfortunately, the concerns about the naval officers did not include any interest in the way they were selected, educated, or trained. In those years, only wartime credentials, Gaullist or Vichy, were important, dividing the navy into two hostile camps with the Gaullists in the minority but also in control.[24] It was extremely difficult, de Gaulle discovered, to find naval officers willing to serve in the Free French Navy. During the war, he managed to commission only one-tenth the number of new naval officers as did Vichy, leaving an enormous imbalance that survived well into the 1960s. Even an attempt to gain control of the navy by retiring all the admirals

23. Peter Novick, *The Resistance Versus Vichy: The Purge of the Collaborators in Liberated France* (New York, 1968), 222–24; Guy Raïssac, *Un combat sans merci: l'affaire Pétain–de Gaulle* (Paris, 1966), 457–58; Haute cour de justice, Stenographic records of the trials of Admirals Jean Abrial, Paul Auphan, and André Marquis, August 14, 1946.

24. Barberot, *A bras le coeur*, 291–92; Admiral Pierre Ortoli, Interview, July 4, 1974.

De Gaulle and His Admirals
Although the postwar trials removed a number of senior admirals from the
active rolls, Charles de Gaulle was never able to claim the French navy as
his own, partly because so few naval officers had served with the Free
French forces in 1940–1942. *U.S. Naval Institute Photo*

who had served Marshal Pétain failed to alter the outlook of the *grand corps*. The new men whom he appointed after 1945 came from exactly the same background as their predecessors. The first two admirals de Gaulle sent to Indochina soon demonstrated how little their policies differed from those of their Vichy predecessor, Admiral Decoux. As high commissioner, Admiral d'Argenlieu thwarted General Leclerc's attempts to reach a peaceful solution with Ho Chi Minh and his strongly nationalist following.[25]

Both d'Argenlieu and Auboyneau, who later commanded the French naval forces in Indochina, were influenced in their conduct of that colonial war by strong religious sentiments and the belief in France as a civilizing race for non-Catholic indigenous peoples. Auboyneau appeared again in Algeria, where his strong belief in the colonial system came into conflict with his support for de Gaulle. He backed the army generals in their 1958 campaign to keep Algeria under French rule. Other than Auboyneau, naval officers were hardly involved in the Algerian War and its political complications in part because of the bad experiences suffered after Vichy and in Indochina. Only one of seventy-three officers brought to trial in 1961 for the military coup came from the navy, and he had served ashore.[26]

Only after civil-military relations reached another breaking point in the 1960s did the French government make a thorough examination of the problem with the view toward dramatic solutions. First journalists and novelists and finally scholars began to examine the reasons why the navy had stepped so far out of line. The director of the Premier bureau (Personnel) opened officer dossiers to scholars looking for clues to this endemic problem. Statistics showed the same imbalance that existed before 1940, showing that the process of recruitment and education had not changed for the *grand corps* and that the officers still had nothing in common with the rest of society. In 1960, one-third of the graduates of the École navale came from the narrow section of the society comprising

25. Theodore Zeldin, *Intellect, Taste, and Anxiety* (Oxford, 1977), 1105–106, Vol. II of *France, 1848–1945*, 2 vols.; *Annuaire de l'Association amicale des anciens élèves de l'École navale* (Paris, 1973), 95–103; Werth, *France*, 330, 333, 342.

26. John Stewart Ambler, *The French Army in Politics, 1945–1962* (Columbus, Ohio, 1966), 242, 338.

high-level bureaucrats, industrialists, and leaders in the liberal professions. By contrast, half the students at Saint Cyr and the École de l'air came from the petit bourgeois and working classes. The navy still did not recruit from these parts of society; the Naval General Staff continued to preserve the elitist image of the *grand corps*. If the novels of Michel de Saint-Pierre are an accurate indication of what the navy was like, then the aristocratic element in the post-1945 navy remained as unreconciled with the Fourth Republic as their fathers had been with the Third.

Entrance exams for the École navale remained more difficult than any but those of the École polytechnique. Midshipmen remained motivated by chivalrous ideas about their careers, while contemporaries in other military schools had become technocratic in their outlook. In the fifteen years from 1945 to 1960, 87 percent of all midshipmen at Navale expected the navy to serve as the moral guide for the country. One scholar found that men who fit the naval officer's description shared a strong belief in the "dialectic of evil," requiring a class of the morally correct to preside over the less fortunate. Boys who received traditional Catholic education saw good and evil in very absolute terms. For them, the most dangerous thoughts were those that questioned conventional beliefs in God, country, and class structure.[27]

The results of these studies divided the Naval General Staff into two hostile camps. Minutes of their meetings remain closed, but impressions that have leaked out reveal long and bitter arguments over the necessity for social reform of the officer corps. These meetings did produce some positive results; changes occurred, but very slowly. While the fleet was rebuilt for the second time in fifty years from the bottom up, the aristocratic and *haut bourgeois* domination of the *grand corps* slowly gave way to boys from the working classes, seeking naval careers as a means of obtaining a technical skill and social advancement.

27. *Ibid.*, 134; Centre d'études et d'instruction psychologiques de l'armée de l'air, "Attitudes et motivation des candidats aux grandes écoles militaires," Jacques Maître, "Le Catholicisme d'extrême droite et la croisade anti-subversive," both in *Revue française de sociologie*, II (April–June, 1961), 133–51, 106–15; Guy Michelat and Jean Pierre Thomas, "Contribution à l'étude du recrutement des écoles d'officiers de la marine, 1945–1960," *Revue française de sociologie*, IX (April–June, 1968), 51–70.

By the summer of 1965, the French naval officers could look back on their recent past with enough objectivity to warn their American counterparts about the dangers of repeating old mistakes in Indochina. At social gatherings, officers no longer spoke of their longing for a restored monarchy or the threat posed by the British fleet. Instead they discussed the Russians and the dream of one day having a larger part of the defense budget than the French army.[28] The scrapping of the last British aircraft carrier, leaving the French navy superior in European waters, did not go unnoticed by these men. Today, a few carry-overs from an earlier period remain. The old families are still represented in the *grand corps* and exert a far greater moral influence than their numbers would indicate. Many retain a marked preference for parochial education. Sainte Geneviève remains top on the list of preparatory courses for the École navale, and a majority attending the École de guerre navale in the mid-1970s sent their children to Catholic schools.[29]

There are also those who have trouble adjusting to the loss of the French empire and who remain attached to the spiritual heirs of Charles Maurras. Though their numbers are small, they represent a tendency that merits the close monitoring for extremism that is routinely done in the West German military. As for the old retired officers, they now read the centrist *Le Monde* for their news if only because they claim it is "well written." They follow this with their favorite "opinion" papers, such as *Aspects de la France*, successor to *Action française*. Although these men acknowledge that social changes have led to improvements, foreign scandals like Watergate and the evacuation of Saigon in 1975 cause relapses into the paranoid thinking of the Vichy era.[30]

28. Commander André Sauvage, Interview, September 10, 1977.
29. Commandant Jacques Vernet, Interview, May 2, 1975.
30. Gleaned from conversations during numerous meals and evenings spent among French officers at their messes in Paris, Toulon, Brest, and Vincennes, 1974–77.

Conclusion

Officers serving in the French navy between the world wars managed to preserve the traditional habits of their profession, which in the other armed forces had given way to modernizing influences. Deployments away from home and geographic isolation from the mainstream of French life in the port cities permitted the navy to survive with a minimum of public scrutiny over its internal affairs. Able to rely on hand-picked sailors to man the fleet, the navy also avoided the problems of having to integrate people from outside their special milieu. Moreover, there were no outsiders trying to break in, for the sea and the colonial empire were never attractive to any but a specialized group of Frenchmen. Although the public did not trust the army's intentions after the Boulanger and Dreyfus affairs, they had no such reasons to distrust the navy. And so, Parliament supported the navy unquestioningly throughout the 1920s and 1930s.

Naval officers believed that the 1872 law denying them the vote also protected them from getting involved in politics. When the military received the suffrage in 1945, these same men and their parliamentary supporters were dismayed.[1] It is, however, arguable that denying these men the franchise forced them to express their frustrations about economic and social problems in clandestine or even illegal ways. In 1906 Edouard Lockroy, then minister of marine, warned of the potential dangers of denying the vote to career military personnel. Evidently, no one heeded his warning.[2] Without constructive ways of channeling their political energies, naval offi-

1. Jean-Michel Renaitour, Interview, July 13, 1974.
2. James Brewer, "Politics in the French Army: The Aftermath of the Dreyfus

cers expressed their frustrations by turning to extremist movements like the Action Française.

As cabinet after cabinet failed to deter this activity, officers became more brazen in the way they conducted themselves, hardly fearing reprisals. Consequently, by the mid-1930s, right-wing political activities were in full view of the officials and the public; yet there were still no objections. Officers could defend themselves by claiming to be a chivalrous corps fighting at home to keep their government out of danger.

The evolution of the navy from its classical political role of "la muette" in 1918 to "engagé" under Darlan in 1940 came in three stages. The first began when officers realized in the early 1920s that the romantic and carefree life they recalled from before 1914 would not return after the armistice. The second phase followed in the 1930s when private grumblings about poor standards of living turned into a serious and growing support for the Action Française in the officer corps. Although the ministers of marine knew of the antirepublican tone in the wardrooms, neither conservatives nor progressives did anything to ease tensions. Finally, the Popular Front victory in 1936 followed soon after by the Spanish Civil War pushed the navy into a clear position of opposition to the government.

Civilian control over naval matters rarely extended below the level of grand strategy and public relations. Only one minister of marine, François Piétri, expressed concern about officers engaging in partisan politics. But even his words of caution had no lasting effect. To find a minister before Alphonse Gasnier-Duparc who tried to keep the officer corps in harmony with republican values, we have to look back to the end of the nineteenth century. At that time, the Radical party used a heavy-handed approach to apply the social and secular legislation to the navy. These efforts failed because of miscalculations and mismanagement. The political awakening of the officer corps took many years to reach the point of no return in civil-naval relations. The separation between the navy and the nation grew as public attitudes diverged slowly from the

Case, 1899–1905" (Ph.D. dissertation, George Washington University, 1967), 112; Edouard Lockroy, *Le Programme naval* (Paris, 1906), 166.

Cartesian and antirepublican beliefs that survived as a way of life in the fleet. Although the naval officer corps caused its own demise, some part of the blame clearly rests with the political leadership, specifically with the sixteen men who served as ministers of marine between the world wars. They did very little to attempt a reconciliation between the navy and the state while it was still possible to do so. Recalling that public faith in government had reached a new low point by the 1930s, it is probably unrealistic to think any one man could have repaired the damage just within the navy.

It was Léon Blum's minister of marine, Gasnier-Duparc, who took the first steps to reconcile the naval officers with the cabinet and the political process in general. His seminars tried to show the officers why they had no reason to fear the policies of a cabinet that was providing the navy with twice the budget of prior administrations. The next minister of marine, César Campinchi, took the first steps to alleviate the officers' personal economic problems with a proposal for higher wages. Unfortunately, neither measure had any appreciable effect on the officers' distrust of the regime. When war came in 1939, it took some attention away from the immediate ideological and economic difficulties, but these remained just beneath the surface in the wardrooms. We can only guess how different the future of the navy and the country might have been if Maurice Gamelin's army had held along the Meuse or, failing there, if Darlan had sailed to North Africa in June, 1940.

Political leaders in France, as in other European countries, failed to understand the danger or magnitude of the radical Right between the world wars. Government after government in Paris treated royalist activities as a harmless form of "platonic monarchism," which many thought would fade in time.[3] Meanwhile, naval officers sought ideological relief in several causes, from traditionalist solutions—spiritual heirs perhaps of Marshal MacMahon—to more radical ones modeled after fellow Latins like Franco and Mussolini. In the *petits corps*, a new technocratic mentality was blossoming, forerunner of what eventually flourished in the 1960s. Meanwhile, the *grand corps* remained inseparably linked to the status quo and

3. Jacques Godechot, Interview, June 25, 1975.

to memories of things past as a solution to France's political dilemmas. In the navy, at least, it was this attitude which prevailed.

The traditionalist officers supported the Action Française, but they largely avoided the more violent Camelots du roi and the Cagoule even though their goals were the same. While Admiral Schwerer spoke of a Bourbon restoration, men like Deloncle and Decoux sought more tangible solutions through vigorous political action.[4]

Although the frustrations of the naval officers after 1918 are understandable, their failure to cope with them is not. Neither the political authorities nor the military leaders seriously addressed this gap in the civil-naval fabric until the late 1930s when it was almost too late to apply any corrective measures. The case of these Frenchmen is living proof of what happens when a professional officer corps manages to isolate itself from its social and political foundations. Scholars have argued this point for several decades but in using American institutions to prove the point, the dangers of military elitism in democratic societies have not been clearly shown. If anything, the French navy from 1918 to 1945 is a classic example of an armed force turning on its parent society after its officers have built a wall between themselves and the institutions they are sworn to protect.[5]

The absence of responsible reaction to naval seizure of power in France was not looked into in 1940 or 1945, when a government commission might have examined the issue in its broadest context. Only in 1962 when the public was forced to view a military coup as a distinct possibility did the politicians and intellectuals start asking why things had gone so far. Even the Gaullist naval officers supported the colonial empire when forced to choose be-

4. Robert J. Soucy, "The Nature of Fascism in France," in Walter Laqueur and George L. Mosse (eds.), *International Fascism, 1920–1945* (New York, 1966), 35–36; Wolfgang Sauer, "Fascism as the Revolt of 'the Losers,'" in Gilbert Allardyce (ed.), *The Place of Fascism in European History* (Englewood Cliffs, N.J., 1971), 172–73.

5. See Morris Janowitz, *The Professional Soldier: A Social and Political Portrait* (New York, 1960), who argues against an isolated military, and Samuel P. Huntington, *The Soldier and the State: The Theory and Politics of Civil-Military Relations* (New York, 1957), who argues that military competence even in democratic societies is best served by a detached, isolated military establishment.

tween it and a European-oriented France. The scene in the film *Battle of Algiers* showing the fictitious Colonel Mathieu denying his "fascist" methods before the French press could have depicted any number of real naval officers.[6]

These men dreamed about the "bon vieux temps" between the world wars. They spent their years romanticizing about the past which no longer existed but which they could read about in the novels of Marcel Proust and other authors of the period. Abroad, they identified with other elite groups facing the same dilemma of preserving the past in the face of social change. *Gone with the Wind* was one of their favorite stories. The only way they could achieve this kind of life was by imposing it from the top through authoritarian leadership.[7] Edward Tannenbaum explained why this sort of Frenchman had difficulties adjusting to rapidly changing situations. "A person may have been hindered in some way from working out his own problems, hence prevented from developing a feeling of confidence in his ability to adjust to new problems and situations. He is afraid of himself, his impulses, his responsibilities and his ability to act freely. Though he does not like to be alone, he fears society and the world, for they require adjustments and sacrifices that he is not prepared to make."[8] Perhaps this is why so many felt the need to stick together in the summer of 1940 and why two years later they scuttled their fleet rather than escape with it while they had a chance. Their dream world was already shattered, and they dared not go back on their oath of "independence" taken at the time of the 1940 armistice. Realization that the naval problems were social and psychological as well as technological finally dawned on the political leaders in the mid-1960s when genuine peace for the first time in twenty-five years permitted some introspection.

Why was the navy so different from other French institutions? Both friends and foes agree on this point, that the naval officer corps was a unique group of Frenchmen. Supporters of this separate

6. Gillo Pontecorvo (dir.), *The Battle of Algiers*, 1973, Scene 112, p. 125.

7. Admiral Louis de La Monneraye, Interview, July 23, 1975; Commander Loïc Abrial, Interview, July 28, 1975; Bernard Paquet, Interview, June 30, 1975.

8. Edward R. Tannenbaum, *The Action Française: Die-Hard Reactionaries in Twentieth Century France* (New York, 1960), 268.

naval identity firmly believed that the officer corps needed to preserve its social and professional isolation to protect the interests of the navy, which no one else really cared about. They believed that the navy could not function without a homogeneous group dominating the officers and the enlisted men, both groups recruited from traditional homes and trained in special schools. Many of the qualities peculiar to the Breton and Provençal ways of life found their way into the fleet. The emphasis on piety, superstition, independence, and strong nationalist values were cherished in the navy as they were in Breton society. Officers tried to preserve as much of these habits as possible because they complemented what one skeptic called "that infernal spirit of the Navy."[9] Two French naval officers-cum-novelists, Pierre Loti and Victor Ségalen, lived and described the uniqueness of Breton maritime life as only true believers could.

Suitable manpower for the navy was always at a premium. The Naval General Staff stabilized its requirements for trained personnel by avoiding mass conscription through the use of trained sailors from the fishing and merchant fleets. Home life and family stability, which were so important elsewhere in French society, were subordinated in the navy to a tradition requiring men to spend much of their time at sea or stationed overseas. In the place of a stable domestic environment, naval officers substituted adventure, travel, and the ego-satisfying jobs of administering vast overseas possessions and laying claim to command of the seas. The list of French naval tragedies from 1715 to 1918 made these officers all the more obsessed with the need to maintain a good fleet and expand the navy's influence at home.

From the Midi came the officers' outspoken preference for other Latin peoples, the belief that the Mediterranean was at the heart of French strategic interests and, perhaps, their reputation for volatile political behavior. This mixture of widely differing habits from two distinct regions, Brittany and Provence, had no counterpart in any other part of the French bureaucracy or society as a whole. The combination was originally established by Colbert, who organized the navy in the mid-seventeenth century around officers and seamen

9. Charles Braibant, *Un bourgeois sous trois républiques* (Paris, 1961), 340.

recruited from these two areas. Although not bad in themselves, these traditions became a hindrance when they blinded officers to the realities of the twentieth century.[10]

An old retired naval officer who always dined alone at the Paris Officers' Mess explained how he and many of his friends devoted their lives to the navy. The gentleman always wore a dark suit with a fedora, grey chamois gloves, and a shirt with a detachable collar, and he carried a brass-tipped cane. He would sit facing a window that looked out on the place Saint Augustin. There, next to a statue of Joan of Arc, many Action Française supporters gathered at the start of their political rallies in the 1930s. In the basement of the mess he and others still spent their afternoons in fencing matches, playing according to Louis XIII's dueling rules posted on the door. The old gentleman did not use his age as an excuse to forget his polished manners or his instinctive belief in what was right and wrong. He explained how his father had been a Bonapartist. This did not deter the son from becoming a royalist, devoting his life to the navy and to the cause of the Action Française as well. With a sigh of resignation one evening, while looking out the window at the tarnished statue of Saint Joan, the old man said, "but now, I suppose we are all, by default, republicans." Perhaps he and others like him are better for having gone through their unique ordeal.

10. *Ibid.*, 325–37; Theodore Zeldin, *Intellect, Taste, and Anxiety* (Oxford, 1977), 43–47, 54–56, Vol. II of *France, 1848–1945*, 2 vols.

Appendix

Composition of the French Naval Officer Corps in 1936

Corps	Schools Leading to a Commission	Number on Active Duty
Officiers de marine (grand corps)	École navale École polytechnique (5–10 vacancies a year) École des élèves-officiers (1–10 vacancies a year)	2,340
Ingénieurs méchaniciens (shipboard engineers)	1/2 from École des arts et métiers followed by École des élèves-méchaniciens 1/2 from other engineering schools followed by École des élèves-mechaniciens	516
Génie maritime (naval architects and shipbuilders)	École polytechnique	225
Santé (doctors and pharmacists)	École de santé de la marine	464

Commissariat (administrative, supply, and legal officers)	1/2 from École des arts et métiers 1/2 from École centrale	231
Génie de l'artillerie navale (ordnance engineers)	2/3 from École polytechnique 1/6 transferring from the *grand corps* 1/6 from other engineering schools	155
Génie hydrographique (geographers and chart makers)	École des arts et métiers	31
Musique et train (music and supply)	École polytechnique Competitive exam offered to enlisted men and civilians	392

Bibliographical Essay

I never thought much about how I uncovered my material until a French officer asked me. Until then, I followed each lead to the point where it ran dry or produced information about the social history of the French navy. Normally, I worked on several leads at the same time, which meant that I was researching several parts of my story simultaneously. Interviews generated further leads on numerous topics during a single taped session. At the end of my second research trip to France, I found that my material fell into three major categories, which became the three subdivisions of the book. Acquisition of this material was far easier than its synthesis, and it took me several years to digest it all properly. Finding a place for everything in this story and making sense out of it all was like putting a large puzzle together without knowing what the finished product would look like.

Basic ideas on how to approach my subject came from Theodore Zeldin's two-volume history, *France, 1848–1945* (Oxford, 1973, 1977). His emphasis on behavioral problems, from bourgeois pretensions to attitudes about marriage were most useful in helping me explain the life-styles of the naval families. Zeldin led me to examine the French naval officers from the perspectives of their social structure, group psychology, and political behavior. I was also inspired by several biographies of French military leaders who served under the Third Republic. Philip Bankwitz' study of Maxime Weygand (*Maxime Weygand and Civil-Military Relations in Modern France* [Cambridge, Mass., 1967]) proved indispensable to my study of the navy. The author shed crucial light on the delicacy of the civil-military balance between the world wars, and he explained better than anyone else I know of why relations between these two groups of Frenchmen continually degenerated after 1918. Robert Paxton was quite helpful in exposing the unique role of the French naval leaders after the armistice of 1940 in his *Parades and Politics at Vichy: The French Officer Corps Under Marshal Pétain* (Princeton, 1966). Of all the authors I have read, he has the best explanation of why the naval elite played such a disproportionately large role at Vichy. Among French authors, the journalist Paul-Marie de La Gorce (*La République et son armée* [Paris, 1963]) provided the best analysis of how the military caste in his country turned to right-wing politics during the 1930s. He understood the way isolation from the rest of society molded the attitudes of a professional officer corps that claimed to be politically neutral throughout these years of crisis. De La Gorce believed that this isolation, combined with the financial impoverishment of the officer corps, created an atmosphere ripe for fascist ideology.

Other helpful books on the French military include the biography of General Maurice Sarrail by Jan Tannenbaum (*General Maurice Sarrail, 1856–1929: The French Army and Left-Wing Politics* [Chapel Hill, 1974]) and the political study of the French army after 1945 by John Ambler (*The French Army in Politics, 1945–1962* [Columbus, Ohio, 1966]). Sarrail's personal difficulties with political leaders helped explain why naval officers with Freemason or left-wing ties had difficulty in pursuing their own careers. Ambler demonstrated the remarkable durability of the traditional habits of the French military leaders, surviving both World War II and the purge of the Vichy collaborators in the trials following the liberation. From the field of behavioral science, Morris Janowitz developed the method I used to analyze the social dynamics of the French naval officer corps. His thesis in *The Professional Soldier: A Social and Political Portrait* (New York, 1960) is that the career military services are natural adversaries of the democratic societies that spawn them. This theory fits the French experience better than the American one which Janowitz used to test his hypothesis. The widespread rejection of the French republic by an aristocratic officer corps had no real counterpart in the United States.

Historical monographs on the modern French navy are few and

have been written largely by partisan authors. Retired officers have produced many of these in the past few decades, setting this field of study apart from the mainstream of French history. The problems of the interwar years and of the Vichy era stimulated a large number of publications by naval officers who served during those difficult years. Admiral Darlan's son Alain, for a while a naval officer himself, put together a collection of the admiral's papers in diary form (*L'Amiral Darlan parle* [Paris, 1953]). This and a similar work by Admiral Jules Docteur (*Darlan, amiral de la flotte* [Paris, 1949]) are the closest things we have to a memoir by François Darlan. The information about Darlan's career that these two sympathetic writers reveal is generally confirmed by the official records of the Ministry of Marine. Darlan's overwhelming importance in the reshaping of French naval policy during the middle and late 1930s and his close association with Georges Leygues are evident in both private and official records. Unfortunately, we still do not know enough about the relationship between Darlan and Leygues and we remain generally ignorant of the admiral's private life. His secret dealings with the French government and with Marshal Pétain on the eve of the armistice of 1940 are just now coming to light.

Admiral Paul Auphan is probably the most prolific contemporary writer on the French navy. His *Mensonges et vérité: essai sur la France* (Paris, 1949) is a statement of the author's bitter feelings after his compulsory retirement in 1945 and several years in seclusion. Auphan's numerous books and articles explain the sense of personal isolation and anger that many of the conservative Catholic naval officers felt in the mid–twentieth century. In the last years before his death, he became quite philosophical about his experiences and granted me two very interesting and enjoyable interviews, which were very important to me in my search for an understanding of the French naval officer's mind. Although many disapprove of his actions and disagree with his thinking, Auphan provides the best inside explanation of conservative naval opinion. Admiral Jean Decoux expressed his resentment toward the Third Republic in his autobiography, which appeared in two volumes— *Adieu marine* (Paris, 1957), covering the period up to 1940, and *A la barre de l'Indochine* (Paris, 1949), which covers his war years in the Pacific. He and his mentor, Admiral Schwerer, represent the stereotype of the naval officer raised in a traditional family who had difficulty accepting a secular and republican form of government. The biography of a more typical naval officer and his wife by their daughter Hélène de David-Beauregard (*Souvenirs de famille* [Toulon, 1970]) provides rare insight into the personal hardships faced by many of these families in trying to live on very meager incomes. The conflict between the Catholic values of the de David-Beauregard family and the burden that the navy imposed on them all offer a perspective on daily life in the *grand corps*, warts and all, that few others have articulated so clearly. Stanislas de David-Beauregard devoted his life to the French navy, often at the expense of his family's welfare. He eventually turned to the Action Française to vent his personal frustration with a life-style and political system he could neither manage nor comprehend.

In the past few years, some of the younger officers of the 1920s and 1930s are coming forward in print to explain what it was like to undergo the indoctrination at the École navale and to work for men like Schwerer, Decoux, and Darlan. Georges Débat (*Marine oblige* [Paris, 1974]) and Roger Barberot (*A bras le coeur* [Paris, 1972]) are two of these former officers, who came from atypical homes but enjoyed successful careers in the navy. Each tried to explain in his autobiography how all midshipmen were forced to conform outwardly and intellectually to the traditional image of the *grand corps*. Both Débat and Barberot revealed their independence of character when they broke ranks with the majority of their comrades in order to continue the war effort in 1940.

The best surveys of French naval history are the short work by René Jouan; (*Histoire de la marine française* [Paris, 1950]), the three-volume history edited by André Reussner (*La Puissance navale dans l'histoire* [Paris, 1964–71]), and the excellent historical study of naval policy under the Third Republic by Admiral Henri Salaün (*La Marine française* [Paris, 1934]). *La Puissance navale dans l'histoire* is the only work I have found that places French naval history in the broader context of competing European and American interests worldwide. In effect, it is a multivolume survey of western civilization from the French maritime point of view. The authors try to show how the Ministry of Marine struggled to maintain a fleet and an empire while having to compete with rival domestic as well as foreign interests. René Jouan, a reserve naval officer and faculty member at the École de guerre navale, relied on student research papers in his book, which reveals the depth of anglophobic sentiments in the French navy of the 1950s. These strong feelings stemmed from a professional inferiority complex toward Britain after centuries of rivalry in which the French navy often came out second best. This was also a major theme in the courses on maritime strategy and history taught at the École navale and the École de guerre navale between the world wars.

On the other hand, Admiral Salaün's work is a thorough and well-balanced study of decision making within the Ministry of Marine from 1870 to 1935. This book is a must for a good understanding of the problems the Naval General Staff and the ministers of marine faced in trying to modernize the fleet without serious parliamentary interest or enough money to make significant progress. Although he participated in many of the top-level decisions of the interwar years, Salaün remained as objective in discussing his years as naval chief of staff as he was in talking about the years before his naval career began. Several of the ministers of marine whom he wrote about also published memoirs of their years at rue Royale. Edouard Lockroy (*Le Programme navale* [Paris, 1906]) and Jean Marie de Lanessan (*La Lutte pour l'existence et l'évolution des sociétés* [Paris, 1903]) were two of those appointed by Radical governments at the turn of the century, when the secular state first clashed with the very Catholic naval officer corps. Both, as ministers of marine, sided with the republic in favoring social reform and technological modernization within the navy.

Four other authors have written excellent works in English on the French navy and colonial empire in earlier periods, explaining how these two institutions were so closely tied for centuries. Paul Bamford's *Fighting Ships and Prisons: The Mediterranean Galleys of France in the Age of Louis XIV* (Minneapolis, 1973) describes Colbert's system of recruiting officers for the two separate French navies of that era. Colbert preferred Bretons to men from the Midi because of their traditional reliability under stress. When he could not find enough of them, he turned to the Knights of Malta for officers to man his more prestigious but less seaworthy galley fleet in the Mediterranean. Geoffrey Symcox wrote an excellent companion work entitled, *The Crisis of French Sea Power, 1688–1697: From the 'Guerre d'Escadre' to the 'Guerre de Course'* (The Hague, 1974). He analyzes the transition from a strategy of competing for control of the seas to one of commerce raiding and limited fleet engagements against larger British squadrons. The attitudes that Symcox examined in the French navy of the seventeenth century changed very little over the following three centuries. Two other works on French colonial policy—Henri Brunschwig's *French Colonialism, 1871–1914: Myths and Realities*, trans. William Glanville Brown (London, 1964), and Raymond Betts's *Assimilation and Association in French Colonial Theory, 1890–1914* (New York, 1961)—show how much of the empire fell under naval supervision and how much the colonial residents depended on the fleet for survival. These two authors also show the continuity of attitudes and bureaucratic relationships from earlier periods when the Ministry of Marine oversaw both the fleet and the colonial territories.

Unlike their counterparts in other navies, the French officers had very sound academic foundations in creative writing and in the humanities. Some have suggested that emphasis on the liberal arts was one reason for their technological backwardness. The humanities formed the core of their curriculum at the École navale and at the schools officers of the *petits corps* attended, and mechanical training tended to be deficient. The strong Catholic influence on young men aspiring to naval careers meant that these boys read many seventeenth-century classics and nineteenth-century romances but neglected eighteenth-century free-thinkers and twentieth-century existentialists. Officers I spoke with relished every volume of Marcel Proust's *A la recherche du temps perdu*, seeing in it the story of their own families. Proust explained the distance that the naval elite of this era set between themselves and all of French society except for a few old aristocratic families in Paris who were spiritual if not blood kin. This tradition of social isolation remained very strong well into the 1960s when the Fifth

Republic by decree forced assimilation of the navy's *grand corps*. The conservative Catholic novelist Michel de Saint-Pierre explained more recently how naval officers tried to preserve their old ways after 1945 in three of his novels: *La Mer à boire* (Paris, 1951), *Les Nouveaux Aristocrates* (Paris, 1960), and *Les Aristocrates* (Paris, 1954). These books were also the favorites of many officers whom I spoke to. On numerous occasions, officers explained points of naval behavior and tradition by using analogies from works by Racine, Molière, La Rochefoucauld, or Proust, to name only a few.

Although only a small number of naval officers wrote full-length books, many frequently contributed to general literary magazines and to specialized naval journals as well. They wrote most often for *La Revue des deux mondes, Écrits de Paris, Revue de France, Revue politique et parlementaire, Revue politique et littéraire*, and a few others that appealed to conservative tastes. In these periodicals, naval writers explained their desire to preserve the status quo to a sympathetic audience. They also voiced some of their more specialized opinions in the *Revue nautique*, journal of the French yachting crowd, and in the official *Revue maritime* where personal opinion remained somewhat muted. In this last publication, the editors from the Naval General Staff provided monthly commentary on maritime affairs in France and abroad. These were often unclassified versions of reports prepared by the Deuxième bureau (intelligence), giving readers a glimpse of top-level concerns of the day from the Parliament to the Spanish Civil War. René La Bruyère's quarterly articles in the *Revue politique et parlementaire* dealt with similar issues while focusing on the disarmament talks and naval budget legislation. La Bruyère had more latitude to interpret events as he saw them than did the officers writing for the *Revue maritime*. His annual evaluations of the naval budget debates are excellent introductions, which a novice in this area can read without any difficulty. These should be attempted before the actual debates in the *Journal officiel*. La Bruyère also wrote for the extreme right-wing weekly *Gringoire*.

During the two decades preceding World War I, the *Revue politique et littéraire* provided one of the clearest pictures of naval opinion on the emotional political and social matters that divided naval and civilian opinion. This journal became a popular forum for naval officers to express their dismay and outrage over the separation of church and state in 1905. Elsewhere in the political press, naval officers turned to the *Action française* after retiring or resigning from the service. The satirical column by John Frog (pseudonym for Jean Gautreau) in this newspaper expressed the raw emotions of the naval officer corps on a wide range of political issues extending well beyond purely maritime affairs. Admiral Antoine Schwerer's contributions to the *Action française* expressed many of the same views but with less coherence and without a trace of humor. In all this commentary on politics and society, I have never found an officer corps in any other country matching these Frenchmen for their breadth of interest and talent for creative writing.

Eugen Weber provided a great deal of detail on the close family ties between the navy and the royalist cause in his exhaustive work on twentieth-century royalism in France, *Action Française: Royalism and Reaction in Twentieth Century France* (Stanford, 1962). Edward R. Tannenbaum's book on the same subject, *The Action Française: Die-hard Reactionaries in Twentieth Century France* (New York, 1960), offers a better explanation of why French authoritarians became so psychologically dependent on Charles Maurras' movement. Of all the anthologies on the subject of right-wing extremism, I found Gilbert Allardyce's *The Place of Fascism in European History* (Englewood Cliffs, N.J., 1971) to be the most helpful. He has chosen material showing how people from all social classes turned to these extremist movements when they were unable to reconcile their political frustrations.

As for libraries, good naval collections in France exist in the port headquarters from Toulon to Brest. Most valuable, however, is the central Bibliothèque de la marine in Paris. The navy's holdings in the capital city are actually under three roofs, with the most important collection now located at the Chateau de Vincennes. The Bibliothèque nationale also has some interesting periodical literature and a few monographs by naval officers that I found nowhere else. In the provinces, the holdings in the port cities are quite extensive and are as old as the central collection in Paris. The French navy's chief librarian, J. P. Busson, has direct control over the Vincennes holdings and supervisory authority over the outlying ones. Recently, he revised the cataloguing system at Vincennes, filing all holdings by subject, title, and author. One of his most interesting classifications, called simply "Esprit de Marine," covers a diverse collection of articles and books by officers who shed light on customs, traditions, and behavior unique to the French navy. Busson is also keeper of the Ministry of Marine's collection of manuscripts, which now takes up more of his time than all seven libraries do. The discovery and acquisition of personal papers from French naval families are difficult but rewarding tasks for Busson, who has only just received official support for this important effort. His assistant in Brest is Admiral J. J. Nielly. Not only does Nielly know the local collection thoroughly, he is one of the best informed sources on French naval biography and genealogy. His knowledge of naval society both past and present needs to be transcribed by some historian or anthropologist, for I am sure much of what he knows is nowhere written down. His knowledge and insights come from the seven generations of his ancestors who were career officers in the French navy. Within his family, the traditions of the *grand corps* live on.

Scholars have not, by and large, devoted much attention to primary source research on the modern French navy. Some feel that the years between the world wars are too recent for serious analysis. In addition, many important official documents pertaining to the 1940s are still protected by the French secrecy laws. Recently, these laws have been liberalized, permitting fairly unrestricted access to material prior to June, 1940, although personnel dossiers remain sealed for 120 years after the birth of an individual. The question of nationality arose when one French officer told me that only a foreigner could do contemporary research on his navy. Even in the late 1970s, he believed any Frenchman would be denied access to private source material because of a "Gaullist" or a "Vichyite" label he would wear, if only through family association.

Even the relatively new colonial and air ministries attract more interest than does the Ministry of Marine. This means that in studies of the French military, the navy's role is not well known. One of the most difficult things to explain is the breadth of power and influence that the minister of marine exercised up to 1940. Except for embassies, the navy oversaw virtually all French government activities abroad, including consulates, until the end of the nineteenth century. Even though some of these varied responsibilities gradually fell into the hands of other government agencies, the navy's power remained far more extensive overseas than was the army's authority in the *métropole*. The best way to grasp the difference is to read the naval archives to see what the ministers of marine had to supervise on a daily basis.

In the field of published material, the diplomatic papers of France, Britain, Germany, and the United States were helpful in my work but only as supporting evidence. For anyone interested in French naval history, these diplomatic documents are useful on topics such as disarmament between the world wars and the formulation of allied maritime strategy during these great conflicts. The unpublished dossiers at the quai d'Orsay were somewhat more helpful than the published *Documents diplomatiques français* in showing the navy's special interest in foreign policy. By comparison, the French parliamentary debates give a much clearer view of the evolution of naval policy from 1919 to 1940. Both houses of Parliament continually demonstrated how much better the vast majority of legislators supported the navy than either the army or the air force. The full house debates expose more of this interest than do the recently declassified naval committee papers from both houses, just the reverse of what one finds in the American Congress. In naval matters, as in most other areas of politics, Frenchmen preferred to work out details of their future in public debate, relegating the parliamentary committee to a lesser administrative status than in either Britain or the United States. Moreover, the French debates were published in unaltered form with the names and votes of each legislator recorded for each roll call vote. This facilitated the quantitative analysis in Part III of this book, where I used the techniques in Charles Dollar and Richard Jensen's *Historian's Guide to Statistics: Quantitative Analysis and Historical Research* (New York, 1971). I used their roll call and clustering techniques for measuring parliamentary agreement, likeness, cohesion, and success on naval legislation. These methods and formulas are the basis for the Guttman scaling technique frequently employed in larger roll call analyses. I determined from the start that the quantification would be used to support my central thesis rather than the other way around because so much of what I looked at did not lend itself to this very valuable but specialized methodology. Dollar and Jensen helped very much in this regard as well.

My heavy reliance on published debates should not be considered a disparagement of the naval committee papers from the Senate and the Chamber of Deputies. These bodies met rather informally, and in the minutes of their sessions it is possible to see how the executive and legislative branches of French government could work together in harmony to produce a coherent naval policy. In a few instances, the ministers of marine used these hearings to test new ideas before presenting them on the floor of either house. My work on these committee documents at the Palais Bourbon and the Palais de Luxembourg permitted me to meet four important staff members who were of great help in guiding me through the maze of legislative paper. The archivist of the Chamber of Deputies, Maurice Daroussin, added those extra touches of reality to the debates by telling countless stories from the *petite histoire* of naval politics in the lower house. In the afternoons there, Madame Michel-Danzac provided a running commentary to the ongoing debates, broadcast live throughout the Palais Bourbon, while she edited the final volumes of the *Dictionnaire des parlementaires français*. In the Senate across town, I received equally fine treatment from the assistant archivist, Georges Bourgeois, who liked to discuss Molière with me in the surroundings of his magnificent baroque office. His superior, Jean Bécarud, met with me often to discuss his country's navy and the merits of Theodore Zeldin's new interpretation of France.

From American sources, the U.S. naval attaché papers (National Archives) were excellent primary source material on the French navy from the 1890s until World War II. These documents provide the only survey of French naval opinion on domestic politics during the 1930s when the American attachés worried about the lack of military support for the Popular Front. The American officers who wrote these reports were well informed and wrote very competently on a wide range of political and social matters as they pertained to the navy. Unfortunately, the converted gun factory in the

Washington Navy Yard housing these papers was no match for the rehabilitated palace at Vincennes where the Ministry of Marine archives are now stored. Ironically, the building housing them and a twin pavilion across the courtyard, housing the army's archives, served as General Gamelin's headquarters during the "phony war" of 1939–1940.

Like the naval libraries scattered across France, the naval archives there are divided among the four naval prefectures and the central collection at Vincennes. Documents in the Toulon collection date from the Crusades, when a fleet was organized to transport soldiers to the Middle East. The main collection in Paris was partly destroyed on the eve of the German occupation. The holdings for the interwar period, therefore, are incomplete, and even today the archivists are struggling to reconstruct the full inventory of what was burned in 1940. Fortunately, copies of some destroyed papers have been uncovered in both the army and the navy archives when representatives of both services attended joint meetings. All naval documents predating the Third Republic are in the Archives Nationales at the Hôtel de Soubise where an excellent French naval historian, Étienne Taillemite, works as a senior archivist.

For the 1920s and 1930s, the bulk of top-level naval papers have found their way into two series of documents amounting to eighty-seven cartons at Vincennes. The first fifty-three boxes contain papers of the Naval General Staff and of the ministers of marine from 1919 to 1930 under the title of "Ca," or "Cabinet du Ministre." These cartons include the working papers from the Washington Naval Conference, the internal staff disputes over modernization and special studies by officers on how to rebuild the fleet and retain skilled manpower after World War I. This series ends in 1932 and is succeeded by another entitled "FMF-SE" or "Forces Maritimes Françaises—Section d'Études" of thirty-four cartons. This one is even more lively. These boxes contain the papers of the "think tank" put together by Admiral Durand-Viel and later expanded by Darlan. This office, the so-called Section d'études, became the political studies group which Darlan took with him to Vichy. These papers show how he evolved from the ranks of the unknown to become a leading political voice in France by the end of 1939. Two lesser series of documents deal with the naval schools and personnel, and I used them in my social profile of the *grand corps* in Part I. The social registers of the French bourgeoisie and aristocracy, notably the *Bottin mondain* (Paris, 1919–39) and *Tout-Paris: annuaire de la société parisienne* (Paris, 1919–39), proved invaluable in making a statistical profile of the naval officer corps. The late Reverend John Bush, S.J., shared my interest in the links between the Jesuit schools and the French elite and guided me in this part of my work. He also served as the advisor to John Langdon whose "Social Implications of Jesuit Education in France: The Schools of Vaugirard and Sainte Geneviève" is work still in progress.

I found all eleven transcripts of those French naval officers placed on trial after 1944 for alleged collaboration with the enemy. Though all were extremely interesting, I was always skeptical of the contents, particularly when I could not confirm evidence in the testimony by outside sources. As I read them, I wondered what information might have been suppressed by either the prosecution or the defense for the sake of making a stronger case before the judges. Fortunately, very little of the evidence of these transcripts dealt with prewar affairs. The material used by both sides in preparing their cases would have been far more interesting than the transcripts, but unfortunately, these remain under lock and key at the Archives Nationales for an indefinite period. The trial records served me best in preparation for interviews with retired naval officers and politicians, especially when questions about individual motives came up.

The thirty interviews that I conducted with many of the chief subjects of this book cannot stand on their own as *prima facie* evidence. Nevertheless, the hours which I spent with these men and women provided me with my best insights into the behavior of the French naval officer corps of some fifty years ago. Time has dulled some of the pain that many of these families still feel about that period of their history. Success or failure in these interviews depended heavily on my research in advance and on the first impressions that my wife and I made during our initial encounter with these very proud people. The way we dressed and our desire to mix business with social talk made a great deal of difference in the way these sessions evolved. In many cases, exploratory discussions opened up in-depth interviews later on, which frequently led to access to personal papers. The search for these retired officers and their relatives took us everywhere in France except to the Alps. Even for the navy, the administrative center remained Paris, to which many of the officers flocked in retirement. Others congregated in their hometowns on the Breton coast and along the Midi with a scattering of others from Toulouse to Dunkerque. We even had occasion to deal with two rival clans from Corsica—one Bonapartist, the other conservative republican. Between comments about the navy, they spoke of life back home as though Prosper Mérimée's Colomba were alive and well. What I expected to be only a regional search for material turned into a nationwide dragnet for missing papers, people, and clues, all made possible by the Eurail Pass and the bicycle.

Two of the most helpful institutions for tracking down these families were the Association amicale des anciens élèves de l'École navale, the alumni society of that school, and the central officers' mess in Paris known simply as the Cercle Militaire. The latter was a gold mine for personal contacts. When in Paris, I made sure to eat there as frequently as possible and this habit led to an introduction to several officers and their families and to those who lived through the events reconstructed in the film *La Bataille d'Alger*. Discussions at the dinner table there turned often to the ongoing "Affaire de Watergate" which made me appreciate the extensive coverage of this story in the *International Herald-Tribune*. Somehow, stories about Dreyfus and Vichy mixed well with those about Deep Throat and Watergate and my willingness to speculate on the outcome of this American *affaire* stimulated interest in my research by Frenchmen whom I met. Though I made an incorrect prediction about Nixon's fate in 1974, my reputation survived untarnished enough for me to continue my research the following summer without loss of face.

I found out early in my research that the Association amicale des anciens élèves de l'École navale had its headquarters only one block from the Cercle Militaire. There in the attic of a Second Empire town house, I discovered the untouched archives of the association, which dated from 1920. These papers are the kind of gold mine that historians dream of but rarely find. The president of the association, Admiral Raymond Frémy, gave me free run of the collection on condition that I brief him on what I uncovered at the end of my research. I had the pleasure of several conversations with him while he assisted me in mentally sorting the mass of information in his files. Along with Admiral Nielly, he is one of the best informed on the social history of the French navy. Unfortunately, many of the documents I found there were disintegrating; I hope the admiral and his staff have sought a way to preserve this valuable material before it is too late.

I discovered firsthand what other French scholars have complained about for decades: the problem of getting at private papers. This is even a dilemma for the Bibliothèque de la Marine, which is now trying to obtain collections from many families before the papers are lost or destroyed. In my particular case, the normal proclivity of Frenchmen to guard their private correspondence was aggravated by the involvement of the French naval leaders in the Second World War, which many would like to forget. Some families denied me access; others put restrictions on the use of material which I could not accept. Still more had already destroyed family papers and some I couldn't locate at all. The finest collections I found were the Abrial and Violette papers. These admirals had overlapping correspondence. The naval officer corps was a small tightly woven community and they stood very much together, in spite of ideological differences such as those dividing these two men. In both cases, we have excellent commentaries on the times by two well-read officers, a running commentary on the French navy that I found invaluable and general confirmation of positions and opinions expressed in the official Ministry of Marine papers. Abrial's papers cover his entire career, while Violette's date from the post-1918 era only. Earlier letters from his days on General André's staff would have been fascinating but, alas, they were blown up when a stray American projectile destroyed the Violette home during the wartime landings in southern France. Other lesser collections added bits of information which I could not have found elsewhere. Perhaps someday, other private papers will emerge to confirm the impressions gathered from these two fine collections.

Acknowledgments

The author gratefully acknowledges the assistance received from the following: Colonel Raymond Abrial and his brother Commander Loïc Abrial for permission to quote from the correspondence of their late father, Admiral Jean Abrial; the late Mr. Charles Audouy for permission to microfilm documents in the official naval collection at the Service historique de la Marine; Madame Ulane Bonnel for introducing me in French naval circles at the start of my research; Madame Claudine Bordas for permission to quote from the correspondence of the late Admiral François Darlan; les Musées Nationaux, Paris for permission to use the painting *Neptune offrant à Louis XIV l'empire de la mer* by Pierre Mignard; the United States Naval Institute for permission to use two photographs from their collection; Madame M. T. Varillon-Dupuy for permission to use photographs and to quote from the correspondence of her late father, Pierre Varillon; Colonel Jacques Vernet for access to the libraries of the École de guerre and the École de guerre navale; Madame Jean Violette for permission to use photographs and to quote from the correspondence of her late father-in-law, Admiral Hector Violette.

I wish to thank the many dozens of French politicians, naval officers and their families, other government officials, and scholars who gave me their time, their thoughts, and in many cases access to additional documentation, all of whom are cited in appropriate places throughout the text. Their assistance was indispensable.

Index

Abetz, Ambassador Otto: comments on Darlan, 182
Abrial, Admiral Jean: social origins, 53, 69; anglophobia, 97
Abrial, Commander Loïc, 69
Action Française: attraction to naval officers, 122–26, 148, 151–52; naval support of 191; mentioned 194
Action française, 90; placed on papal *Index*, 120; appeal to naval officers, 125; and Pierre Varillon, 148–49; successor newspapers, 187
Air Force: service rivalry with navy, 91–92; budget, 139–40
Algerian War, 185
Alienation: naval officers from society, 165
Alliance de l'Action Française, 152
Amis de Darlan [A.D.D.], 158
André, General Louis: *l'affaire des fiches*, 113
Anglophobia, 96–98, 170; expressed by Darlan, 156
Anglo-Saxon menace, 96–98. *See also* Anglophobia
Anticommunism: expressed by Decoux, 155–56
Anti-Semitism, 119; expressed by Decoux, 155–56
d'Argenlieu, Admiral Thierry, 179–80, 185
Aristocracy: naval ties with, 33–38
Armée Coloniale, 24, 177
Armée d'Afrique, 177
Armée Métropolitaine, 24, 177
Army: service rivalry with navy, 90–94; budget, 139–40
Association amicale des anciens élèves de l'Ecole navale [A.E.N.], 4; guardian of social traditions, 40–41; pre-

paring boys for Ecole navale, 45; role of secretary general, 73; annual ball, 88–89; mentioned 149
Aube, Admiral Théophile: on naval reforms, 108
Auboyneau, Admiral Philippe, 179–80, 185
Auphan, Admiral Paul: inspired by Pierre Varillon, 149
Auriol, Vincent, 135
Aviation, naval, 90–92

Bainville, Jacques, 148
Baker, Joséphine: at the A.E.N. ball, 88
Barberot, Ensign Roger: June, 1940, pp. 178–80
Barrès, Maurice: on uprooted Frenchmen, 108
Battle of Algiers: film by Gillo Pontecorvo, 192
Black Sea: French naval operations in, 105–106
de Blois, Countess, 90
Blum, Léon, on naval expenditures, 128; selects Darlan as chief of staff, 156; mentioned 190
"Bon vieux temps," 173, 192
Braibant, Charles: on royalist sentiments in French navy, 147
Briand, Aristide, 129
Brittany: recruiting ground for naval officers, 29–31, 193
de Broglie, Duchess, 90
Budget: naval funding between world wars, 128

Cagoule, 191
Camelots du roi, 191
Campinchi, César, Minister of Marine, 160, 190

217

Candide, 90
de Castelnau, General Noël: influence on sex education, 40
Castex, Admiral Raoul: on curriculum at Ecole de Guerre navale, 83; association with Admirals Salaün and Violette, 114; anti-Semitism, 119; anti-parliamentary views, 143; mentioned 174
Catholic Church: rituals practiced in French navy, 84–87
Chamber of Deputies, 130–42 *passim*
Chaplains, in French navy, 85
du Chesne, Captain Georges Mabille: on inseparability of church and state, 85
Le Cid, 73
Civil-naval relations: anti-parliamentary views of officers, 126, 142–47; popular image of, 140–41; absence of "man-on-horseback" tradition in navy, 140–41; naval isolation from society, 141, 191–92; civilian indifference to naval behavior, 147; collapse of, 189–90
Colbert, Jean-Baptiste, Minister of Marine: role model for naval officers, 8; plan for officer recruitment, 14, 46, 193–94; mentioned, 1, 99, 138, 177
Colonial Army. *See* Armée coloniale
Colonies: naval involvement in, 10
Combat readiness: comparison of army and navy, 171–72, 173
Combes, Premier Emile: naval policies, 12
Commissariat, corps de: aristocratic tradition in the navy, 38; social origins of officers, 49; royalist sympathies, 169
Commissions de marine [parliamentary naval committees], 131–33
Communist party, 135; influence on naval legislation, 136–37
Contrôleurs, corps des, 78
Cot, Pierre, Minister of Air, 90

Darlan, Admiral François Xavier: creates new rank for himself, 94; anglophobia, 97, 178; rise to power, 109; association with Admirals Salaün and Violette, 114; on naval readiness, 142; ties with center-left politicians, 156–57; centralizes power in navy, 157–60; officers loyalty to him, 160; anti-parliamentary sentiments, 160–61; on weakness of democracy, 171; defeatism, 171, 174; secret visit by Pétain to Hq., 175; crisis of June 16, 1940, pp. 176–78; brings officers to Vichy, 180–82; mentioned, 127, 189, 190
Daudet, Léon: on Washington Naval Conference, 121
Daughters of naval officers. *See* Dynasties, naval
David-Beauregard, Commander Stanislas: attracted to the Action Française, 123; naval career, 54–55
Débat, Commander Georges: on royalist sentiment in navy, 124, 149–50; on intellectual mold of officer corps, 146; on attraction to fascism, 162; collapse of, 179–80
Decoux, Admiral Jean: friendship with Bourbon pretender, 34; on Latin solidarity, 95; head of Section d'études, 153–56; pro-Italian policies, 154–55; mentioned, 116, 145, 185, 191
Degouy, Admiral Jean Degouy: anti-parliamentary sentiments, 144
Delcassé, Théophile: as minister of marine, 13
Deloncle, Eugène: as head of Cagoule, 153, 191
Docteur, Admiral Jules, 171
Doriot, Jacques: his Parti Populaire Français avoided by naval officers, 153
Dreyfus Affair: effect on civil-naval relations, 35–36, 144; mentioned, 101
Drug habits, 59–60
Duperré, Admiral Victor: and the Ralliement, 11
Durand-Viel, Admiral Georges: family ties with August Le Normand, 116; relations with Admiral Decoux, 153; pro-Italian policies, 154; mentioned, 119
Dynasties, naval:
—Daughters: traditional life-styles and careers, 63–64, 68
—Families: Foillard, 67; Saint-Raymond, 67; Lesqueru, 68; Nicolas, 68; Quesnel, 68; Requin, 68; Rouvier, 68; Saint-Cyr, 67–68; Savidan, 68; Truc, 69; O'Byrne, 72; Peltier, 74
—Homes, 70–71
—Marriage patterns, 41–42, 122
—Sons, 73
—Weddings, 64–66

—Wives: reluctance to travel abroad, 54–55; role in family, 60–62, 71; career aspirations, 62n; birth control, 62; guardians of family legacies, 70n; financial inexperience, 71–72; role in education of children, 75

Ecole de l'air, 186
Ecole des arts et métiers, 21
Ecole de guerre navale, 83–84, 187. *See also* Ecole supérieure de guerre navale
Ecole des élèves-officiers, 26
Ecole navale: academic preparation for, 41–46; status of graduates in navy, 77; curriculum, 79–81; mentioned, 21–30 *passim*, 185–86, 187
Ecole normale supérieure: curriculum, 80
Ecole polytechnique: multiple paths to naval commission, 66–67; and *corps de génie maritime*, 66; mentioned 21–28 *passim*
Ecole supérieure de guerre navale, 82. *See also* Ecole de guerre navale
Economy: post-1918 conditions in navy, 27–29, 106–107
Entertainment, official: importance in Paris, 88
Estéva, Admiral Jean-Pierre, 174
Ethics, 87
Ethiopian War, 155
Examinations: entrance hurdle for Ecole navale, 80–81

Factionalism: in naval officer corps, 108–18
Families, naval. *See* dynasties, naval
Family papers: how handled, 70–71
Fashoda crisis: naval officers' reactions to, 12
Fernet, Admiral Jean: friend of Pierre Varillon, 149; pro-Italian policies, 155; on Spanish Civil War, 161; political frustrations, 163–64
Ferry, Jules, 1
Fifty-year law: document declassification, 3
Le Figaro, 90
La Flèche, preparatory course for Ecole navale, 43
Force de frappe, 1
Force structure: reliance on volunteers and *inscription maritime*, 20–21
Franco, General Francisco, 190

Freemasonry, 116, 178
Frog, Captain John [pseud. for Jean Gautreau]: anglophobia, 97–98, 148
Funerals, naval, 70

Galley fleet, French navy, 33
Gamelin, General Maurice, 190
Gasnier-Duparc, Alphonse, Minister of Marine: relative of Admiral Darlan, 157, 189–90
de Gaulle, General Charles: dealings with navy, 183–84
General Staff, naval, 22 ,25, 108, 121, 159
Génie maritime, corps de: elite social traditions, 38–39, 49; comfortable life-style, 66–67; royalist sentiments in, 169; mentioned, 26, 153
German naval officers: social origins, 31–32
Godechot, Professor Jacques: on naval attraction to Maurrassism, 150; naval reaction to Spanish Civil War, 161–62
Godfroy, Admiral René, 179
Goude, Emile: on naval legislation, 136
"Grand Corps." See *Officiers de marine*
Grandes écoles. *See under* names of individual schools, Ecole navale, etc.
de Grasse, Admiral François, 1
Grasset, Admiral Maurice: caste system in officer corps, 118
Gringoire, 90
Guilbaud, Commander René: attracted to the Action Française, 124

Haut Cour de Justice: trials of naval officers after World War II, 182–83
Ho Chi Minh, 185
Homes, naval, 70–71. *See also* Dynasties, naval

Ingénieurs méchaniciens, corps des, 78–79
Isolation, naval: reasons for, 192–93
Italy: naval bid for alliance with, 154–55. *See also* Latin solidarity

Jaurès, Admiral Louis: brother of Jean Jaurès, 115; sponsorship of naval legislation, 135
Jesuit schools: ties with the Ecole navale, 43–45

Jeune Ecole: officers interested in doctrinal reforms, 110–12; ties with anticlericals, 115–16
Joan of Arc, 194
de Joinville, Admiral Prince, 33
de Jonquières, Admiral Eugène: role model for naval officers, 59
Le Journal des débats, 90

Knights of Malta: recruited for naval service, 15, 46

de Laborde, Admiral Jean: royalist ties, 124; pro-Italian policies, 155; scuttling of fleet in 1942, p. 180; mentioned, 174
Lacaze, Admiral Lucien: and factionalism in officer corps, 109; royalist ties, 124; mentioned, 116
de La Gravière, Admiral Jurien: member of the Académie française, 116
de La Monneraye, Admiral Louis: service under Admiral Violette, 114; anti-parliamentary sentiments, 144; on Spanish Civil War, 161; mentioned, 145–46
de Lanessan, Jean-Marie, Minister of Marine, 12; on Fashoda crisis and naval reform, 112–13
de La Rochefoucauld, Duchess, 90
Latin solidarity, 95, 120
Lavigerie, Charles Cardinal: the Ralliement and the French navy, 11
Leclerc, General Philippe: and the Vietnam War, 185
Le Cour Grandmaison, Jean: conservative support for naval budget, 138
Legends, naval, 7–14
Legislation, naval, 131–42, 136–38
Leygues, Georges, Minister of Marine, 129–31; sponsorship of naval legislation, 135; budget debates, 141; godfather to Admiral Darlan, 157
Ligue de l'Action Française, 152
Lockroy, Edouard, Minister of Marine: naval modernization, 12; Fashoda crisis, 112; denial of suffrage to military, 188–89
Loti, Pierre, 193
Louis XIII, 194
Louis XIV, 7–8, 19
de Loÿs, Commander Pierre: royalist sentiments, 147

MacMahon, Marshal Patrice, French president, 190

Mahan, Admiral Alfred Thayer, 1
"Marianne," 7
Marriages, naval. *See* Dynasties, naval
Maurras, Charles, 123, 148, 187
Mers-el-Kébir, 180
Metropolitan Army. See *Armée métropolitaine*
Midi: officers recruited from, 29–31, 193
Mignard, Pierre, 98–101
Millerand, Alexandre, French president, 130
Ministry of Marine: state within a state, 138–39
Moch, Jules, 135
Morinaud, Emile: Algerian interest in the navy, 136
Mothers, naval. *See* Dynasties, naval
Moysset, Henri: postwar trial, 183
Muselier, Admiral Emile, 179–80
Mussolini, Benito: naval admiration for, 154–55, 190

NATO, 1
Neptune, 98–100

Oaths: effect on professional behavior, 87
Officer corps, naval: structure, 19–22; delayed reform, 192
Officiers de marine, corps de: social origins, 20–32 *passim*; aristocratic heritage, 37–38, 46–49; economic status, 39–40; social isolation, 39–40; Catholic education, 40, 42; links with *corps de santé*, 66; esprit de corps, 74; changing recruiting patterns, 75–78; prejudices, 101; royalist sympathies, 168; post-1945 changes, 186–87; mentioned, 26
Ollivier, Commander François: and Action Française in Toulon, 152

Paquet, Bernard: on the Action Française, 125; mentioned 152
Paris: officers' social life, 55
Parliament: on political activities in navy, 170
Pelletan, Camille, Minister of Marine, 12, 113–14
Pétain, Marshal Philippe, 175, 185
"*Petits corps.*" *See under* names of officer corps, *génie maritime*, etc.
Piétri, François, Minister of Marine, 148, 183, 189
de Polignac, Princess, 90

Political activity: growth in military, 189
Political attitudes: post-1930, pp. 126–27
Popular Front, 189
Proust, Marcel: comments on naval officers, 34, 192

Radical-Socialist party, 135
Ralliement: naval officers reactions to, 11. *See also* Cardinal Lavigerie
Ratyé, Admiral Jean: on officer caste, 77
Reading habits: of officers after 1918, p. 124
Rearmament, naval, 141–42
Renoir, Jean: *La Grande illusion*, 75
Revue française de sociologie, 3
Robert, Admiral Georges: on social composition of A.E.N., 78
Roosevelt, Theodore, 145
"La Royale," 7
Royalist sentiments: U.S. naval attaché report on, 162–63, 165, 167–68; lack of official interest in, 169–70. *See also* Parliament
Russian Revolution: French naval involvement, 106. *See also* Black Sea

Saigon: U.S. evacuation from, 187
Saint-Cyr, 21–29 *passim*, 186
Sainte-Geneviève, 43–45, 187. *See also* Jesuit schools
Saint-Maixent, 25–26, 68
de Saint-Pierre, Michel: novelist, 186
Salaün, Admiral Henri: on naval reforms, 109; ties with Pelletan Briand and Herriot, 114; opposes officer caste system, 118
Santé, corps de: social origins, 49; access to, 66; royalist sentiments in, 168
Schwerer, Admiral Antoine: links with Bourbon pretender, 34; on economic conditions of officers, 107; factionalism in officer corps, 109; conservative spokesman, 116–17; anti-Semitism, 119; mentioned, 145–46, 148, 191
Section d'études: role in policy formulation, 153–56; at Vichy, 180–81
Ségalen, Victor: life overseas, 58, 193
Senate: on naval legislation, 132–33

Service rivalry, 90–94
Sexual relations: of officers, 55–58
Sims, Admiral William S.: observations of French anti-Semitism, 119; on Washington Naval Conference, 121
Socialist Party [S.F.I.O.], 135
Sons of officers. *See* Dynasties, naval
Spanish Civil War: Darlan's position, 156; U.S. naval interest, 162–63, 189
Suffrage, military: law of July 29, 1872, p. 146

Tardieu, Premier André, 129
Thiers, Adolphe, French President: on the Commune, 140
Thought habits, officers, 81. *See also* Officiers de marine
Titles, aristocratic: claimed by officers, 36–37
Toulon, 56–58
Trafalgar, 141
de Trogoff, Admiral Jean, 165–66

United States Navy: southern influence in officer corps, 145n

Varillon, Pierre: with *Action française*, 148–50; on Spanish Civil War, 161–62
Vietnam War, 185
de Villeneuve, Admiral Pierre, 1
Violette, Admiral Hector: naval reform, 109; masonic ties, 113; association with General André, 113; ties with Briand and Herriot, 114; ties with Georges Leygues, 115

Washington Naval Conference: French reaction, 120–21, 139; influence on civil-naval relations, 142
Watergate, affaire de, 187. *See also* Dreyfus affair
Weddings, naval, 64–66. *See also* Dynasties, naval
Weygand, General Maxime: on separation between *pays légal* and *pays réel*, 166; crisis of June 16, 1940, p. 176
Wives, naval. *See under* Dynasties, naval
World War I: bitterness over results, 13–16, 105